Treacherous Subjects

TREACHEROUS SUBJECTS

Gender, Culture, and
Trans-Vietnamese Feminism

LAN P. DUONG

Temple University Press

PHILADELPHIA

Temple University Press
Philadelphia, Pennsylvania 19122
www.temple.edu/tempress

Published 2012

LIBRARY OF CONGRESS CATALOGING-IN-PUBLICATION DATA

Duong, Lan P., 1972–
  Treacherous subjects : gender, culture, and trans-Vietnamese feminism /
Lan P. Duong.
    p. cm.
  Includes bibliographical references and index.
  ISBN 978-1-4399-0177-9 (cloth : alk. paper)
  ISBN 978-1-4399-0178-6 (pbk. : alk. paper)
  ISBN 978-1-4399-0179-3 (e-book)
  1. American literature—Vietnamese American authors   2. American literature—
20th century—History and criticism.   3. American literature—21st century—History
and criticism.   4. Vietnamese diaspora.   5. Authorship—Collaboration.   6. Motion
pictures—Production and direction.   I. Title.
PS508.V54D86   2012
810.8'089592073—dc23

                                                                              2011043062

  ♾ The paper used in this publication meets the requirements of the American
National Standard for Information Sciences—Permanence of Paper for Printed
Library Materials, ANSI Z39.48–1992

Printed in the United States of America

2 4 6 8 9 7 5 3 1

A book in the American Literatures Initiative (ALI), a collaborative
publishing project of NYU Press, Fordham University Press, Rutgers
University Press, Temple University Press, and the University of Virginia
Press. The Initiative is supported by The Andrew W. Mellon Foundation.
For more information, please visit www.americanliteratures.org.

CONTENTS

ACKNOWLEDGMENTS

A book on collaboration must acknowledge all of those collaborators who have helped make this book possible. At UC Irvine, I worked with a number of professors who were formative in shaping my intellectual inquiries from the beginning, guiding me toward the career path I am on today. They are Gabriele Schwab, Ketu Katrak, and Jane Newman. Among my committee members, Laura Hyun Yi Kang has been a forceful presence in my academic life then and now, providing me with ready advice, encouragement, and support. Animated conversations with Glen Mimura at UCI have also inspired many ideas that later took root in this book. In Asian American Studies, Linda Trinh-Võ always offered a place in her office for me as a graduate student. Now, as colleagues working on various collaborations, I appreciate even more than before Linda's strength and wisdom.

At UC Riverside, I have the pleasure of being among very generous colleagues. When I first arrived to UCR, Women's Studies was a most welcoming department. Alicia Arrizón, Piya Chatterjee, Christine Gailey, Amalia Cabezas, Chikako Takeshita, and Tracy Fisher have been a constant source of mentoring and good wishes. My home department is now Media and Cultural Studies. In this department, I appreciate the allies I have in Toby Miller, Keith Harris, Andrea Smith, Ruhi Khan, Wendy Su, Derek Burrill, Ken Rogers, Tim Labor, and Setsu Shigematsu. I also thank Carole-Anne Tyler, Michelle Bloom, Vorris Nunley, Katherine Kinney, and Traise Yamamoto for the snippets of advice they have doled out to me throughout these years. While writing and researching the book,

I have relied on the faculty in the Southeast Asian Studies Program for their warm conviviality and intellectual vivacity. They include Deborah Wong, Henk Meier, Sally Ness, David Biggs, and Rene Lysloff. I would like to especially thank my colleagues Christina Schwenkel, Tamara Ho, and Freya Schiwy, who have integrally helped to see this book through, providing invaluable feedback on my work and so much encouragement throughout the process. Beyond UCR, other colleagues from whom I continue to learn a great deal are Dorinne Kondo, Bliss Cua Lim, Jim Lee, Jane Iwamura, erin Khuê Ninh, Adam Knee, Gaik Khoo, Sophia Harvey, Nhi Lieu, Caroline Kiều Linh Valverde, Quan Tran, Jane Hseu, Wilson Chen, Arnold Pan, and Nguyễn Tân Hoàng.

Shepherding me through the publication process was my editor, Janet Francedese, and series editor, David Palumbo-Liu, whose insightful comments meaningfully shaped the book. I would also like to thank my editor, David Martinez, for working on the manuscript with me until the very end. I am grateful to Hong-An Truong for allowing me to use her stunning artwork for the book cover. And special thanks go to Việt Lê for designing the book covers. My heartfelt thanks are also extended to all the people whom I interviewed in the book. Nina McPherson, Dương Thu Hương, Đặng Nhật Minh, and Vũ Ngọc Đãng have opened themselves up to me, allowing me to pore into their documents and peer into their lives. For this I am very grateful.

With generous support from a number of institutions, the research for the book was conducted from 2001 to 2007. A Fulbright-Hays Dissertation Fellowship, a Vietnamese Advanced Student Institute Fellowship, and a University of California of the President's Pacific Rim mini-grant funded many trips to France and Việt Nam during my time as a graduate student. In 2006, a Pacific Rim Faculty Grant from UCOP allowed me to do archival research in Hà Nội. Through UCR, I received a Regents Faculty Grant in order to visit the Southeast Asian archives in the south of France in 2007. As a fellow at UCR's Center for Ideas and Society, I had the good fortune to work with colleagues Jacqueline Shea Murphy, Michelle Raheja, Erika Suderberg, and Patricia Ploesch. There I found the kind of intellectual engagement that assisted me in thinking through questions of embodiment and otherness, central themes in my research.

In other "places" outside of academia, I have found other "wonders," to paraphrase Daniyal Mueenuddin's book title *In Other Rooms, Other Wonders*. I am indebted to a group of scholars and friends who come together every now and then for good food and good company. They are cô Kim-Loan Hill, cô Lan Phó, Việt Lê, Như-Ngọc Ông, Mariam B.

Lam, and Chương-Đài Võ. Within this group, however, Yen Le Espiritu, Thu-Hương Nguyễn-Võ, Thúy Võ Đặng, and Cẩm Nhung Vũ have been particularly supportive during very trying moments. I truly appreciate their presence in my life. Even though we came together initially as colleagues, we now leave these gatherings as close friends. In my community work, I work with a wonderful group of women. Through the Diasporic Vietnamese American Network, I have had the great pleasure of working closely with Isabelle Thuy Pelaud, whose charm and good cheer never seem to be exhausted. Vietnamese American Arts & Letters Association collaborators like Trâm Lê, Ysa Lê, Ann Phong, and Jenni Trang Lê have definitely influenced this book, especially in terms of the collaborative feminist vision that it upholds.

Another "place" from which I draw strength is San José, California. My friends from San José inspire me with their stories of courage and fight. The rough-and-tumble ways that we grew up underlie the feminist sensibilities of *Treacherous Subjects*. They are Claire L. Phan, Tam Phan, Trang Le, Odine Bui-Ludwico, Tina Deruntz, Lan Phan, Ae Langsaveth, Kalainy Chen, Thi Le, and Monica Gallegos. In ways both implicit and explicit, this book also commemorates my family's experiences and the stories we used to tell one another. With all my heart, I thank Ba, Má, chị Tuyết, anh Thạch, chị Trang, chị Hương, chị Lee, chị My, anh Khắc, and chị Mỹ-Lệ for all of your acts of bravery.

Finally, I wish to thank Việt Thanh Nguyễn whose boundless support has been extremely critical to the book, both its writing and research. From the beginning of our relationship, Việt has always helped me to see the beauty in possibility. I would not have persevered in finishing the book had it not been for him and his encouragement. But more than this, he and his family (Ba, Má, anh Tùng, chị Huyền, and especially Minh, Lực, and Linh) bring so much joy to my life. With Việt, I have truly found my most wondrous place.

Parts of Chapter 1, titled "Manufacturing Authenticity," were published in *Amerasia Journal* 31.2 (2005): 1–19. Parts of Chapter 5 were included in the anthology *Transnational Feminism and Film*, eds. Áine O'Healy, Katarzyna Marciniak, and Anikó Imre (New York: Palgrave Macmillan Press, 2007), 163–84. My work on *Souls on Swings* in Chapter 5 was previously published in *Journal BOL: Special Issue on Vietnam and US*, eds. Viet Le and Yong Soon Min 7 (winter 2007): 126–37. Sections of Chapter 4 on Trinh T. Minh-ha's *Surname Viet Given Name Nam* were published in *Discourse: Journal for Theoretical Studies in Media and Culture*, ed. Bliss Cua Lim 31.3 (fall 2009): 195–219.

Introduction

With a flash of light, a newspaper photographer's camera captured the moment of my family's arrival to the United States in Butler, Pennsylvania, in 1975. This grainy, black-and-white image accompanied a story that detailed how my family members had become the wards of a Catholic Church and the first refugees to arrive in this small town. The photo shows my father, my five siblings, and me. A lieutenant colonel in the Southern Vietnamese army, my father had been forced to flee before April 30, 1975, the day Sài Gòn fell to the communists in the war with the Americans. My father was among those South Vietnamese who had served with the US government and the southern military and who were evacuated or fled for fear of communist reprisal. Had he stayed, as did some of his friends, he would have been reeducated because of his perceived collaboration with Việt Nam's colonial and Cold War enemies. From the communist perspective, he was a traitor, and this picture of him in America was evidence of his betrayal.

The photograph attests to something else: my mother's absence. Not until I was much older did I realize that she was missing from the picture. She stayed behind when my father took the children and escaped from Sài Gòn. In the eyes of the communist regime, my mother might have been perceived as loyal to the national family because she stayed. From the war years through the postwar years, betrayal and loyalty would be important terms for both communists and noncommunists as they struggled over control of Việt Nam. Both sides often used charges of collaboration and betrayal to redraw the bounds of nation. But by the late 1980s, those contentions had abated somewhat, at least in Việt Nam. In 1990, my mother was able to leave for the United States to be reunited with her grown children; conversely, overseas Vietnamese, including myself, began returning home. The staggered pattern of immigration and return that marks my family history is not unique. It demonstrates in concentrated form the kinds of jagged reunifications that took place for diasporans, as well as for those in Việt Nam, as families tried to reunify through multiple migrations and various homecomings in the postwar era.

This incomplete family portrait speaks to the fractures of war and displacement, recalling the trauma of betrayal writ large for the postwar national family of Việt Nam. As my family history suggests, the Indochina wars are imbricated with charges of treason and collaboration, charges that might be reversed with a shift in the political wind. Indeed, the government condemned overseas Vietnamese, like my father, as traitors and collaborators after 1975, but following its embrace of economic market reforms began in 1986, the government slowly opened the country's doors, welcoming overseas Vietnamese as part of its transnational family. Diasporans now return home as tourists, investors, scholars, and artists. After denouncing collaboration as betrayal, the state has recently imbued the term with a positive connotation of joint endeavors and creative productions. While overseas Vietnamese are still seen as potential collaborators, the meaning of "collaborator" itself has changed from someone like my father, who betrays the country, to someone who aids the country.

Given this history, *Treacherous Subjects* examines collaboration's doubled meanings in the cultural politics of Việt Nam and its diasporic populations, particularly those who settled in the United States and France. *Treacherous Subjects* asks: What does it mean to be a collaborator? How has collaboration been represented in history and culture? And how have collaborative practices been narrativized as acts of betrayal or loyalty? The book pivots on the word *collaboration* because of its vexed resonance within a modern Vietnamese history marked by French colonialism, US imperialism, Japanese occupation, and the economic role of foreign powers in postwar Việt Nam. This history shapes how Vietnamese subjectivities, both national and diasporan, are characterized by divided loyalties and shifting alliances. These treacherous subjects have been caught between opposing forces: nationalism, communism, occupying powers, and domestic states with competing claims to the name of

Việt Nam. Indeed, the aftereffects of colonialism and foreign occupation in Việt Nam have led to an anxiety about betrayal and its inverse, loyalty, embodying what Timothy Brook calls "collaboration's haunting of the postwar world."[1]

My claim is that this haunting remains present not only for the Vietnamese in Việt Nam, but also for those who have made their way abroad and who identify as Vietnamese Americans or Vietnamese French. From Việt Nam to the United States and France, this legacy is particularly evident in film and literature, as artists grapple with the political and thematic meanings of collaboration today. *Treacherous Subjects* thus focuses on the term's cultural significance, demonstrating that collaboration shapes the ways that major filmic and literary works have been produced and received. The book analyzes several postwar Vietnamese and Vietnamese diasporic cultural productions that are collaborative in nature or that use the notion of treasonous collaboration as a motif. It exposes how accusations of collaboration are contingent upon what is named collaborative, who is named collaborator, and who names her as such, depending on the dominant regime that has the power to define such terms.

Most expressly, the book interrogates the practices and themes of collaboration in order to elaborate on the term's gendered dimensions. My close readings elucidate upon the discursive power of naming those who are "traitors" and "heroes," "enemies" and "friends,"[2] in the formation of community and nation-state. In the postwar era, charges of collaboration score the anxieties involved in the work of nation-building and community-making. In cultural form, the collaborator is often figured as a female traitor, an "outsider" who enables collective solidarity against the menace of the treacherous subject that she embodies. Centralizing the figure of woman, *Treacherous Subjects* delves into the politics of collaboration to ultimately challenge the braided ideology of patriarchy and nationalism that undergirds denunciations or celebrations of collaborative acts. *Treacherous Subjects* develops a mode of analysis I call trans-Vietnamese feminism, which decenters nationalist notions of the family and familial notions of the nation, both dependent on each other and on circumscribed roles for men and women. Trans-Vietnamese feminism especially finds its inspiration in the works of writers and directors in Việt Nam and the diaspora, who have used their art in order to challenge traditional notions of gender, family, and nation.

Traitors and Heroes: Remaking the National Family

The ways that artists deploy the notion of family in their works relate to Việt Nam's postcolonial narratives of resistance and liberation, which consistently use rhetoric about family and filiality.[3] Like Patricia Pelley, I read this discourse of heroes and traitors as productive and prescriptive,[4] but I further argue that these constructs are deployed in both national and diasporic discourses, allowing for these formations to demarcate outsiders and insiders within their borders. The subject positions of "traitor" and "hero" within the bounds of a family imagined as the nation, and the nation itself as a family, are not only interpellative, they are also crucial to the disciplining of subjects in Việt Nam and the diaspora in terms of gender and sexuality.

Discursive terms such as heroes and traitors also work dialectically in narratives about how Việt Nam was either won or lost, in ways that commemorate the past and fundamentally shape the future. In contrast, historians of collaboration have mapped a more complex moral topography of the difficult choices the colonized and occupied had to make during and after war.[5] In so doing, they point to a profound ambivalence underlying the story of colonialism, rejecting the moralizing and teleological framework that accompanies the narrativization of anticolonialism. This book adds to such discussions by focusing on Vietnamese and diasporic narratives about collaboration and the metaphorical family. More saliently, the book marks out the discursive effects that narratives of collaboration produce: gendered figures of heroism and treason whose symbolic significance lingers today.

To fully understand the implications of these terms, it is important to briefly chart Việt Nam's collaborationist history, beginning with the most well-known group of collaborators during French colonialism: the Constitutionalist Party. This political organization was considered "the most powerful native Vietnamese group operating at the time, and the most influential."[6] To use Jay Carter's words, this "subject elite" was composed of an educated, intellectual class of men, later denounced by the anti-colonial resistance movement. *Collaborateurs*, such as Pétrus Phạm Kỳ and Phạm Quỳnh, began as Catholic translators for the French colonial administration and employed the Romanized alphabet of *quốc ngữ* to disseminate colonial documents.[7] As Milton Osborne observes, collaborators believed that *quốc ngữ* would help to eradicate Chinese traditions. As such, these "interpreters" took charge of educating the youth in the colonial metropolis and exercised their limited power as intermediaries to try to achieve Vietnamese autonomy through Franco-Vietnamese collaborations.[8] They used explicitly familial language, viewing France as "father to a Vietnamese son."[9] But their proposals for reform were limited and aimed at obtaining French citizenship for their own class, since they saw themselves as exceptional to the colonized masses.[10]

Anti-French agitator Phan Bội Châu, regarded as "the first great modern Vietnamese nationalist,"[11] strongly opposed the Constitutionalist Party and its ideals. For enlightened scholars like Phan, as Walter Vella argues, the goal was not to leave Western modernity behind but to transform Việt Nam into a modern Western-like nation: "progressive, economically prosperous, socially liberal and politically independent."[12] Phan's imagined Việt Nam was modeled on America and a national lineage that included "Confucian heroes who knew the path of social evolution and used their conscious will to guide society through it."[13] His celebration of heroism extended to women, as Phan was also known for championing the rights of women and advocating for women's self-motivation within the terms of national revolution. Advancing the idea that women play the role of "mother to the nation,"[14] Phan famously declared that when a woman was asked for her name by a courter, she should reply that her "surname is Việt, given name Nam." Within the revolutionary imagination, women could be maternal heroines only when married to the country, pledging their patrimonial allegiance to the national family.[15] These gendered and heteronormative metaphors about the national family found their apotheosis with Hồ Chí Minh's familial rhetoric.

At the helm of this national family, as an "elderly Vietnamese sage,"[16] Hồ Chí Minh based his political identity on the role of an ascetic, patriotic statesman who expounded on his protection of Vietnamese tradition and the reunification of the family as nation.[17] Sharpening his rhetoric about national unity, Hồ used the trope of the family, likening it to a hand, to describe Việt Nam. The inhabitants of the country—though unequal—were adjoined like fingers for a common cause.[18] In the war with the Americans, Hồ's regime named as "traitors" those Vietnamese nationals who betrayed the fatherland (tổ quốc) by cooperating with the American government. For Hồ Chí Minh and his followers, the ultimate traitor to this family and the figurehead for the "puppet regime" was the president of South Việt Nam, Ngô Đình Diệm. Characterizing the South as its militarily and morally weaker counterpart, the Hà Nội regime bolstered its own position as Việt Nam's political stronghold through Hồ's image as an avuncular head of state and his devotion to the country (he once called himself Nguyễn Ái Quốc, literally, "Nguyễn the Patriot").

For the North, the most troubling aspect about South Việt Nam, or the Republic of Việt Nam, was its collaboration with the French and then the Americans. Sài Gòn, South Việt Nam's capital, rapidly gained a reputation for corruption during the 1960s and 1970s, and it was regarded by the regime in Hà Nội as the "enemy within," the country's most vulnerable aperture to foreign contamination because of its openness to capitalism.[19] Consequently, Hồ Chí Minh's regime portrayed the Army of the Republic of Việt Nam (ARVN) as feminized, decadent, and cowardly, particularly in contrast to the determined soldiers of the Democratic Republic of Việt Nam (DRV) and the National Liberation Front (NLF).[20] The rhetoric of treason, conjoined with the term "puppet regime," denoted a southern submission to the power and seduction of US currency.[21] Within this context, betrayal is gendered feminine and stems from a treacherous false consciousness, which was treated with ideological conditioning after the war ended.

Kinship metaphors and the trope of loyalty abound in the postwar diaspora as well. In the introduction to his translation of *Truyện Kiều*, or *The Tale of Kiều*, the beloved nineteenth-century epic poem by Nguyễn Du,[22] Huỳnh Sanh Thông argues that Vietnamese diasporic subjects are "victims of a perverse fate" similar to the poem's main character, Kiều, a wandering prostitute.[23] Thông appropriates female suffering by arguing that the term for overseas Vietnamese, *Việt Kiều*, is based on the character of Kiều, who eventually returns home after many trials. As errant subjects dispersed globally in the postwar era, diasporans always look homeward, according to Thông's reading. Forging an identity informed by migration and displacement, the exilic community remains a fundamental part of the national family. In spite of having migrated elsewhere, the exiles' true roots are in Việt Nam. These popular notions of kinship, family ties, and nationalistic sentiment reinforce a sense of transnational cohesion through the production of "a fictive ethnicity."[24]

The Vietnamese state continues to hail the family today, but in different ways. In Việt Nam's transition to a market economy, with the "downsizing of the socialist welfare system, and return of the household as a unit of production and consumption," families occupy a central role in the country's political and economic structure.[25] Along with the reconfiguration of the family, the meanings of collaboration, betrayal, and loyalty have also changed with Đổi Mới, or "Renovation,"[26] in 1986. Đổi Mới was itself preceded by a chain of events that demonstrated how the national family had been fundamentally altered after the war ended. In 1975, North and South Việt Nam were reunified, but the country also faced grave crises at the national and international levels. The state's attempts to collectivize land and reform agricultural output had disastrous results. Two years later, following Việt Nam's invasion of neighboring Cambodia, the United Nations and the United States imposed a trade embargo on the country. Because of Việt Nam's border wars with China in the late 1970s, support from communist China ceased as well. During this time, refugees fled Việt Nam in successive waves.[27] As a result of so much political and economic instability in the postwar years, the reformers who established Đổi Mới had several goals: "improve lagging productivity, raise living standards, and curb rapid inflation."[28] In more symbolic terms, Đổi Mới became an ideological compromise between the forces of globalization and the anti-colonialist, nationalist spirit Việt Nam was founded on. The advent of Đổi Mới also set in motion intense anxieties about opening the country to the global market, along with its related impurities and impact on gender roles.[29] Within the context of the country's new economy, the state now attempts to reform its subjects according to "neotraditional" constructs of family and filiality.[30]

On the cultural front, the market reforms of Đổi Mới created the conditions for the Vietnamese film and publishing industries to develop, allowing for greater cultural exchange between Việt Nam and other countries. Việt Nam's foreign policies permit diasporic artists to return to the homeland and work collaboratively with the government to produce their work. Once denounced for having abandoned the homeland, Vietnamese diasporans are now "an inseparable part of the community of Vietnamese nationalities."[31] The state's embassy webpage has recently described this community as exerting "political and economic influence" on Việt Nam but notes that they are also essentially stateless. Because of their statelessness, as the state observes, they would do better to invest in Việt Nam's future. In service of this idea, new immigration laws allow for five-year visas for returning Vietnamese, and recently instituted dual-citizenship laws also ensure that diasporans can become not only naturalized citizens but also cultural workers of and for Việt Nam.

Aspiring to be an Asian Tiger like some of its Southeast Asian neighbors, the country positions itself as a major geopolitical player within the region. In so doing, the state constantly refurbishes its relations with France, the United States, and its own diaspora, parts of which still agitate for regime change and thus severely test the model of affiliative relations that the state envisions for itself and the overseas community. Neoliberal economics, nonetheless, trumps political ideology and determines the methods by which the Vietnamese state manages its relationship with its past enemies, including those within the diaspora.

For the diasporic community, the act of naming collaborators and traitors within the symbolic family is influenced not only by a Cold War discourse but also by Việt Nam's recent ascension in the global economy, as well as the international stature and geopolitical visibility that WTO (World Trade Organization) membership endows on the Vietnamese government. After the war ended, the overseas community often labeled those diasporans who returned to the homeland and/or worked with the Vietnamese government as "traitors" to the southern Vietnamese regime. In a newspaper commentary written after the 1994 lifting of the US-led trade embargo, for example, a Vietnamese American writer lists the numerous ways in which one is a traitor to the overseas community because of his/her relationship with the government in Việt Nam.[32]

Within the Vietnamese American community, the most notorious traitors have been both male and female,[33] but as I show, anticommunist discourse uses familial rhetoric to specifically position women as sexual collaborators. In culturally nationalist terms, women prostitute themselves when they disavow the diasporic community and its politics. As a result of the normalized ties between the United States and Việt Nam since 1994, however, more and more Vietnamese diasporans have returned to the homeland for touristic, familial, and work-related reasons. The use of "traitor" to describe those who return is less frequent as Vietnamese American calls for reform have become more moderate.[34] But the charge of treason can still be used to discredit a person's reputation. For example, Le Ly Hayslip, who is the subject of Chapter 2, is a woman who was branded a "traitor" in the early 1990s by some members in the Vietnamese American community for her charity work in Việt Nam.[35] More recently, the controversy surrounding naming a business district "Little Saigon" in San José, California, and Councilwoman Madison Nguyễn's involvement is similar. Nguyễn is also seen as a traitor in the eyes of the Vietnamese American community because she has allegedly nurtured business ties with communist Việt Nam.[36] Furthermore, there are continuing protests and demonstrations against Vietnamese officials and nationals who travel to the United States. When Vietnamese President Nguyễn Minh Triết came to the United States in 2007, he was met with protests in San Diego, California, and Washington, DC. More recently, in 2010, at singer Đàm Vĩnh Hưng's concert in San José, California, war veteran Lý Tống dressed up as a woman, approached the singer on stage, and sprayed him with mace.

Of course, homeland and diaspora are not equally capable of pros-
ecuting and persecuting those labeled traitors, dissidents, and terrorists
in their midst; yet, cotemporally, both formations must deal with the
unruly subjects found within their communal and national borders, as
well as the traffic of people, goods, and funds traveling between them
today. As a result of these transformations, cultural and national boundaries are extremely hard to maintain, but some forces are still working
hard to do so. These efforts are articulated as cultural nationalisms that
circulate in the homeland and diaspora, resulting in the marginaliza-
tion of certain bodies and the imposition of the meanings of home and
homeland on gendered subjects.

My proposal for trans-Vietnamese feminism critiques a form of
heteropatriarchal nationalism that underpins not only the recriminations against collaborators-as-traitors, but also the discourse surrounding heroism and treason that celebrates loyalists. M. Jacqui Alexander
describes heteropatriarchy as the "twin processes of heterosexualization
and patriarchy."[37] Spike V. Peterson further adds that heteropatriarchy,
grounded in a familial discourse, works in conjunction with nationalism to establish a power rooted in "a systematic and heterosexist gender
inequality."[38] Heteropatriarchal nationalism especially manifests itself
via the demonization of collaboration and the denigration of women's
artistic work as being collaborative and treasonous rather than auteurist and worthy of acclaim. A trans-Vietnamese feminist way of reading
not only challenges these denunciations of women's work but also insists
upon seeing collaboration as an important feminist practice.

Transnational Family Politics and the Figure of Woman

In postwar literature and film, both national and diasporic, the Vietnamese body politic appears in the form of a transnational family rup-
tured by the politics of collaboration, a metaphor that has a historical
precedent. According to Heonik Kwon, wartime collaboration resulted
in brutal forms of punishment and retaliatory violence amongst real and
symbolic kin in postwar Việt Nam.[39] While Kwon documents Việt Nam's
painful history of collaboration in order to probe its ethical dimensions,[40]
Treacherous Subjects is concerned with how the cultural discourse of collaboration takes place on the rhetorical ground of the (national) family,
and particularly via the figure of the treasonous woman. The family is a
powerful trope in Vietnamese and diasporic cultural production, with
collaborative acts portrayed as a form of treason against a family that

demands loyalty. The texts I examine depict the dissolution and reconstitution of family bonds at both the personal and national levels, staged via sexual, military, literary, and political collaborations and expressed through the Manichean terms of betrayal and loyalty.

Some Vietnamese cultural producers in the homeland and the diaspora figure the collaborator as a woman, a traitor who enables the cultural policing of imagined borders during colonization and in the era of globalization. Consequently, betrayal—as a form of collaboration—usually becomes tethered in the nationalist imagination to the supposed moral inconstancy that women embody, signaling not only their political treachery but also their sexual infidelity to the nation. The recurring figure of the prostitute in the literature and films studied here is an example of this treachery; she symbolizes how women's subjectivities are tied to commerce, the body, and sexuality. While state collaboration takes on a neutral cast, and the artistic collaborations authored by men retain the original duality of meaning, more often than not treachery tinges female collaborations, whether personal or aesthetic, symbolic or actual. In contrast to male directors who are viewed as "auteurs," women artists are often seen as collaborators and traitors to the national family, or represent themselves as traitorous to the same family.

Tracing the complex meanings of collaboration, this book captures the aspects of gender that structure how cultural works are both produced and received. I point to the division of labor in the writing of literature and filmmaking between women and men as well as the historical, material conditions that shape how these works are produced. While it is mostly men who have dominated the making of films in terms of directing and producing, many women have found more opportunities for themselves in literature, either as authors or cowriters. Looking at some of the most popular writers from each country, I examine the market demands for minority women's literature within a globalized publishing industry, exploring the processes by which women writers cowrite, produce, and are translated. Along the same lines, I also analyze the networks of support that enable the most successful male filmmakers in Việt Nam and the diaspora to shoot on-location, produce, and distribute their movies. Such structures largely determine how these filmmakers treat the question of gender in their films, which are often celebrated for their representations of gender. These gendered concerns condition whether collaborations in the texts, and the collaborative acts that produce these texts, are read either as acts of feminine betrayal or masculine loyalty to a nation that the Vietnamese at home and abroad imagine in familial terms. *Treacherous Subjects* argues that in collaboration lay the grounds for a trans-Vietnamese mode of analysis, one that deconstructs notions of family, nation, and community in the cultural discourses of collaboration.

The Art and Politics of Collaboration: Negotiating Gender in Films and Literature

Like the cultural productions and producers it studies, *Treacherous Subjects* pivots upon dual definitions of collaboration. The word signifies either the act of working together, usually in terms of an intellectual and artistic endeavor, or working treacherously against one's country. Collaboration's value as a term shifts subject to its currency within a specific context and history. Within the contemporary United States, for example, collaboration is often associated with entrepreneurial modes of research and development, whereas it remains a highly fraught term in the French context, conjuring memories of the Vichy collaboration during WWII. Although its largely negative charge in colonial and wartime Việt Nam survives in the contemporary Vietnamese diaspora, in today's Việt Nam, collaborations (*sự hợp tác*) now describe joint-ventures (*liên doanh*) with foreign countries in the era of economic reform inaugurated by *Đổi Mới*. These relations are at once political (as the Vietnamese government works with its former enemies) and economic (as the state welcomes capitalism). Unlike scholarship that deals chiefly with the ethics of collaboration politics, this book focuses on the rhetorical ambiguities of collaborative practices in multiple contexts.[41] This fluidity is vital to the way collaboration shuttles between the categories of art and politics.

In terms of practice, colonized subjects and disempowered minority communities who wish to see their stories translated, written in a dominant language, or produced on screen, have had to collaborate. This continues to be the case in Việt Nam, as writers negotiate with foreign presses to have their works translated in another language and directors must cooperate with the Vietnamese government for permission to film. While collaboration also shapes cultural production in France and the United States, particularly for minority writers and for film production, the nature of collaboration in Việt Nam or with Việt Nam is much more politically sensitive and contentious. For Vietnamese American and Vietnamese French writers and filmmakers, the practice of collaboration with the Vietnamese government might be perceived by their diasporic communities as working with the "enemy." The theme of collaboration that emerges in many postwar cultural productions is no less controversial. Here, collaboration gestures toward a history of colonial governance and warfare where subjugated natives have sometimes been complicit with colonizers. This history continues with Việt Nam's current "open-door policy," which some understand as a collaboration with former enemies and a capitulation to foreign capital, both being acts of betrayal.[42] In sum, the practice and theme of collaboration for Vietnamese and diasporic artists is enmeshed with the politics and economics of it for the nation itself.

Today collaboration is a necessary practice for cultural producers who must make and distribute their work in a global network, one formed through and shadowed by the collaborative practices that were widespread under colonialism. Representing material actions and ethical transactions, collaborative practices traverse transnational boundaries within the global marketplace. In so doing, these practices become entrenched in an interdependent network of mutual support and investment that is emotional as well as financial. Situated in this larger context, *Treacherous Subjects* insists that artistic collaboration is necessary in the making of culture, and that cultural texts should be read in a way that accounts for how they are conceived, constructed, and circulated through modes of collaboration. Interrogating collaboration in this fashion sheds light on how artists *labor*—the Latinate root of the word collaboration—in imagining Việt Nam and the diaspora in the postwar period. They imagine their subjectivity in relation to the nation and manage their gendered identity within the family *qua* nation. Reading through the prism of collaboration, *Treacherous Subjects* asserts that artists act as agents when they negotiate their gendered positions within not only larger structures of power but also the confines of a national culture.

Trans-Vietnamese Feminism: Remapping Việt Nam and the Diaspora

In her book *Betrayal and Other Acts of Subversion*, Leslie Bow writes that betrayal and loyalty are most often pinned on women's bodies, since infidelity is "intrinsic to feminine nature."[43] Bow focuses on Asian American women's bodies because they represent the duality of treachery and virtue most clearly within the American imagination.[44] Like Bow, I see charges of betrayal as masculinist and gendered; such charges are fundamental to the negative connotation of collaboration and the ways that this meaning is most often directed toward women. While Bow's work shapes my analyses, the paradigm I use here enlarges Bow's frames of reference to look at the constructs of femininity and masculinity in texts from Việt Nam and the diaspora. The nature of the diasporic formations and nation building that have resulted from the wars carried out on Vietnamese soil necessitate a transnational scope for this book. Vietnamese gender relations have and continue to form across regions, forged and enforced by successive wars, migration, and displacement. Much of the research about Việt Nam and the diaspora has focused on either a French or American perspective, or on singular aspects of the Vietnamese or the diasporic experience.[45] In contrast, this book's transnational and interdisciplinary frame allows for a broader understanding of the contexts of power within which the artists and their audiences are historically located.[46]

As part of this transnational commitment, this book resists Western and Vietnamese scholarship that discusses women's rights, or *nữ quyền*, solely within a Western liberal discourse.[47] In a text on Vietnamese women's revolutionary movements, for example, Arlene Eisen defines present-day struggles for equality in Việt Nam within a framework of Western liberalism, which includes "having control over a woman's body; women's rights to health care; the freedom to live without threat of rape and violence; equal access to jobs and political leadership; and the freedom to define one's own sexuality."[48] Eisen uses such criteria to define Vietnamese women's lack of rights and to serve as the basis for the idea of global sisterhood.[49] By focusing on the formal rights that "long-haired warriors"[50] lack in the present moment, nonetheless, Western feminist scholarship on Vietnamese women not only treats the category of women as unified and essential, but also it fails to account for their negotiations with the present conditions of modernity. Collectively, these texts form a narrative about Vietnamese women as heroic and loyal revolutionaries that fossilizes their sense of agency in the past.[51] This agency also stands in implicit contrast to those who collaborated with outsiders against the nation.[52] By constructing this narrative of heroic Vietnamese women, these Western scholars inadvertently align themselves with Vietnamese state narratives that already fetishize both revolutionary womanhood and nationhood.[53] As important as some of this Western feminist scholarship is, it also overlooks how both women and men offer competing notions to this official history within the shifting domains of Vietnamese culture.[54]

In a similar fashion, Vietnamese women's scholarship praises women because of their adherence to family and Confucian notions of loyalty, values that enable them to build the nation and resist collaboration.[55] This body of work relies upon the same founding moments used by Western feminist scholarship in the narrativization of the women's movement, beginning with women's oppression under Confucianist patriarchy and concluding with women's wartime participation in the twentieth century.[56] Laying out the distinct nature of Vietnamese women's history, especially in comparison with that of women in the rest of Southeast Asia and China, Vietnamese women's scholarship deploys "outstanding female figures [to] mark an ostensibly unified national culture that predates and outlasts Chinese cultural influence."[57] The exceptionalism of Vietnamese women and their history draws from a form of cultural nationalism, pointing to what Nhung Tuyet Tran calls the "myth of equality" found in both Vietnamese and Western scholarship. Abiding by a linear trajectory, this feminist discourse renders the history of Vietnamese women as a glorious one. Whereas women are commemorated as heroes in the Western feminist imagination, in Vietnamese historiography, women are exhorted to appropriate an exalted past and craft a subjectivity suited for the demands of a neoliberal economy. Indeed, Le Thi Nham Tuyet celebrates Vietnamese heroines in order to refine the three submissions (to the father, husband, and son) and four virtues (industry, appearance, prudent speech, and exemplary conduct). These Confucian precepts, Le argues, must be reworked in the new millennium.[58] Following this revolutionary lineage, Vietnamese women remain loyal to the project of national reconstruction.

The reproduction of loyalist ideology, however, demands the participation not only of women but also of men. By only examining the constructs of femininity, these texts leave Vietnamese masculinity untouched as a point of analysis and focus mostly on women, oppression, and their fight for nationhood.[59] While the four virtues and three submissions dominate discussions of the "woman question" in Vietnamese women's scholarship, these studies overlook the way family, state, and nation call on men to submit to these same structures. David Marr makes clear that in Vietnamese society, concepts of the (male) self and the individual have been influenced by a Confucian model that depends on the "relations between ruler-subject, father-son, husband-wife, elder-brother-younger-brother, friend-friend."[60] The performance of citizenship and community membership within the public space is therefore gendered for men as well. How masculine and feminine subjects are interpellated should be equally important to analyses of gender in Việt Nam and the diaspora.[61]

Further, as studies on queer identity and the nation-state have shown, issues of normative sexuality are also affixed to state citizenship and community membership.[62] Confucian and neo-Confucian ideals explicitly make relationships within families to be homologous for the relations between the ruler and the ruled in society. Loyal subjects are those who follow patriarchal rule and reproduce the nation and its ideologies. Adhering to these models, both the Vietnamese nation and diaspora include or exclude members on the basis of their ability to practice compulsory heterosexuality, particularly because ideological and biological reproduction is necessary for the longevity of nation and community. Spike V. Peterson writes about national and communal formations similarly; social groups like these abide by heterosexism when there is a presupposition that "heterosexual coupling [is the] basis of sexual intimacy, family life, and group reproduction."[63] In upholding an ethnically homogenous and heterosexist familial ideal, the nation and diaspora restrict the behavior and discipline of the bodies of women, minorities, and queer subjects, who are often rendered in nationalist discourses as potentially traitorous and likely to collaborate. Countering narratives of uniformity, this book posits that tandem analyses of gender and sexuality must reveal the interrelated aspects of power and agency in such contexts.

This method of analysis, which I call trans-Vietnamese feminism, ensures that nation, diaspora, gender, and sexuality are not treated as "discrete and autonomous constructs."[64] Trans-Vietnamese feminism is a historically informed, feminist inquiry that understands gender and sexuality as interlocking processes in the transnational formations of both nation and diaspora. Like Chandra Talpade Mohanty's notion of a "feminism without borders," trans-Vietnamese feminism is not the same as "border-less feminism"; rather, it is a feminist politics that "[acknowledges] the fault lines, conflicts, differences, fears and containment that borders represent."[65] These differences serve as the foundations for a trans-Vietnamese feminist analysis and are catalyzed by the affective dimensions and lived realities of Vietnamese subjects in multiple places. Trans-Vietnamese feminism privileges collaboration and emphasizes that while collaboration has been stigmatized as a woman's practice or a treacherous practice gendered as feminine, collaborative practices between women have been central in their economic, political, and artistic endeavors.

Exploring differences across fault lines, trans-Vietnamese feminism's methodology investigates Việt Nam and the diaspora in the same coordinates of time and space. A cotemporal focus on the homeland and the diaspora dispels the notion that the latter is an inauthentic representation of the former, that only the diaspora is saturated with feelings of affect, exile, and nostalgia, or that the diaspora is traitorous to the homeland.[66] In the book's analyses, neither homeland nor diaspora is perceived as being "behind the times" in the reconstitution of the national family, the members of which are "equally decadent participants in contemporary world culture."[67] Moreover, the prefix "trans" and its definition highlight how trans-Vietnamese feminism must query the "geopolitics of knowledge production"[68] in reference to works about "Vietnam" that are "carried over" and "across" spatial geographies. Literature and film, works in translation, and critical reviews and essays comprise such bodies of knowledge. Vis-à-vis a historicized understanding of the texts' refractions across regions, this interpretive framework places in relief the gendered relations of power and shifting political contexts within which artists produce and are received.

The book signals these uneven relations of power through typographical means. By placing quotes around the word "Vietnam" throughout the book, and distinguishing it from Việt Nam, I delineate how "Vietnam" pertains to a gendered and racialized discourse about the country that circulates widely in the West and maintained as such in Western culture. Ethnic studies and French cultural studies scholars note that "Vietnam" is a still-resonant, ever-powerful discourse about wounds and loss, victims and victors. Writing on the media's coverage of the twenty-fifth anniversary of the "Fall of Saigon," Yen Le Espiritu explains, "the United States war in Vietnam is renarrated as a noble and moral mission in defense of freedom and democracy, rather than as an attempt to secure United States geopolitical hegemony in Southeast Asia and by extension Asia."[69] Post–Cold War revisionism within US culture, Loan Dao argues, is an "intricate lattice—delineating the quagmire of an imperialist war as a Manichean tale of democracy against communism, good versus evil."[70] Within the French imaginary of its colonial past, as Panivong Norindr points out, the phantasm of "Vietnam" as "Indochine" replays as a spectacular narrative of loss and mourning.[71]

Overwhelmingly, this discourse links "Vietnam" to war and the "Vietnamese" to victimhood, not only in the United States and France but also within the diasporic Vietnamese imagination, since Vietnamese diasporic artists feel beholden to respond to and revise such constructions. In contrast, "Việt Nam," when broken down into two words in this book, alludes to the ways that the country spells its name. I do not use "Việt Nam" to reference the country for linguistic or nationalistic authenticity. Nor do I claim that Vietnamese nationals represent themselves more accurately than those in the diaspora do; they, too, are influenced by a discourse about "Vietnam," and these influences invariably limn their cultural productions. Rather, I employ the different spellings to mark the various ways in which the country has been perceived differently by those at home, abroad, and in the West.

Elaborating upon these differences in perception, *Treacherous Subjects* shows how a Western imagination has viewed the Vietnamese primarily as refugees and survivors to whom a kind of symbolic capital has been endowed. Pierre Bourdieu defines symbolic capital as "the degree of accumulated prestige, celebrity, consecration or honor" given to an individual and is "founded on a dialectic of knowledge and recognition."[72] In this context, symbolic capital describes the situated powers and recognition that some Vietnamese cultural producers possess as supposedly authentic knowledge producers about the Vietnam War and its aftermath. A trans-Vietnamese feminist analysis details how major diasporic and Vietnamese artists have wielded this form of symbolic capital variously during the postwar years. This reading practice illuminates the gendered nodes of power and agency underlying dominant narratives about "Vietnam" more than thirty-five years after the American War has ended.

Through the mode of trans-Vietnamese feminism, *Treacherous Subjects* advocates for historical specificity and cultural precision, signal imperatives for feminist researchers working in and on the global South.[73] My work is especially influenced by feminists whose research challenges the efficacy of applying Western paradigms to women in the global South. Critiquing global and international feminisms, Caren Kaplan and Inderpal Grewal, for example, define a feminism committed to an interrogation of the transnational flows of culture within the "historically specific social formation of 'postmodernity.'"[74] As they argue, in an era of global economic restructuring, a transnational feminist analysis must be comparative in order to highlight the linkages between multinational corporate strategies and dominant nationalist agendas that work collaboratively to oppress gendered subjects.[75] Against the master narratives of nationalism, especially since they serve "various patriachies in multiple locations,"[76] transnational feminism also grounds the historically specific differences between women, deploying these acknowledged differences as the foundation for a critical praxis vivified by women's collaborations.

Dovetailing with Kaplan and Grewal's work, this book weaves together two theoretical frames: transnational feminism and collaboration. As other feminist theorists have argued, analyzing collaboration and engaging in a collaborative praxis is critical work. Linda Karell writes that locating "the traces of collaboration is both a politically subversive and an avowedly political act."[77] At stake in the devaluation of collaboration is a conservation of the authorial subject himself.[78] To study collaboration, then, is to uncover this problem in patriarchal systems of knowledge, revealing disparities of power and highlighting the decentering of authority that collaborations can enact.[79] More recently, Amanda Lock Swarr and Richa Nagar argue for a transnational collaborative dialogue, particularly within the realms of art, activism, and the academy, to "radically rethink existing approaches to subalternity, voice, authorship and representation."[80] Drawing upon such interconnections between transnational feminism and collaboration, a trans-Vietnamese feminist approach, first and foremost, critiques the disciplinary logic and familial rhetoric that fortifies Vietnamese national and diasporic discourses. Trans-Vietnamese feminism also invests collaboration with a positive valence, one that serves as a touchstone for aesthetic and political endeavors.

Treacherous Subjects: The Films and Literature of the Vietnamese and the Vietnamese Diaspora

In the chapters that follow, *Treacherous Subjects* investigates some of the most well-known films and literary works by postwar Vietnamese artists in the homeland and the diaspora. I have chosen to analyze controversial and commercial works that have been produced within a key time period—after the war ended and at the onset of Việt Nam's Đổi Mới. Against this historical context, I look at how constructs of gender and sexuality constitute these artists' subjectivities and are inseparable from the ways that the texts have been produced and received. Each chapter centralizes the representations of gender and sexuality within a film or literary work and reveals how women often play an especially important role in these texts, serving as either heroes or traitors to the national family. The dialectic of heroism and treason—in which women collaborators, writers, translators, and directors are especially caught—underpins the book's close readings. Interwoven in these chapters is a trans-Vietnamese feminist analysis that reveals the ways betrayal and loyalty operate differently for men and women in Việt Nam and the diaspora.

The book begins by establishing the terms for how Vietnamese women are often represented in male-directed films. The movies of Vietnamese French director Tran Anh Hung (*The Scent of Green Papaya* and *Cyclo*) and Vietnamese American filmmaker Tony Bui (*Yellow Lo* *Seasons*) provide excellent examples of critically celebrat represent women as self-sacrificing figures for the nation. of Hung's and Bui's films is a feminized Việt Nam, partic ...., at the moment when the country opens its markets to capitalism. Standing in for Việt Nam is the compromised figure of the female prostitute. If women's betrayal is signed by the country's collaboration with foreign capital, however, the "problem" that women represent is covered over when the films end spectacularly—with the restoration of feminine virtue and the prostitute's redemption. But when it comes to these films, and the others that I analyze in the rest of the book, the films' characters are not the only collaborators. By emphasizing these texts and their reception, this chapter also examines how the directors themselves are collaborators in the making of diasporic films. The politics of filmmaking and collaboration we see here lay bare an important distinction in the ways men's films and women's writings have been received. Even though they collaborate with the Vietnamese government to produce and circulate their work, male filmmakers are not subject to charges of collaboration in the same way women writers are.

Unlike the way Bui and Tran privilege feminine ideals, Vietnamese American writer Le Ly Hayslip and Vietnamese French author Linda Lê treat the representation of the feminine in more unseemly terms. They employ the image of the concubine and prostitute to criticize the national family and its idealization of women. This move has led to their notoriety as collaborators and traitors in the pejorative sense. Chapter 2 interrogates how issues of collaboration undergird the production of Hayslip's co-written works and the thematic concerns of Lê's texts. Exploring Hayslip's controversial autobiographical works (*When Heaven and Earth Changed Places* and *Child of War, Woman of Peace*), this chapter focuses on how Hayslip's cowritten texts operate within the constraints of nationalist, patriarchal, and conservative political discourses. Novelist Lê writes in a similar semiautobiographical mode, but within a Vietnamese-French context. For Lê, the fluent use of the French language in her novel *Calomnies* underwrites her female protagonist's cultural betrayal of Việt Nam and illegitimacy in relation to her birthright. Juxtaposed, these two women writers and their works demonstrate that accusations of treason and allegiances of fidelity function differently not only for women and men in the diaspora but also for various classes of women.

Continuing the trope of female heroism and treason, Chapter 3 looks at the films and literature of Việt Nam's most famous male director, Đặng

Nhật Minh, and the country's most infamous woman writer, Dương Thu Hương. This chapter examines the issues of familial and political betrayals as they are found in Dương's novel, *Paradise of the Blind*. Comparing the Vietnamese, French, and English versions of this book, the chapter emphasizes how the translations are part of a collaborative practice that allows for a broader readership. As her book gains wider distribution, though, so does Dương's notorious persona as a "Communist traitor," positioning her as a highly symbolic figure for the Vietnamese state to monitor in the post-*Đổi Mới* era. The reception of Dương's novel stands in stark contrast to that of Đặng Nhật Minh's film, *Woman on the Perfume River* (1987). Along with Đặng's other films, which often feature suffering heroines, *Woman on the Perfume River* is an essential part of the country's film canon. Similar to Bui's and Tran's films, this acclaimed film also centralizes a prostitute, a former collaborator, who is ultimately disciplined and reformed by its conclusion. The chapter compares the ways that Đặng and Dương produce their works in Việt Nam, and how their identities as heroines and traitors lead these artists to be received differently by both the state and Western audiences. It ends by further interrogating Dương's troubled relations with the state and the implications of her expulsion from the Communist Party as grounds of inquiry into the nature of complicity and resistance in Vietnamese politics today.

As with Dương's book, the collaborative films of director Trinh T. Minh-ha, *Surname Viet Given Name Nam* (1989) and *A Tale of Love* (1995), bring the politics of translation to the fore and undo the representational bind of female virtue often yoked to Vietnamese womanhood. Trinh's important works, well-known in Western academic, feminist, and avant-garde film worlds, exemplify my formulation of trans-Vietnamese feminism. Through a collaborative effort with Vietnamese American women who act out the lives of Vietnamese women and then narrate their own stories in *Surname Viet*, Trinh exposes the documentary mode's over-reliance on oral testimonies and voice-giving claims, revealing the true artifice of the scaffolding upon which the genre is built. Rather than reify the film's theoretical innovations and Trinh as an auteur, however, the chapter scrutinizes the collaborative acts that constitute the film's core, an aspect of *Surname Viet* that is often overlooked in the critical scholarship surrounding Trinh's work. The film displaces the author as auteur by elaborating on women's collaborative acts. I demonstrate how a multiply-layered, women-authored collectivity decentralizes the function of the auteur and his/her objectification of the ethnographic subject in the film and its surrounding discourse. Through this reading I elucidate the

broader theoretical implications of *Surname Viet*, as th
also extend to her second film on diasporic women, *A*
chapter underlines how women's acts of translation a:
constitute the political and aesthetic grounds for trans-\
inism, which examines not only the exchange of ideas ~~ges out~~
also the power differentials overlaying such a passage.

This feminist practice extends to an examination of how Vietnamese films are increasingly collaboratively produced and transnationally
consumed. As a rejoinder to the first chapter, the last chapter of the
book investigates Vũ Ngọc Đăng's *Long-Legged Girls* (2004) and Nguyễn
Quang Dũng's *Souls on Swings* (2006), two films in which women's virtues are not tragically dramatized but playfully resituated. Exploring
the ways that scripts of gender and sexuality are being rewritten in contemporary Vietnamese films, Chapter 5 first investigates the circuitry
of gazes enacted by the women and queer characters in Vũ's hit film.
Through the film's youthful subjects who are impelled by desires for
upward mobility, not familial belonging, *Long-Legged Girls* expresses a
desire for modernity on the part of the members of a fractured national
family. In similar terms, the chapter then interrogates the body-switching
thematics found in Nguyễn Quang Dũng's popular film comedy, *Souls
on Swings*. More precisely, I analyze the performance of a Vietnamese
American actor—Johnny Trí Nguyễn, arguably Việt Nam's best-known
leading man today—who plays a gay character in the film. I investigate
the implications of his queer performance for both homeland and diaspora. The two films oppose the idea that the performance of gender and
sexuality is tied to a fetishistic identification with the national family,
the members of which can only be traitors or loyalists. On the contrary,
these directors and their work envision different subjectivities for men
and women, subjectivities that trespass the imagined borders of the
national. By ending with these texts from Việt Nam, *Treacherous Subjects* gestures toward the formation of queer identities founded within a
burgeoning, transnational Vietnamese popular culture.

The book's Conclusion takes a cue from Trinh's experimental films
and the popular movies of Vũ and Nguyễn to consider how artistic collaborations can reconfigure the dynamics of family in alternative ways.
Positing a need to rethink community politics, the Conclusion briefly
investigates the work of Vietnamese American artist Hanh Thi Pham
through collaborative practices. Pham is an example of a feminist collaborator whose artworks have drawn ire from a Vietnamese American
community. Here, I point to a pattern of how community politics often

accuses women of being traitors because they do not fulfill the role of the dutiful daughter. I examine the familial rhetoric used within an anticommunist Vietnamese American community, arguing that a trans-Vietnamese feminist mode of inquiry must consider the deep sense of loss that marks these communities and their histories. At the same time, community politics must be subject to a feminist critique for the ways that community discourses are often exclusionary in their attempt to enforce normative behaviors, especially in relation to women. Ultimately, collaborative acts are necessary in order to form communities of activists and artists that speak to the increasingly complex transnational politics underlying Việt Nam and the diaspora today. In the end, trans-Vietnamese feminism enables us to reject the binary of betrayal and loyalty entrenched in culturally nationalist discourses, rethink the accusation of collaboration, and imagine the formation of other political kin.

1 / Manufacturing Feminine Virtue: The Films of Tony Bui and Tran Anh Hung

In the mid-1990s, Hồ Chí Minh City and Hà Nội banned the use of cyclos on their main thoroughfares, restricting the vehicles to the cities' key tourist zones. Despite the prohibitions, sightseeing in a cyclo remains the tourist commodity par excellence, lavishly described in travel brochures and on websites as an obligatory experience when traveling in what is still designated as "Indochina."[1] The cyclo is a product of the colonial era, a tri-wheeled vehicle consisting of a wide, reclining chair for the passenger, slung low to the ground between the front two wheels, pedaled by a driver (always a man) mounted behind and above the passenger. While cyclos have been used by locals, they hold a particular fascination for tourists, for whom the ride can evoke a sense of colonial romance and the lingering desire to master an alien and urban landscape through an imperialist gaze. Contemporary filmmakers, well aware of the symbolic meaning of the cyclo for tourists, have used the cyclo and its driver to comment on tourism and the contradictions of Việt Nam's socialist-capitalist economy, caught at the intersections between technological advancement and devolution. This chapter examines the films of Tony Bui and Tran Anh Hung, where the cyclo and its driver have been used to drive home the wretchedness of poverty in postwar Việt Nam.

Tony Bui was a briefly lauded Vietnamese American director, while the highly acclaimed Vietnamese French director Tran Anh Hung is the most prominent director in the diaspora. Tran's *Cyclo* (1995) and Bui's *Three Seasons* (1999) are parallel films that reflect the themes and practices of collaboration, and are themselves examples of the fraught process of collaboration. To make their points, these filmmakers deploy not only the cyclo and its male driver but also the figure of the female sex worker who serves, like the cyclo driver, as a sign of wretchedness. More than this, the prostitute's sexual relations with her clientele—essentially her collaboration with foreign capital—metaphorize the country's own entrance into a market economy at the start of Đổi Mới, the era of capitalist market reforms that began in 1986. Situated in this historical context, women's bodies in such films are symbols of exploitation that critique the capitalistic forces at work in Việt Nam. My readings of these films further reveal that women's bodies are used to buttress a patriarchal ideology in which it is men who produce art and culture, while women labor to reproduce the nation and tradition. As laboring subjects, female sex workers are especially negated in this equation and must be transformed by the films' conclusions in order for them to become productive workers for the national family.

In contrast to women's bodies, men's bodies in the same films are associated with an enlightened and artistic subjectivity and do not carry a moral valence in relationship to labor. The cyclo driver is made central in these films; through his ability to see and drive the narrative, he reterritorializes for spectators the space of "Vietnam." Vis-à-vis these gendered figures, diasporic male directors recreate a "Vietnam" strongly inflected by nostalgia. With such strikingly similar characters in both films, this chapter argues that *Cyclo* and *Three Seasons* articulate a masculinist sensibility expressed at the expense of Vietnamese women's subjectivity. It analyzes *Cyclo* and *Three Seasons*, as well as two other films by these directors that take up the themes above (Bui's *Yellow Lotus* and Tran's *The Scent of Green Papaya*) to underline a specifically masculinist pattern in the ways Vietnamese womanhood has been represented in diasporic films. In these films women oscillate between the polarities of purity and impurity, depending on the nature of their sexual and domestic labors.[2]

Tran and his films use an ahistorical pattern of commemorating women's labor and discourse against the "reality" of Vietnamese quotidian life, paying visual homage to women's work along a trajectory unmarked by any changes in time and space despite the changing historical moments in which the films are set. As the director moves from a studio setting of 1950s Sài Gòn (*The Scent of Green Papaya*) to on-location shooting in present-day Việt Nam (*Cyclo*), a suspension of time-space occurs: neither women's relations with different classes of women nor their relationship to their household labor changes. *Scent* and *Cyclo* restore men and women to essentialized gender roles demarcated by

static and ahistorical concepts of feminine domesticity a
line public. They underline how the sign of woman (the en
la douceur, or softness, as Tran puts it) secures the home as
eternal haven against Vietnamese modernity's anomie.[3]

Bui's two films—a short, *Yellow Lotus* (1995), and a critica..y successful feature, *Three Seasons* (1999)—attempt to critique capitalism during
the time of Việt Nam's embrace of global capitalism. Through the use
of gendered metaphors such as the prostitute and the cyclo driver, Bui's
films also portray a country that is arrested in its development, one that
has failed to become part of the new global order in the postwar era.
The implications of this portrayal are especially troubling, as his films
often crystallize the conflation between woman and nation. Việt Nam
is an imperiled feminized nation once the forces of capitalism invade.
At the same time, these gendered metaphors illustrate how Vietnamese
Americans, in particular those in the 1.5-generation of which Bui is part,
struggle to cope with the historical weight that "Vietnam" represents.[4]

A theorization of collaboration in Bui's and Tran's films not only
exposes the relations of labor that produce the films, but also it demonstrates that the mobility of capital and the (male) diasporic subject
are historically continuous. The diasporic subject's ability to return to
the homeland, the frequency of these travels, and their relationship to
cinema is made possible by the state policy of *Đổi Mới*. I contend that
the figure of the collaborator and traitor in their works is not merely the
female sex worker but is also represented by the director himself. Bui and
Tran act as potential collaborators when they direct films in Việt Nam,
countering the anticommunist dictum from the Vietnamese diaspora
that disallowed and continues to forbid diasporans from collaborating
with the government, including touristic returns home, small business
ventures, and acts of reconciliation. The chapter emphasizes the historical and cultural import of their films while probing the contradictory
and gendered ways their films have been received. As the book contends
throughout, the critical acclaim that directors like Bui and Tran receive
stands in direct opposition to the ways in which women writers and
filmmakers must always contend with the accusations of collaboration,
a highly charged representational politics of betrayal and loyalty whose
terms for women are much more contentious than they are for men.

Interpreting Bui's and Tran's work through a trans-Vietnamese feminist lens, this chapter further critiques the deployment of gender and
sexuality by diasporic male artists. The study of collaborative practices
underlying their films makes visible the masculinist manufacturing of

feminine virtue in Vietnamese diasporic film. The chapter recognizes the critical productivity of marginalized artists like Tran and Bui who must work within dominant nation-states (the United States, France, and Việt Nam). At the same time, it emphasizes the limits of their visions, particularly in terms of their representations of gender. My trans-Vietnamese analysis investigates the use of gendered tropes and the particular investment in them within a key historical era—after the end of the war and when Việt Nam figures prominently within the West as a site for economic collaboration. The momentous opening of the homeland to the global market becomes a source of anxiety for diasporic artists, especially around the question of gender roles and laboring bodies, not the least of which are their own.

The Postcolonial Imaginary and French National Cinema

From directing in a closed-set studio in France (*The Scent of Green Papaya*) to the city streets of Việt Nam (*Cyclo* and *Vertical Ray of the Sun*), Tran Anh Hung has made major films in the context of Việt Nam's economic reforms, and he has done so with the collaboration of the Vietnamese and French national governments.[5] One outcome of Đổi Mới after 1986 was that more film projects were increasingly shot in Việt Nam, thus providing the diasporic Vietnamese subject more opportunities to make movies in the homeland. That Tran is a *Việt Kiều*, or overseas, filmmaker lends an aura of a "native" sensibility to his body of work, even for Vietnamese audiences. Thus his first film, *The Scent of Green Papaya,* was nominated by the Vietnamese government for an Oscar in the "Best Foreign Film" category upon its international release in 1994, even though it was shot entirely in a French studio. Celebrated in France as well, Tran's films have established him as the "cinéaste de la vietnamité," or the "director of Vietnamese-ness," as Sylvie Blum-Reid notes.[6]

Tran's reception and acclaim are partially due to his immigration history and France's colonial legacy, which shape how his films are produced and their visual poetics. After the war ended in 1975, Tran and his family immigrated to France. Tran's family's migration was one among many during this time. France was second to the United States in the number of Indochinese refugees it received. Because of the country's postcolonial obligation to Indochina as well as the country's own history as *une terre d'asile,* or a land of asylum, the French government constructed Indochinese refugees as "victims" and received their immigration rather favorably, which stands in contrast to France's reception of other post-colonial minorities.[7] According to cultural critic Nicola Cooper, the gesture to receive forty thousand Vietnamese refugees [in 1975] was also a way to mask the concurrent tightening of controls upon the Algerian community, whose presence and colonial legacy have been more troubling to the French nation.[8]

Two decades after the historic influx of Indochinese refugees into France, the French reception of Tran's films is crucially related to France's colonial histories and contentious racial politics, which hierarchize its ethnic minorities according to class, assimilability, and immigration history. It is impossible to speak of the Vietnamese French without referencing the ways they are positioned relative to other postcolonial populations within a racialized hierarchy, one that is marked by notions of visibility and assimilability. During a time when French immigration and citizenship laws are more exclusionary,[9] especially in their targeting of France's more "visible" minorities,[10] such as Muslims and those of Maghrebi descent, French films about Indochina reinstate the image of the Vietnamese immigrant as docile, collaborative, and grateful. Evidenced in the tremendous popularity of films like Régis Wargnier's *Indochine* (1992) and Jean-Jacques Annaud's *L'Amant* [*The Lover*] (1992), "Indochina" retains a powerful currency in the French cultural milieu as a site for ethnographic consumption and the exotic background for illicit love. As Panivong Norindr contends, the French imaginary still mourns the melancholic loss a "phantasmatic Indochina" represents for the collective psyche.[11]

French "heritage films" like *Indochine* and *L'Amant* carry symbolic and material weight within the international arena.[12] They work to resuscitate the romantic, glorious years of the French empire during a time when French national identity underwent a crisis, a situation Ien Ang diagnoses as a general European malaise.[13] Responding to a troubled French hegemony, Jack Lang's negotiations in the 1993 GATT agreements, one year after the release of *Indochine* and *The Lover*, resulted in the designation of French films as "cultural exceptions" in the face of "continuing Americanization and an encroaching Europeanization."[14] Consequently, French films are linked to France's national identity and represent unique commodities derived from French culture and history.[15] As such, they hold an ambassadorial status for French cinema and are "exceptional" to the free market in cinema.[16] In this context, wherein France's national cinema is partially subsidized, minority filmmakers find it difficult to compete and realize their projects. In order to make films, Tran must collaborate with these centers of power and funding, drawing upon a certain idea of "Vietnam" as his subject matter and relying on a unique use of camera work, color, and music as the signature for his oeuvre.

Part of this signature is Tran's use of "aesthetic distancing," whereby he recreates an intimate world in which the spectator peers into the everyday lives of the Vietnamese. A framing strategy, aesthetic distance refers to a set of filmic practices that allow a filmmaker like Tran to reproduce "the illusion of physical depth and distance in the frame and, ultimately, in the movie theater. The size of a shot, from an extreme close-up to a long shot, places the audience in a physical relationship with the subject that has psychological and, ultimately, moral implications."[17] The technique of aesthetic distance can provide an impassive gaze and foreground emotional detachment. With a seemingly objective camera, Tran creates distance between his subjects and subject matter, perhaps doing so in order to avoid *misérabilisme*, an aesthetic pejoratively associated with ethnic cultural productions produced in France that "[appear] to wallow in the disadvantaged background from which they come."[18] Film theorist Carrie Tarr maintains that filmmakers like Tran Anh Hung and Rithy Panh must contend with the issue of misérabilist representations.[19] She makes clear that the critique of French culture and its colonial history is thus a challenging project for postcolonial directors,[20] who often have to rely on government funding to make their films in an industry that sees its films as "objects of national pride."[21]

In his feature films, Tran's use of aesthetic distance is an important technique to distill excess emotionalism within the filmic frame, but it also works to set the contours of Vietnamese female subjectivity in highly aestheticized terms. What results is an idealized construction of Vietnamese femininity in such films as *The Scent of Green Papaya* and *Cyclo*. The following analysis examines these two films to underscore how Tran's films offer a masculinist expression of anxiety about gender order in the era of Đổi Mới. Tran's films often pay tribute to tradition through the figure of woman, while they simultaneously commemorate the production of art in Việt Nam's commercial economy through the male artist. Women in his films are docile workers who serve the national family or sex workers who cannot find their place in the national family. Tran's representations of gender, and specifically of motherhood, inadvertently collude with state discourses about women's roles in the postwar era.

Exploiting the Feminine Ideal in *The Scent of Green Papaya*

Due to logistical miscalculations and problems with on-location shooting, Tran directed his first major film entirely in a French studio—without the collaboration of the Vietnamese government. The movie won the prestigious Prix de la Camera d'Or for Best First Feature Film at the Cannes Film Festival in 1993, firmly establishing Tran as a major director. In France, it registered 340,958 entries in movie theaters when it opened.[22] The film grossed $1.91 million in the United States, a significant amount for a foreign film.[23] Claiming the film as a Vietnamese product because of the director's national origins, the Vietnamese government nominated the film in the Oscar's "Best Foreign Film" category, but it did not win. *Scent* remains Tran's most successful film in terms of box-office receipts and awards. Because of its critical acclaim, the film paved the way for him to later shoot his next two films, *Cyclo* and *Vertical Ray of the Sun,* in Việt Nam. The film's success in France and Việt Nam can be attributed at least partially to Tran's neutralization of political history, roughly two decades after the trauma of the American War. Aligned with this impetus, the film posits an eternally youthful and feminine ideal; she is the ideal laboring subject who works for the cohesion of the (national) family and understands her place within the domestic space.

A narrative about female maturation, the film centers on the story of Mùi (her name means "scent" in Vietnamese), an inquisitive young girl sent to work in a middle-class household in Sài Gòn. Except for the occasional sounds of air raids and allusions to military curfews, Tran's movie literally represents a closed set that does not directly deal with the anticolonial resistance. It presents an idealization of wartime Việt Nam from the perspective of a member of the peasant class in the 1950s. With its tight narrative focus on the family, the film ideologically contains the historical conflicts between the Vietnamese peasant and elite classes. Refusing to retell the history of the Franco-Vietnamese war, which culminated in the 1954 Điện Biên Phủ victory, the film traffics instead in the images of Vietnamese femininity and female bonding. A sense of enclosure surrounding the women, for example, operates through the camera's focused compositional framing of its subjects. Most of the film is shot in slow pans, the camera moving from left to right and vice versa within the confined space of two middle-class homes. Tran uses a technique of *plan-séquence* in an attempt to relay "the connections between things and the passing of one idea to the next—softly."[24] Bathed in symbolic coloring (greens, blues, and yellows) and artificial lighting, his simulacrum of Vietnamese everyday life is registered through a stationary camera and a series of balanced shots emphasizing the film's focus on interiority and intimacy.

Narratively and visually, *The Scent of Green Papaya* emphasizes an instinctive closeness between women, which transcends class and age. Though the film includes an understanding of class structure and tries to orient camera angles to approximate the servants' perspectives, *Scent* also undermines this focalization, positing women's suffering as universal and transcendent of class boundaries. In an interview, Tran says he tried "to make a film based on the experiences of my mother. I wanted to show how the servitude of women transforms itself into a form of self-sacrifice."[25] Indeed, Tran's film pays tribute to Vietnamese women laboring, suffering, and submitting to their tasks gracefully. This is true for both the peasant women in the household and for the family's middle-class matriarch. After her profligate husband abandons the family, the dignified mother suffers silently, awaiting his return. The film aestheticizes the silent suffering women undergo and essentially ties suffering to the loss or pain of romantic, heterosexual love. Though Mùi's suffering differs from the matriarch's because of their class differences, their suffering is fundamentally the same: love represents servitude for women of any class. After Mùi reaches adulthood in the second half of the film, she becomes essentially mute, remaining innocent and defined by her love for Khuyên, a young classical pianist, who later employs her. In the rare moments when a subjectivizing perspective sutures the spectator's viewing to Mùi's gaze, the object of that gaze is the food she devotedly prepares to serve her lover, their relationship representing the (literal) fruit of her labor.

In the film women also undergo a process of reeducation by the film's conclusion. The nature of women's education, marked by an entrance into language and narrative, is a key element in Tran's film. Mùi's transformation in the conclusion occurs when Mùi's lover teaches her how to read and write, the extended sequence stressing her induction into voice, narrative, and discourse. Here, Tran emphasizes the power imbalance between the two lovers. The dictation of Vietnamese texts and her lover's correction of her posture while they sit—teacher and student, master and servant—reinscribe the pedagogical act of teaching gender *and* class performance (see Fig. 1–1). The final image shows how this form of instruction is complete, featuring Mùi, who wears a traditional yellow *áo dài*, Việt Nam's national costume. Reading aloud from a Vietnamese textbook, the pregnant Mùi seems delighted with her condition as she reads from a poem by Natsume Soseki. When the camera pans up to end the film, she becomes a reflection of the smiling

FIGURE 1.1. Teaching Mùi class and gender performance. From the film *The Scent of Green Papaya* © 1993. Lazennec Films, SFP Cinema, La Sept Cinéma, Canal+, Centre National de la Cinématographie (CNC), Procirep, Fondation GAN pour le Cinéma, Ministère de la Culture et de la Communication, Sacem.

religious deity above her. The abrupt ending of the film alludes to a sense of mysticism about womanhood. In a singular fluid camera movement, Tran emphasizes the pregnant and placid beauty inherent in women's bodies.[26]

Tran's predominant themes are about women's transformations. In his films' conclusions, women are re-formed either bodily (as in *Scent*) or existentially (as in *Cyclo*). For women, Tran's films map a return to innocence, a return that is situated within the domestic space. Central to the concept of domestic femininity is the figure of woman, played by Tran's wife, Trần Nữ Yến-Khê, the ingénue in most of Tran's films. Her casting remains crucial, because she visually reiterates the themes of pleasure and desire unifying his work.[27] An eroticized object, the simply coiffed actress is swathed in silk and performs a language of gestures on film. The camera habitually gazes upon her in medium and full close-ups. Its impassive, frontal angles emphasize the flatness of the painterly tableaux centrally featuring her as a narrative subject. The objectivity of the camera's monocular perspective is sustained and lends an anchored but idealized focus to the narrative. According to Steven Neale, the camera's perspective provides stability to both the real and the ideal. He writes, "What must be crucially emphasized is that the ideal of a steady position, of a unique embracing center is precisely that: a powerful ideal."[28]

Because this ideal is often situated in the home, Tran's films reinforce the domestic containment of women and strip their labor of political content.[29] During the major wars marking twentieth-century Vietnamese history, female labor was a deeply political construct, particularly in rural settings where some women participated in the workplace, the household, and sometimes on the battlefields. In postwar Việt Nam, the role of women's labor in both private and public spaces has had an enormous impact on the country's socioeconomic development, as women constitute 60 percent of the labor force,[30] and they perform an overwhelming majority of household tasks within the home.[31] In times of war and peace, Vietnamese women, as generals of the home, or nội tướng, are doubly charged, obligated to manage the household finances as well as defend against the invasion of foreign influences and forces. The metaphor of political participation about women (as "ministers of the interior") is ironic because of the decreasing rates of women in political office. But the metaphor is also fitting, describing women's proscribed roles in the space of the private and public for the (national) family. Though these details about women's historical conditions are not meant to reveal a truer reality to which Scent is diametrically opposed, I expose, nonetheless, a reliance on authenticity in Tran's use of women's bodies and the Vietnamese quotidian. Referents for the "real" are mostly rooted in women's procreative abilities and the unchanging nature of their domestic work.

With Cyclo, however, Tran disrupts the theme of women's work to stage a radically different portrait of contemporary Sài Gòn as a place of capitalistic desire and violence, where modernity and tradition are jagged counterparts. Nonetheless, a preoccupation with the division of gendered spaces still predominates. While Trần Nữ Yến-Khê's embodied presence in Scent is a signifier for an idealized construction of tradition, in Tran's next film, Cyclo, her body is more of a passive site for the acting out of perversion and fantasy against the backdrop of a Vietnamese xã hội đen, or Mafioso society. Because of the degradations she undergoes as a sex worker, she must also be spiritually reborn by the end of the film. At the crux of both Scent and Cyclo Vietnamese women and their bodies are freighted with the symbolism of purity.

Cyclo and the Body-in-Transition

Released in 1995, *Cyclo* was a highly anticipated film, but it opened to mixed reviews in several national contexts. In France, it registered only 167,298 entries nationwide; in Paris, it was in only thirteen theaters for a total of fourteen weeks.[32] Even so, the film won the Golden Lion Award in Venice in 1995. The Vietnamese government, however, after authorizing the on-location shooting of the film, banned its release because of its graphic depiction of the "social ills" plaguing Vietnamese urban life.[33] Việt Nam's acclaimed director Đặng Nhật Minh[34] and film critic Ngô Phương Lan both argue that Vietnamese audiences find Tran's films to be inauthentic and marked by a Western sensibility.[35] The lack of critical acclaim and the Vietnamese government's rejection of the film are not the only ways in which *Cyclo* contrasts with *Scent*: *Cyclo* had a bigger budget, was shot on location, and used a distinctive mélange of filmic styles. Tran leaves behind the static camera technique of his first film, utilizing instead some neorealist techniques—hand-held cameras, nonprofessional actors, and on-site location shooting—to relay the energy of Sài Gòn's urban life. Juxtaposed against *Scent*, *Cyclo* shows the effects of collaboration, which failed to garner praise from many in or outside Việt Nam. Despite such differences, these two films share a striking continuity in the ways that women are portrayed in his films; they are laborers whose purity pivots on their sexuality.

Cyclo is also dedicated to Tran's father, while *The Scent of Green Papaya* was dedicated to his mother. The film explores the loss of paternal and, by extension, state authority. Its narrative traces the moral devolution of three principal characters, named for their occupations in the film: Cyclo, Prostitute, and Poet, all of whom yield to the lure of money, specifically American dollars. The film opens with close-up shots of the cyclo driver while he bicycles through the city. His father's voice-over informs us of the father's death in a traffic accident several months earlier. A cyclo driver himself, the father left nothing for his family as an inheritance. These introductory narrative details set the stage for Tran's scathing criticisms of the capitalistic forces at work in Việt Nam and the socialist bureaucracy that does not help its people and youth. Tran's critique exposes the gaps between the country's market economy and the socialist values upon which the country was founded. The film effectively reveals the US dollar's corrupting effects on the bodies of sex workers and common laborers. Although capital may be fluid in the new economy, Tran demonstrates that laboring bodies are not mobile, exemplifying this point in an unedited long take showing the transfer of a dollar bill in a flowing circuitry of hands and crime.[36]

Cyclo's suffering body most succinctly delivers Tran's point about the alienation of the young, postwar generation of Việt Nam. The further he involves himself with Sài Gòn's underbelly, the more deformations his body undergoes; the urban corruption exacerbated by Đổi Mới is externalized through Cyclo's body. Comparable to Bui's version of the cyclo driver in *Three Seasons*, Cyclo's boyish body is revealed half-nude in key scenes as a central visual leitmotif and embodies Việt Nam during its period of renovation. Yet, unlike the main character in Bui's movie who serves as the moral center of a Manichean film, Tran's version of a cyclo driver is visibly scarred and underdeveloped. This further reinforces how the character, played by a young, nonprofessional actor, functions as a visual metaphor for Việt Nam's arrested development: he represents the desires of Vietnamese youths struggling to survive within the commodity-oriented economy of Sài Gòn.

Displayed in various states of unnaturalness, Cyclo's body is painted blue, dipped in black, grainy mud, smothered, contorted, and tortured throughout the film by a vicious gang of thugs. In several scenes dealing with small animals, the character places goldfish and geckos in his body's orifices; done in objectifying extreme close-ups, the scenes attempt to visualize the alienation and deviancy he experiences under capitalism. As a sign of the oppressed laboring masses, however, he mostly lacks individuality throughout the film. The camera tends to gaze directly downward upon his figure or frame him against the bustling city, rendered in faraway angles to underscore his anonymity and the objectification of his labor. Yet it is through the privileging of Cyclo's body and the reification of the tools of his labor (his cyclo and dirt-encrusted slippers are magnified in key scenes) that we apprehend the value of labor and the decline in morality marking Việt Nam's momentous transition to a market economy.

As a parallel to Cyclo's moral decline, foreign currency, in its multiple exchanges, becomes the breeding ground for sadistic perversions. The Prostitute (Cyclo's sister) undergoes a series of bizarre encounters with her fetishistic customers, culminating in a sadomasochistic interaction with a Chinese-Vietnamese customer who lacerates her wrists and robs her of her virginity. He rapes her for a large amount of money, an act that precipitates a drawn-out murder sequence between her pimp and the john. The different corporeal transformations that Cyclo and Prostitute experience under capitalism reveal how Tran aestheticizes violence differently, according to essentialized notions of gender. With the character of the Prostitute, Tran emphasizes how her character is not uncontradictorily both pure and impure. Such is the ideal of femininity that aligns this film with *Scent*.

Key shots in the film exemplify this stylization of the gendered forms of violence that Cyclo and Prostitute undergo. After engaging in a brutal criminal act, Cyclo submerges his face in a fish tank. When he pulls away from the water, the movement glides from right to left because Tran's camera is positioned so that Cyclo's vertical movement reads horizontally on the screen (see Fig. 1–2). Executed in slow-motion, the scene shows the water's pull of gravity as it flows from the right side of the screen to the left, which works to disorient and defamiliarize the viewer's sense of perspective. Symbolically, the unnatural action marks the character and his acts as aberrant within the diegesis, but the scene also signals Tran's own deviation from a neorealist mode of filmmaking and establishes his unique visual style. Following this shot, which stressed the horizontal design of the fish tank on the right of the screen, is a match cut with the body of the Prostitute, engaged in a fetishistic fantasy with one of her customers. In contrast to Cyclo's criminal behavior, Prostitute's actions are still rendered wholesome; she wears white underwear and moves in a halo of light in this scene (see Fig. 1–3).

The match cut delineates the gendered spaces of violence and harmony operating in the city. Up until her rape, Prostitute, played by Trần Nữ Yến-Khê, is central to the film's realization of innocence and harmony. Tran's images of female bonding also relay this sense of harmony, illustrated in the relationship between Prostitute and two other sex workers. In an extended sequence, underpinned by a return to childish innocence, the three women frolic in the small room where they are kept, dousing one another with buckets of water. The sequence of scenes follows the trio to a bed where they eat papayas, at which point one of the women declares she may be pregnant. She quickly denies it, but her statement elicits ecstatic cries and laughing between the women. (Not coincidentally, *Vertical Ray of the Sun* also features similar scenes with a trio of sisters, one of whom falsely declares herself pregnant.) Tran's films often feature recurring images of young women who find themselves on the brink of maturation. Visualized through the leitmotif of ripe, exotic fruit, the scenes with the three prostitutes relay women's desires for a return to innocence but also for procreative maturity.[37]

As performed by Trần Nữ Yến-Khê, the youthful muse in most of Tran's films, Prostitute is imbued with sexual innocence and purity, even though she is a sex worker. Within much of Tran's work, feminine labor performed by women is celebrated as deeply fulfilling and naturalized as maternal

FIGURE 1.2. The character of Cyclo and the gendering of spaces in Việt Nam. From the film *Cyclo* © 1995. Canal+, Centre National de la Cinématographie (CNC), Cofimage 5, Cofimage 6, Giải Phóng Film Studio, La Sept Cinéma, Les Productions Lazennec, Lumière, Salon Films, Société Française de Production (SFP).

within the home's confines. But for those characters who are engaged in sex work, like the prostitutes in the film, they are women who can return to innocence in their childlike play with one another. For Prostitute most particularly, she is transformed in the film's concluding frames wherein the loss of her feminine virtue is reinstalled. As prostitutes, Vietnamese women symbolically represent a capitalist Việt Nam that has opened itself to a market economy. For women to be redeemed within this new economy, they must return to a prior, purer state. In *Cyclo*, Prostitute's final scenes speak to this impetus. Shot in blues and grays, these haunting scenes take place on the morning after Poet has immolated himself. Prostitute mourns Poet at a public park after she has been praying at a community altar and was pick-pocketed. At the park, Prostitute meets a mother and her son in a scene that sutures both past and present together. The boy is a reminder of the boy that Poet used to be. More importantly, serving as an evocation of a melancholic but nostalgic past, the figure of the mother is dressed in a traditional *áo dài* and coiffed with a slight bouffant hairstyle (see Fig. 1–4). This mother is the appropriate feminine ideal for Prostitute. Seeing this woman, the spectral substitute for all the loving mothers in the film, provides the necessary

FIGURE 1.3. From violence to harmony: the character of the Prostitute and the match cut. From the film *Cyclo* © 1995. Canal+, Centre National de la Cinématographie (CNC), Cofimage 5, Cofimage 6, Giải Phóng Film Studio, La Sept Cinéma, Les Productions Lazennec, Lumière, Salon Films, Société Française de Production (SFP).

closure for Prostitute to reconcile with her loss and sets up the premise that she will perhaps leave sex work behind.

Looking at the other characters in the film places in relief the moralizing imperative of Prostitute's transformation. The emotional and material linkage between women in the film is Poet (played by Hong Kong actor Tony Leung Chiu-Wai), who serves as the prostitutes' pimp and embodies the true flâneur of the city. Oscillating between scenes of lush beauty with women and scenes of brutal violence with men, the film establishes the domains of gender that dichotomize the city and further stresses that it is only Poet who is able to negotiate and trespass these oppositional spaces in what Do and Tarr argue is "Tran's Manichean vision of the city."[38] It follows that Poet's sacrificial death--through the dramatic act of immolation--is necessary for the film's narrative closure. Concentrating upon the figure of the male poet here, I find a striking symmetry between this film and Bui's *Three Seasons*. In the latter, the leper poet is also anguished about the commodification of art and literature in Sài Gòn. With *Cyclo*, despite the ambivalent morality of the Poet, his tragic melancholia and martyrdom are similarly underscored, so that his death symbolizes rebirth and renewal as well. In both *Cyclo* and

FIGURE 1.4. The Prostitute and the maternal ideal. From the film *Cyclo* ©
1995. Canal+, Centre National de la Cinématographie (CNC), Cofimage
5, Cofimage 6, Giải Phóng Film Studio, La Sept Cinéma, Les Productions
Lazennec, Lumière, Salon Films, Société Française de Production (SFP).

Three Seasons, the figure of the poet eloquently argues for the role of art in
the marketplace and mourns its death. An estranged figure that must be
gendered male, the poet consolidates the critique of capitalism for the two
filmmakers, standing as a marker of true art in an era of globalization.

Like Poet, Boss Lady, who controls the employment of Poet and Cyclo,
is also able to transcend the boundaries of class. In contrast to the paternal spiritual presence of Cyclo's father, images of her effectively banish the
soft maternal imagery found in *The Scent of Green Papaya*. Played by Như
Quỳnh, a well-regarded Vietnamese actress, this matriarch is strongly
figured as an emasculating mother, her transgressions signaled when she
smokes a cigarette, brutalizes a male servant, and has sexual relations with
Poet. As punishment for her transgressive behavior, however, she must
struggle to care for a mentally handicapped son as a single mother and is
firmly restricted from moving outside of the private domain to the public.
Constantly framed within the home, she is such an anomalous figure that
her illegal and morally corrupt actions only make sense in the underworld,
rendering her character ultimately confined to this unnatural space. Her
containment emphasizes the freedom that Cyclo and his family experience
at the end of the film when he is released from her grasp. Consequently
the film's dreamlike conclusion ends where it begins—with an homage

to the legacy of the father. The last scenes of the film feature images of movement that guide viewers into the future, albeit an uncertain one: the reborn Cyclo undertakes to lead his family (grandfather and two sisters), all of whom are dressed in white, on his cyclo into an open urban space, free of criminal pollutants and noticeably absent of Boss Lady's influence. If Cyclo embodies Việt Nam's violent transition to a market economy, then the transformation of Vietnamese society requires the reestablishment of a potent paternal heritage. In this final scene, it is clear that the difference between Cyclo and Prostitute's transformations hinges upon gender. While Prostitute is haunted by the ideal mother of the past, Cyclo drives the family and their cyclo toward an uncertain future, one that forecloses the bad mother's malingering force.

Reinforcing traditional constructs of gender, Tran's films praise the dignity of good mothering and thus uneasily align themselves with contemporary Vietnamese political discourses that seek to return women to motherhood following some of their treacherous wartime roles as prostitutes, informants, propagandists, and guerrilla soldiers. Even though his films have had a mixed reception in Việt Nam, they still disconcertingly speak to the official culture's insistence that women's main contribution to the war effort was primarily symbolic as "heroic mothers."[39] Whereas Việt Nam's national culture emphasizes the respected role of the self-sacrificing, older maternal figure, Tran describes motherhood in terms of youthful ignorance and feminine innocence, a figuration of femininity that is found in both *Scent* and *Cyclo*. Operating within a nationalist paradigm that hierarchically assigns symbolic value to men and women and the spheres of labor, Tran's films dovetail with a current reassertion of Vietnamese revisionist sentiment that subordinates the issues of Vietnamese women's labor and emphasizes instead the largely maternal role they play in the reconstruction of the nation.

As I demonstrate in the following section, the image of woman as pure or impure subject is not isolated to the Vietnamese French context and its particular mode of nostalgia. For Vietnamese American director Tony Bui, a gendered construct of Việt Nam is a motif that threads together his short and feature films. Besides the analysis of gender, my readings of Bui's work demonstrate how the mobility of capital and the (male) diasporic subject is historically contiguous. The male diasporic subject's ability to return to the homeland, the frequency of these travels, and their relationship to cinema is made possible by the state policy of Đổi Mới and the changed relations between the United States and Việt Nam in the early 1990s.

Three Seasons: Remaking Masculinity and the Vietnam War Film

Four years after *Cyclo* was released, Tony Bui's *Three Seasons* features a similar cast of characters: prostitutes, poets, and cyclo drivers. But while the film shares the same thematic concerns and preoccupations with gender found in Tran's films, *Three Seasons* positions itself more firmly as a product issuing from a US cultural and political milieu. As a result, the modes of production and spectatorial address are different. Unlike Tran's work, Bui's films directly respond to Hollywood's Vietnam War film and strive to revise past representations of Vietnamese masculine subjectivity. Bui uses both men's and women's bodies to critique Hollywood versions of the Vietnam War but in ways that largely stress how women operate solely as symbols of vice or virtue, authenticity or inauthenticity. In this configuration, female sex workers in *Three Seasons* are traitors to their truer selves, while models of virtuous femininity are docile women laborers.

When *Three Seasons* was released in 1999, the film was promoted as the first American movie shot in Việt Nam since the war's end. The film has been recognized internationally, winning awards at the Sundance, Cannes, and Havana film festivals. When the film was internationally released, the Vietnamese American community also embraced it. The glossy magazine *25 Years of 25 Vietnamese Americans* recognizes *Three Seasons* as an important film for the community, marking the artistic achievements of "one of its own" and representing the community's cultural productivity.[40] In the US context especially, the film serves many ideological ends, particularly relating to the thematic of overcoming adversity. As a necessary counterpoint to American films like *Rambo*, *Three Seasons* gestures toward a humanization of the Other in Vietnam War films and is imbued with a post–Cold War logic. Spliced together, the film's four stories instruct a Western audience about the defeat of communist ideology with the triumph of human will and the possibility of redemption in poverty-ridden Việt Nam, the first country to defeat the United States in its war against communism.

Bui is a member of the 1.5 Vietnamese American generation that perhaps grew up watching highly lauded films like *Apocalypse Now* (1979), *Platoon* (1986), and *Full Metal Jacket* (1987), which routinely featured Vietnamese subjects as faceless victims, prostitutes, and snipers. Bui's own film is inevitably tied to Hollywood's Vietnam War film. Shortly after *Three Seasons* was released, *LA Times* journalist John Balzar brought

Oliver Stone and Bui together for an interview. The article compares the two as filmmakers who share a similar project, but who come from vastly different backgrounds. (Stone's *Heaven and Earth* was released in 1993.) They are asked to give their visions of contemporary Việt Nam. Most emphatically, as Bui argues, his film attempts to "give a different vision of Vietnam . . . to defend it."[41] Bui takes this defensive position to counter Hollywood films that portrayed the Vietnamese negatively. In his films, Bui plots a different trajectory for the Vietnamese. Rather than stage the multiple deaths or the symbolic death of the Vietnamese, his short film *Yellow Lotus* (1995) and *Three Seasons* feature humanist, sensitive, and enlightened male subjects who continue to forge ahead in their future, despite the odds.

Remaking the Vietnam War film, Bui reclaims Vietnamese masculinity in the American imagination. His films stage the vitality of the Vietnamese male body and revise the effeminacy and sense of impotence marking representations of Vietnamese men who stand in contrast to the white soldier.[42] The male characters in his two films represent an embodied anchor for the critique of American capitalism and are played by Bui's uncle, the Vietnamese actor Đơn Dương. In *Three Seasons* especially, the male cyclo driver is invigorated by moral strength and a strong physical presence in opposition to the emotionally disabled and broken body of the American veteran seeking spiritual guidance (played by Harvey Keitel). These two male characters are both pivotal in the movie, yet the Vietnamese male body possesses an enlightened and artistic aura and guides the film along its narrative trajectory. In the film's storyline, he alone helps to enlighten the women workers about their own labor. In contrast to these male characters, women alternate between two types of characters, representing a degraded form of labor (as in prostitution) or an exalted form of menial labor (as in flower trading).

Political contexts also shape Bui's films and their representations of gender, for example the period of Clintonian politics and the reinstatement of US-Việt Nam relations in the 1990s. Within this decade, the presidencies of both George H. W. Bush and Bill Clinton signaled a move away from the swaggering masculinity defined by Ronald Reagan and his celluloid counterpart, Rambo, in the 1980s. As many critics have noted, one of the lasting consequences of the Vietnam War has been the reparation of patriarchy and American political power after losing a war to a third world country.[43] By the early 1990s, a "kinder, gentler" construction of masculinity focused on family values and the role of the father,[44] the vectors of which formed the platform for the conservative Right and its use of the paternal figure of George H. W. Bush. Led by Bush, the first Persian Gulf War was tightly managed and closely monitored in order to avoid the paralysis of the "Vietnam Syndrome." As Marita Sturken argues, this syndrome "was an image of emasculation, a 'disease' that prevented the government from displaying strength."[45] The result was a technologized and sanitized war, importantly choreographed through the media as victorious and swift to counter the images of death and destruction of the Vietnam War.[46] Even so, Susan Jeffords contends that constructs of masculinity did not change during Bush's administration but were merely reworked to better suit the state of world politics in a post–Cold War era.[47]

When Bill Clinton succeeded Bush in 1992, the image of American masculinity shifted to reflect a youthful and dynamic understanding of global economics and post–Cold War geopolitics. After the 1989 demise of the Soviet Union, the Clinton administration strove to establish good relations with its former communist enemy, Việt Nam. In 1994, Clinton lifted the nearly twenty-year-old US trade embargo against Việt Nam, and in the following year, he formally normalized trade between the two countries. In 1999, the United States and Việt Nam signed the Bilateral Trade Agreement, which provided the US greater market access to Việt Nam's industrial and agricultural goods and services and legal protection of US investments in Việt Nam. Advancing global capitalism and publicizing American goodwill at home and abroad, Clinton's trip to Việt Nam in 2000 heralded a new phase of US-Việt Nam relations. Clinton's visit was especially symbolic because he had avoided the draft during the war. Before leaving office, Clinton formalized a historic series of trade agreements with the Vietnamese government, establishing a strong foothold in the country's economy. While Reagan wanted to revive the memory of "Vietnam" to bolster US militarism amid threats of nuclear war with the Soviet Union, the Clinton administration's dealings with the Vietnamese socialist government were deftly ideological and economically motivated.[48] They sought to pave the way for economic collaborations with Việt Nam through the discourse of reconciliation and healing.

In this milieu of post–Cold War reconciliation, Bui's films pivot on the historic regeneration of relations linking the United States and Việt Nam, as they were managed by a younger head-of-state who embodied a vital, political masculinity. This construct of masculinity—as a responsive and introspective masculine figure similar to the ways that Clinton presented himself as a public persona—limns the portrayal of

Bui's leading male characters: they are simultaneously physically capable and deeply concerned with their roles within the family. Revising the hypermasculinity found in the *Rambo* series, Bui creates Vietnamese male characters defined by both masculine strength and sensitivity. This recreation of Vietnamese masculinity is best exemplified in Bui's student thesis film, *Yellow Lotus* (1995).

Yellow Lotus and the Fantasy of the Feminine

Both of Bui's films exhibit masculinist anxieties about the vitiation that Việt Nam undergoes in the period of Đổi Mới and the changes wrought by a profound reorganization of gender roles. At the core of his films is a vision of a pure Vietnamese woman who represents the premarket economy, a nostalgic and pristine notion of the nation-state. Configured by Manichean oppositions, Bui's films represent Western investment and enterprise as evil forces pitted against a vulnerable and feminized Việt Nam. Exemplifying this notion, the preface for *Yellow Lotus* provides the historical context for the film's narrative, as it takes place during Đổi Mới, which Bui represents through a gendered metaphor. The open market becomes a sign of the feminine, signaling the corruption and decadence that accompany American-style capitalism.

Yellow Lotus demonstrates these ideas from the beginning. It opens with picturesque shots of Việt Nam's rural landscape: birds flying across a lake and green, expansive rice fields. The next sequence of images, framed in both medium and long shots, features an anonymous young woman with long, black hair. She is dressed in a white *áo dài*. The mise-en-scène positions her on one side of the screen; her back is to the spectator, while the landscape is imaged on the other side. The tableau flattens out the woman's body against the background, crystallizing her alignment with nature. To render this idea more pointedly, the film never reveals the woman's perspective, nor does she speak or interact with the other characters. As a way to inaugurate and end the film, the woman's images serve as signifiers for a bucolic, timeless "Vietnam," notably before the forces of foreign investment "invade" the country. Following the visually and aurally harmonious scenes of the Vietnamese woman, we cut to a flock of white geese being released at a farmer's gate. Through a visual match, the film's climax in which women in white *áo dài* flow down a street on bicycles will echo the white of the geese.

An integral aspect of this short film is the way that it focuses upon the physicality and strength of the Vietnamese male body. The main character appears half-naked or nude at several points, his unclothed and muscular Vietnamese body pictured in both rest and labor. In marked contrast to the ways in which Hollywood films usually portray Vietnamese men as the faceless enemy, Bui imbues Vietnamese masculinity with an earthy eroticism. Filmed in static medium shots, the male body embodies a resilient force, housing a soul with an artistic vision the protagonist longs to express. The film also asks us to identify with the male character. After the opening scenes of the Vietnamese woman, the film offers a tight close-up of Đơn Dương's face as he plays a recently widowed peasant trying to survive in Sài Gòn as an artist.

An alienated subject, the male artist evokes a wounded but ultimately regenerative masculinity. Mostly the reparation of Vietnamese masculinity, premised on moral courage, responds to American representations of Vietnamese men as feminized. A key scene exemplifies such a dynamic. The protagonist plucks a yellow lotus out of a pond and runs to an all-girls school to give it to a young woman he had seen in the streets several days before, the same woman featured in the film's opening sequence. Indicative of Bui's idealized vision, a flock of women leaving the school trample the bloom at the moment when he accidentally drops it on the ground. With crumpled flower in hand, Dương searches until he finds the woman in a classroom. By positioning Dương in a classroom filled with young women who mock him, Bui portrays the idealized artist, his talents and services wasted in Việt Nam's new economy. The film's last scene offers a dream sequence epitomizing Bui's optimism: the woman in the white *áo dài* accepts the yellow lotus and smiles with gratitude. What was disabled and crushed is restored in the end; the lotus survives, if only in his dreams, reviving many things deemed important for the male artist—his confidence, will to continue, artistic vision, and manhood.

In contrast to his examination of Vietnamese masculinity, Bui constructs a Vietnamese femininity in purely visual terms. Against a lush backdrop, his female protagonist is dressed in a white *áo dài* and exudes a youthful innocence. Because she does not speak, this protagonist remains an enigma and a muse for the main character. She also becomes readily and sexually available. In one of the artist's dream sequences, the camera offers the spectacle of the female body as she bathes in the woods, allowing spectators scopophilic access to the body of a young, nude Vietnamese woman. Ideologically, women's relationship to nature is further epitomized in this extradiegetic fashion. The dream sequences are, lastly, signposts for the protagonist's subjectivity; they not only naturalize our gaze with his but also concretize his active imagination.

Eschewing point-of-view and perspective shots for most of his female characters, Bui reconfigures the Vietnam War movie but disavows women's subjectivity in his films. Following a post-Orientalism critique, Rey Chow argues that much critical work has attempted to recuperate the subjectivity of the once-colonized, a turn that merely reverses the terms of power.[49] Denouncing Malek Alloula's rewriting of French colonialism's appropriative use of Algerian women in postcards, Chow argues that this rewriting only objectifies the women again in Alloula's own discourse. Alloula's images thus allow for a second, penetrating gaze that gives way to a retaliatory gesture between male colonizer and male colonized. As a result a symmetry between imperialist and nonimperialist gazes "cross[es] over onto the images of women as silent objects."[50] Similarly, Bui's representation of the Vietnamese female subject as silent object becomes subjected to an objectifying gaze, one that does not portray them as prostitutes or snipers, but nonetheless performs the same irrevocable damage for the question of Vietnamese female subjectivity.

In both *Yellow Lotus* and *Three Seasons*, the representations of Vietnamese women are integral to the films' citation of the "real." Dressed in either white *áo dài* or simple peasant outfits, these women evoke culturally nationalistic concepts of tradition and heritage, naturalized as part of the films' tableaux. Like Tran, Bui pays tribute to the virtues of female suffering against the backdrop of contemporary Việt Nam. More robustly than Tran, however, Bui invokes women's labor as a vital element in his critique of capitalist exploitation. Women operate as bodies through which Bui enacts a nostalgic elegy for the death of tradition at the advent of *Đổi Mới*. Bui further circumscribes female subjectivity by rarely allowing his women characters to instigate or participate in the "looking relations" of the film.[51] The male character's perspective guides the spectator, melding his view with the privileged eye of the camera. As in *Yellow Lotus*, the point-of-view shots in *Three Seasons* also emphasize the ideological position of the movie in terms of gender. Unlike their female counterparts, male characters in *Three Seasons* undergo extreme crises as laboring bodies, marked by physical exertion and spiritual angst. These men are the moral and emotional focal points with whom viewers are asked to identify and through whom audiences apprehend the realities of postwar Việt Nam. Consolidating a masculinist perspective, the film asks the question: How should men and women labor for the country? *Three Seasons* responds to this question with a patriarchal vision of how gender roles in contemporary Việt Nam should be.

Spectacles of Womanhood: Female Traders and Traitors in *Three Seasons*

After Vietnamese officials granted him permission to film *Three Seasons*, twenty-seven-year-old Bui needed to construct a character's elaborate home, one surrounded by lotus flowers. Unable to find a lotus pond, Bui built one by growing ten thousand lotus bushes in a muddy field. With greater irony, he unrooted the actual blooms and substituted them with white plastic ones when they began withering.[52] This site serves as the home of a leper poet, a character based on renowned Vietnamese writer Hàn Mặc Tử. The film's biographic focus on Hàn Mặc Tử, however, transcends the poet's life to include a fictionalized relationship with Kiến An, one of the many female workers he employs to tend to the lotuses and sell them in the city.

As the only woman endowed with the ability to look in the film, Kiến An's character is fundamental to the film's elegiac denouement. Most importantly, she is mobilized to realize Bui's homage to female filial piety. The film begins when Kiến An, a young peasant woman, is hired as part of a group of lotus-blossom pickers employed by the leper poet. Bui frames Kiến An against the expansiveness and beauty of the pond, in the same way he choreographed the opening scene from *Yellow Lotus*: we are presented with Kiến An's back as she stands against the verdant landscape. This time, however, even with the requisite long, black hair, Kiến An's body signifies more than schoolgirl innocence. She wears peasant clothing: black pants and a shirt called an *aó bà ba*, a simple, collarless chemise made of either cotton or light silk. Represented through her clothing, Kiến An's inherent goodness is squarely located in the countryside, her modest ways signified by her clothing and Vietnamese folk singing.

Kiến An's naive innocence is a symbol contrasting with the allure of the city. Pictured through Bui's camera, she is profoundly disjunctive when placed against the urban space of Sài Gòn. In a prolonged sequence, she appears lost in the bustling city when she finds that no one is buying her employer's flowers; instead, the locals flock to a vendor selling scented fakes. Although we understand that Kiến An's real flowers are not wanted, Bui refuses to invest her with a sense of knowing. As Kiến An looks at her competitor and with an eyeline-match shot, we see the truck selling the fake flowers. In the next shot, she enters from the left side of the frame and buys a fake flower from the same vendor. Smelling the flower, she does not realize the import of what is transpiring until Hải, a cyclo driver, explains that the flowers are not, in fact, real. He adds that they are extremely popular in today's market, and then disapprovingly remarks: "People have been giving into their conveniences. . . . [The fake flowers] won't wilt or die. They even spray the flowers to make them smell real. These days that seems to be the trend for everything."

As this scene unfolds, the camera tracks Kiến An's gaze but displaces it; originating with Kiến An, the filmic gaze does not end with her and most assuredly, does not belong to her. Though there are multiple ways of reading point-of-view shots, the mechanics of film establish that eyeline-match and shot/reverse shots are crucial for setting up a character's active subjectivity. As film theorist Edward Branigan asserts, the "concept of a glance [from an object] implies the existence of a sentient observer in whose viewpoint we may participate."[53] This device is important not only for satisfying the spectator's epistemological desires but also for informing the spectator's quest for knowledge and having that knowledge reconfirmed.[54] Indeed, the demand for the "fake" flowers serves as Bui's allegory for the corroding effects of commercialism in Sài Gòn, the center of Việt Nam's market economy. Those who are "true" subjects in the film instinctively know the difference between the fake and the real, between real art and its false copy.[55] Artificiality, for example, infuses the characterization of the prostitute, Lan, who, by the end of the film, becomes reborn through the cyclo driver's anointment of her new self. If she was "fake" in her materialistic desires before her rebirth, she embodies a "truer" self in the film's conclusion.

Consumers who buy Kiến An's flowers are also more knowledgeable than those who buy and sell fake ones. They are customers like James Hager, an American GI who returns to Việt Nam looking for his Amerasian daughter, and Hải (played by Đơn Dương), a cyclo driver. Privileged by the camera gaze, Hải and James are endowed with the ability to look and have that look fulfilled with an accompanying shot, which permits spectators to see what the characters are seeing and thus make meaning out of the film. Bui primarily uses eyeline matches and shot/reverse shots to narrate the men's stories, thereby creating subject positions for those knowledgeable decoders of the film's themes. As Stephen Heath explains, "The character, figure of the look, is a kind of perspective within the perspective system, regulating the world, orientating space, providing directions for the spectator."[56] Moreover, the spectators' apprehension of the "true" Việt Nam is constituted most often through Hải's gaze as he masterfully navigates the cityscape.

However, the choreography of the shots also differs from one character to another. As Kiến An is part of the natural landscape, her character must authorize the poetry of the country, and consequently her point of view is sometimes privileged in the film. Yet, the construct of her as a knowing subject is noticeably different from that of either Hải or Woody, the little boy who searches for his case of merchandise in another subplot. For Woody's story, Bui is careful to shoot at the boy's eye level in order to approximate his childlike viewpoint. In the rare moments when Kiến An's perspective is composed with a subjective shot, the eroticized object of that gaze is aimed at the disfigured poet, who asks her to transcribe his poetry. When she obliges, her gaze in his home is constructed to affirm only the existence of the male artist or what Bui deems to be the appropriate object of desire for her character.

The parallel between the two artists in *Yellow Lotus* and *Three Seasons* is revealing. The narrative of the exiled leper poet relays the same anguish about commodification Bui poses in his earlier short film. As with *Yellow Lotus*, Bui simultaneously celebrates and mourns the loss of the artist in a capitalistic economy. The figure of the poet serves as a proxy for Bui's own position as an exiled artist in the United States and Việt Nam. This issue speaks to his generation's need to belong, both at home and abroad. The displacement of the male artists in the two films represents the director's own liminal status: although his home is within the United States, he is marginalized as an artist within US national culture. Similarly, although Bui is endowed with financial capital from abroad, he is marginalized within Việt Nam for not being Vietnamese enough. From the Vietnamese perspective, he lacks the cultural capital with which to make authentically "Vietnamese" films.[57] By posing the question of true art versus fake art, *Việt Kiều* director Bui seems to express his own anxieties about the state of *his* art within the global marketplace. Part of these anxieties relate to how the counterpoint to true (male-produced) art is female labor in both its tainted and untainted forms.

The celebration of the leper poet and his art is signed through women's bodies and female labor. After the leper poet dies, Kiến An goes to the floating market and throws white blossoms into the water in order to fulfill her master's lifelong dream. Cued by Vietnamese folk music, a group of women vendors on the market unitarily look on and pay homage to him by standing up in their boats and singing a song (see Fig. 1–5). This scene is strikingly similar to the stream of white female bodies in *áo dài* that serves as the

FIGURE 1.5. Vietnamese peasant women paying homage to the male poet. From the film *Three Seasons* © 1999. October Films, Giải Phóng Film Studio, Open City Films.

climax of *Yellow Lotus*. Both scenes are shot with a fluid camera that echoes the grace and beauty that women are supposed to embody here. Vietnamese female characters in Bui's movies often function as representatives of an eternal Việt Nam, whose labor does not produce art itself, but carries the import of the movie's themes about being true to one's self and ideals.

Given the film's logic, inevitably cast as the virtuous Kiến An's opposite is the corrupt Lan, a highly paid prostitute with whom Hải falls in love. Her story follows a narrative arc that moves her from sin and cynicism to redemption and rebirth; she symbolizes Bui's own hope for Việt Nam. Importantly, Lan's story is not her own; it is told through the perspective of the cyclo driver whose eyes constantly observe Lan's movements. When we first see Lan, the scene is accented by a crash of glass as she is chased out of a storefront. To Hải and to the spectator, she is a moving spectacle in white and sunglasses. When he picks her up, Hải strains to see her true face behind her dark glasses from the back of the cyclo. Bui positions spectators in the same location, so we too struggle to discern her identity. When we are finally presented with Lan's face and eyes, they are seen only through her compact mirror's reflection. The mirror and the makeup are conventionally rendered as women's accoutrements for dissembling. These objects emphasize her unknowability and her doubling: although her consumer desires mark her as crass and betray her true desires, the film struggles to prove that she also doubles as a "good" and decent person. As the narrative continues, it is clear that Lan, in becoming a prostitute, has betrayed her own values, a loss that is spectacularly restored by the end of the film.

The narratives of the prostitute and cyclo driver emphasize that the capitalist system oppresses them both as it exploits their labor. In this new economy, Hải and Lan yearn for life in "air-conditioned, foreign-owned" hotels; however, with Lan, Bui implies that her exploitation as a sexual commodity results from a loss in moral values. In contrast, Hải's physical labor, itself a tourist commodity, is portrayed as manual but not immoral. Hải is wise and literary, reading in his spare time. Lan, by contrast, is a synecdoche for a soulless materialism infiltrating the city during the time of *Đổi Mới*. As a figure of collaboration, Lan is also symbolic of how the Vietnamese and the state have sold out to the global market. Bui uses her character to reinforce his critique of foreign investment and the rampant consumerism found among the youths in Việt Nam. Yet, Lan further represents a patriarchal division of labor configuring this film and *Yellow Lotus*. In Bui's two films, men's work produces "true" art (the leper poet, Hải, and the artist in *Yellow Lotus*), while women's work is either base (Lan's prostitution) or unspoiled (the domestic labors of Kiến An).

Through Lan, Bui also attempts to resuscitate a potent model for Vietnamese womanhood, drawing from *The Tale of Kiều*. The motif of the redeemed Vietnamese prostitute finds its precedent in the beloved nineteenth-century poem. Bui's representation of Vietnamese womanhood is not far from the suffering heroine that Nguyễn Du created and the diasporic subject that Huỳnh Sanh Thông has reinterpreted as embodying Kiều. The figure of the prostitute footnotes Vietnamese classic literature in a culturally nationalistic gesture even as it replays the theme of redemption for women characters. As Thông's interpretation of the poem demonstrates, the narrative has seemingly created a template for the representation of Vietnamese women as heroines who have metaphorically returned home after being wayward for a long period of time.

Although the redeemed prostitute in films can be a regressive figure, some feminist film theorists have shown that she can also be a productive site of critique and ambivalence.[58] The prostitute, as a member of the marginalized, female working class in the global South, is a critical figure for an intersectional analysis of capitalism and patriarchy. Lan, while curtailed in her movements by the cyclo driver's gaze, is, nonetheless, endowed with a vital mobility and financial agency absent in other characters. As such, she is the visual embodiment of the struggles against the entrapping forces of capitalistic exploitation and patriarchal surveillance. Her limited circulations in the city streets and the unlawfulness she represents at the beginning of the film constitute a strong condemnation of the world she inhabits.

Nonetheless, because Lan is comparable to the cyclo image as a metaphor for a precapitalist era, Lan's ability to mean something more is constrained by the allegorical import Bui imposes upon her character, an onus Lan (and other female characters) have to carry, given the film's ambitions and thematic concerns. In the film's conclusion, Lan's redemption is forced in a double sense. In the visual climax of the movie, Hải leads her to a deserted road, where she is showered with red flowers. Significantly, he anoints her rebirth by giving her a Vietnamese self-help book called *Rèn Nhân Cách,* or *Forging personhood,* thereby initiating Lan into the realm of language and social relations. With Hải's proclamation, "You don't have to pretend anymore," the restitution of her former, truer subjectivity is complete (see Fig. 1–6). Similar to the final scene in Tran's *The Scent of Green Papaya,* this conclusion alludes to how men instruct women on appropriate codes of behavior and usher them into the symbolic imaginary. Appropriately enough, the scene is punctuated with swelling Vietnamese heritage music. To stress her newfound innocence, Lan wears a white *áo dài* and remains a fetishized object, as a stationary camera captures the entire female body framed against the natural landscape. In its visual and aural excesses, the scene repeats how Bui imagines his female characters and the natural environment. Usually situated within a primordial scene, the loss that womanhood represents is reconstituted in all its plenitude (see Fig. 1–7).

Cross-cutting between Kiến An's elegy to the poet and Lan's spiritual reincarnation, the film concludes with a kind of exalted visuality that exceeds the limits of narrative. Its ending is ambiguous in an otherwise conventional narrative film: Kiến An's future is undecided, while the two lovers' future together remains unresolved. Uncertainties such as these, however, are covered over by a regime of color, sound, and spectacle. Lan's prowling insistence for security and wealth, expressed throughout the film and which constitute the defining elements of her character, are left suspended in the final frame with a static shot of Lan's house. Notably muted in terms of music and image, this scene domesticates and

FIGURE 1.6. Learning how to see again: the rebirth of Lan, the prostitute. From the film *Three Seasons* © 1999. October Films, Giải Phóng Film Studio, Open City Films.

immobilizes Lan's character within the private realm. At the same time, and contradictorily, it emphasizes her own property, not Hải's small room imaged earlier in the film. The concluding shot emphasizes the place that Lan is positioned, (in)securely inside the home. Lan's sexual and financial independence threatens Hải's economic insecurity and upsets the conservative gender order Bui envisions as part of postwar Việt Nam. Though cast as a figure in need of salvation, Lan actually represents a menace to the hierarchical relations of conventional notions of gender and class. She embodies a threat that needs to be destabilized. Her rebirth in the film's conclusion fails to control the ambiguities of power relations and gender roles exposed in the film.

Collaborative Acts: The Production and Reception of Vietnamese Diasporic Films

Analyses of the representations of masculinity and femininity in Vietnamese diasporic films underscore how gendered bodies convey the

FIGURE 1.7. The female body in its plenitude. From the film *Three Seasons* © 1999. October Films, Giải Phóng Film Studio, Open City Films.

anxieties and aspirations of a young generation of male directors. For Tran Anh Hung and Tony Bui, a construct of womanhood stands in for a diasporic desire for plenitude. Operating mostly at the level of visuality and metaphor, women's bodies serve as ciphers for men's desires. Vietnamese female sex workers, in particular, function as figures of economic collaboration and of the betrayal of a feminine ideal. In the same films, men's bodies also labor for the nation, but they do so differently. Through menial but artistic labor, their exertions within the new economy are invested with a sense of intellectual interiority that the directors do not extend to their women characters. Markers of this authoritative subjectivity are signified in the ways that the men's points of view are privileged and their stories aurally narrativized—through voice-overs and expressions of poetry. In this fashion, Tran and Bui are similar: they both emphasize gendered notions of "servitude" in the reconstruction of the nation. The masculinist strategy of representation is meant to be heuristic, as their works underline the ways in which Vietnamese women and men should serve the family and the nation during the tumult of *Đổi Mới*.

In a book devoted to "accented cinema," a term describing films produced by postcolonial, third world filmmakers in the West, Hamid Naficy argues, "[it is a cinema] in dialogue with the home and the host societies and their respective national cinemas, as well as with audiences, many of whom are similarly transnational, whose desires, aspirations, and fears they express."[59] The multilayered nature of Tran's and Bui's critiques—aimed at the American, French, and Vietnamese political milieus—is aligned with Naficy's formulation here. Close readings of Tran's and Bui's films demonstrate how their works are significant because they critique a negligent Vietnamese state as well as past American and French representations of "Vietnam." This need to revise previous images becomes both the burden and charge of ethnic cultural producers who produce within dominant national cultures. Their reworking of past representations clears a space for the investigation of diasporic thematic concerns and the use of gendered images in film. Their films speak affectively and effectively to diasporic audiences as they attempt to reclaim what has been lost: the time and space of Việt Nam.

Beyond these analyses of representation, however, we must also chart the institutional ways the films are produced in order to see how diasporic directors imagine a gendered notion of "Vietnam," often with the state's cooperation. Indeed, after Đổi Mới, or "Renovation," was implemented, Bui's and Tran's films were shot in collaboration with the Vietnamese government. The state allowed the directors to shoot on location but with some constraints. As part of the films' preproduction processes, the directors had to first submit their scripts to the state and receive state approval and a permit to shoot. For both Cyclo and Three Seasons, a government agent was on the set to ensure the films were shot under censorship guidelines.[60] Việt Nam's censorship policies make it difficult to critique the Vietnamese government while working in the country. The cinematic collaboration of diasporic filmmakers, then, exceeds the collaboration typical of any cinematic production. While cinematic production always requires the collaboration of a team of artists and an adherence to local regulations, for diasporic Vietnamese filmmakers, an added layer of political collaboration—with a Vietnamese state intent on controlling some degree of political meaning in cultural production—is not only necessary but also fraught with problems.

However, the question remains: What does it mean for the Vietnamese state to claim these films as its own? With its recent laws allowing for dual citizenship, the state certainly adds to the repertoire of cultural productions in circulation, bolstering the country's own impoverished culture industry in the process. Since the policies of "Renovation" were put into place, the state has increasingly encouraged artistic collaborations, allowing for more open relations with *Việt Kiều*. Particularly in terms of film, the Ministry of Culture and Information (now under the aegis of the Ministry of Sports and Tourism) has authorized the establishment of private film companies within the country, leading to the transnational funding of films and their marketing.

In the twenty-first century, the government is keenly invested in welcoming returning Vietnamese, who come back not only as venture capitalists and tourists but also as artists and filmmakers. In 2005, Ngô Phương Lan, who was recently made Head of the Cinema Department, noted that for the Vietnamese film industry to flourish, it must cooperate with overseas filmmakers in making films. Ngô exhorts the importance of maintaining "favorable conditions" for *Việt Kiều* to return and advance the development of Vietnamese cinema.[61] As she writes, "Using their experience, *Việt Kiều* directors will be better at flying the Vietnamese flag than directors in the country itself."[62] At the same time, however, the government is not yet ready to cede control to directors, since some subjects are still taboo and subject to censorship, particularly those that deal with the American War, reeducation, Vietnamese refugees, South Vietnamese resentment, and anticommunist feeling. It is still the case that diasporic artists and filmmakers working in Việt Nam must either actively collaborate with the state or passively collaborate by conceding that some topics cannot be broached.

Such traces of economic and artistic collaboration underline how the making of films in Việt Nam is crucially positioned at the political intersections between Việt Nam and its Western Others. From the Vietnamese government's perspective, acts of collaboration are no longer contaminated with the marks of betrayal as when such acts were deemed treasonous in Việt Nam's historically vexed relations with foreign countries. For example, members of the former southern Vietnamese regime were treated to brutal reeducation camps by the communist Vietnamese regime, who labeled them "puppets" for collaborating with the Americans (*những con rối của Mỹ*) during the American War. In the same context, the term *Việt Kiều* was a derogatory classification in the post-1975 era, implying the diaspora's betrayal in abandoning the country. More recently, however, the Vietnamese state recognizes the profitable ways that the diasporic community contributes to the economy and culture. Viewed as mutually benefiting enterprises, such collaborations in this new century are more economically tinted than politically tainted.

These political negotiations between the artist and the state show the mechanisms by which the state disciplines diasporic artists in regulating the artist's work and the circulations of the work both domestically and internationally. These collaborative acts also underline how the production of Vietnamese diasporic film is necessarily a cooperative enterprise, a multilateral process that positions itself in between cultures and among geopolitical alignments in the post–Cold War era.[63]

Though Bui and Tran have been compelled to collaborate with the Vietnamese government to shoot their films on location, an international viewing community has been mostly quiet about the implications of this collaborative act. It may be that the films' critical acclaim often mystifies these relations. The praise for Bui's and Tran's films in the United States and France, for example, has been aided by the ways in which the marks of these male diasporic filmmakers' return to the homeland are erased, signaled by a camera eye aligned with the laboring male subjects at the center of the films. This recentering of the subject allows for the film to be seen as a "Vietnamese" film rather than a diasporic one, a conflation that the Vietnamese government encourages when it lays claim to the same films. As for the diaspora, where once an overseas community labeled those Vietnamese diasporans who returned to the homeland as traitors, Tran and Bui are now considered important directors who have forged a path for other Vietnamese diasporic filmmakers to follow.[64] The next chapter looks at how the receptions of male filmmakers radically contrast to the ways in which women authors are often charged as traitorous daughters within the diaspora.

2 / Colonial Histories, Postcolonial Narratives: Traitors and Collaborators in Vietnamese Women's Diasporic Literature

When Le Ly Hayslip's cowritten autobiographies *When Heaven and Earth Changed Places* (1989) and *Child of War, Woman of Peace* (1993) first came out, US reviewers and reading audiences warmly embraced them.[1] Hayslip's works achieved great commercial success; they were translated in seventeen different languages and reprinted several times over by major publishing houses like Doubleday and Plume. Nonetheless, when Oliver Stone's film *Heaven and Earth* (1993), based on Hayslip's books, reached the theaters, the reception among Vietnamese American expatriates was largely antagonistic. In an article in the *LA Times* details the ways Vietnamese Americans in Orange County, California, launched a protest against the film. Evocatively, the interviewees' comments dwell not only on the film and Hayslip's pro-normalization politics, but also on her gender. Chuyên Nguyễn, editor of the Vietnamese-language newspaper, *Tiếng Chuông* [*Sounds of a bell*], states, "As a movie maker, Oliver Stone used us. As a Vietnamese woman, Le Ly betrayed us."[2] Along the same lines, writer Kim Hà, author of *Stormy Escape*, denounces the portrayal of womanhood in the film. "We have all these honorable women. And who is perceived as a symbol of the beautiful Vietnamese woman but an illiterate country woman who spied for the Việt Cộng and prostituted herself with the American soldiers?"[3] Hậu Nguyễn, a former soldier in the Army of the Republic of Việt Nam, mourns what he considers Hayslip's desecration of the heroic memory of the southern Vietnamese regime: "We fought for freedom from the communists. And in the movie, that woman tells the world that we are bad men, that we plundered villages and killed the peasants, that we tortured innocent women."[4] In the article, Nguyễn emphatically relays the ways in which this group of US allies continues to seek recognition for their participation during the war, efforts that appear to be negated by Hayslip's texts.

Even as these statements gesture toward the straitjacket of representation binding marginalized communities, they also express a belief that Hayslip personally bears responsibility for the grievances she has committed against an exilic Vietnamese American community in the writing of her two coauthored books. The line of critique follows that Hayslip, as a writer, must be held accountable for the historic totality of the Vietnam War. As a woman, she is obligated to uphold the virtues of Vietnamese womanhood. As a Vietnamese refugee, she must honor the memory of southern Vietnamese soldiers and their heroism. I draw upon these directives issued by Hayslip's detractors because they symbolize a barbed thicket around which diasporic women's textual selves are produced and received; that is, a discourse of betrayal. This chapter explores how Vietnamese American author Le Ly Hayslip's and Vietnamese French writer Linda Lê's self-referential works are implicated in multiple registers of treason.

Through a transnational feminist analysis, the chapter argues for an understanding of the collaborationist politics that underlie the fraught position of in-betweenness in which writers like Le Ly Hayslip and Linda Lê find themselves, an aspect Leslie Bow de-privileges as a "potentially radical site."[5] Without celebrating this third space as subversive in the way Homi Bhabha has theorized it,[6] I place the texts within an intricate subset of power relations, which lies at the crosshairs of northern and southern Vietnamese politics, US and Vietnamese ideologies, and indigenous and colonial cultures. Besides interpreting what is represented on the page, however, this chapter interrogates the reading communities that consume these works and the Western publishing industries that help to produce them. Although Bow dismisses the "anxiety about collaboration" shadowing cowritten literatures,[7] the import of collaboration, national allegiances, and familial obligations carries more substantive weight here. The threat of treason women embody is not only scored by anxieties about women's sexuality but also inscribed in the act of writing itself. For these authors, writing represents both symbolic and material collaboration.

Focusing on Hayslip's cowritten autobiographies, *When Heaven and Earth Changed Places* and *Child of War, Woman of Peace*, and Lê's *Calomnies*, I investigate how these daughters of the national family treat the problem of being discursively positioned between and amid competing allegiances. Here the act of collaboration is a manifestation of this positioning; in my reading, collaboration becomes a metaphor for writing as well as a material practice. For Lê, the collaborator is more figural than in Hayslip's texts, a figuration clearly embodied by the character of Madamère. Described as a "killer doll," Madamère was the colonial concubine *par excellence*, bartering her body for status, material goods, and class privilege when she took on foreign lovers during the waning days of French colonialism and the American War. In Lê's allegorical form of writing, in which most of her characters go unnamed, the loathsome Madamère remains that primordial connection between Việt Nam and its Western Others. Emerging from the past, she also symbolizes a haunting figure who demands to be confronted in the postcolonial present. As the coupling of her names, "madame" and "mère," suggests, the maternal concubine collaborates with the West and as a result bears "mad" offspring—the children of empire, both insane and full of fury. Her legacy of sexual collaboration extends beyond the colonial context and accents the difficult conditions surrounding the speaking subject, or the "dirty foreigner writing in French," as Lê puts it, who is producing in the metropole today.[8]

While collaboration is only a theme for Lê, the sole author of her highly literary books, the collaborative acts manifested in Hayslip's cowritten texts are actual. Hayslip was a "traitor" to both the northern and southern regimes, a one-time prostitute, the former wife of two American War veterans, and a mother to two Amerasian sons.[9] Because of these acts, an anticommunist Vietnamese American community calls Hayslip a traitor whose texts represent infidelity to the memory of the southern Vietnamese regime. Additionally, the levels of collaboration Hayslip enacts in the coproduction of her life in print (with Jay Wurts) and in film (with Oliver Stone) may also be why Asian American literary critics dismiss her. They see the genre of autobiography and her relations with white men as problematic and complicated, if not ideologically suspect. While sympathetic to these concerns, I contextualize her work against the conservative milieu in which they were produced and highlight how the controversial nature of the production and reception of Hayslip's works impinges upon the critical issues of class and symbolic capital.

Hayslip's and Lê's respective class and citizenship statuses are radically different, which are reflected in the production and reception of their works. Originating from a rural class in central Việt Nam, Hayslip became a naturalized American citizen only after she married an American GI in 1970. By contrast, because the French government saw them as repatriates, Linda Lê and her family were granted French citizenship before they even arrived in France in 1977. As opposed to Hayslip's third-grade education and lack of English literacy, Lê's elite education and fluency in French, the training of which began in Việt Nam, determine the ways in which she writes. While Hayslip's cowritten autobiographies strive for clarity and legibility, Lê's single-authored works are premised on an elliptical style of writing that resists comprehensibility. Because of these issues of style and form, Lê and Hayslip are received in highly contrasting ways. While Lê's work circulates amongst elite reading publics in the United States and France, Hayslip's texts have less currency within these circles, yet she is widely read by a mainstream audience in the United States. Most importantly, though Lê often writes about being slandered, she is never the target of defamation in the way that Hayslip has been publicly castigated in print. Rather, Lê's self-indictments of treason accrue symbolic capital that positions her as one of the most important writers in contemporary French literature. Meanwhile, Hayslip continues to be branded a traitor because of her books, politics, and activism.[10] These differences in reception point to a system of literary valuation that dispenses symbolic capital in hierarchical ways, according to class, immigration history, and literariness in this postwar moment.

Writer Ha Jin notes that the migrant author is often perceived as a traitor to his country because he chooses to write in another language. Countering this, Jin provocatively proposes the inverse—that we instead accuse the country for having failed and betrayed the individual.[11] Premised on Jin's proposition, this chapter foregrounds the national contexts from which Lê and Hayslip emerge to sharply highlight how the national family betrays these women writers. In this way, we see how matters of reception are densely knotted with the production of diasporic women's textual selves. A trans-Vietnamese feminist mode of analysis places in relief that uncanny relation between "woman" and the written word, a vexed affiliation that has been born from a history of colonialism and war for Việt Nam and the diaspora.

Text and Context: *Le Monstre* in Linda Lê's *Calomnies*

The editors of the anthology *Postcolonial Subjects: Francophone Women Writers* observe that writing in French for postcolonial writers is a challenging project, a problematic explored in writings produced in and outside of France. Green and colleagues further argue, "For a woman writer from Guadeloupe, New Brunswick, or Algeria, the act of writing in French is, of necessity, an attempt to make a place for herself in that elite, male-dominated, white European literary tradition."[12] The onus of writing in French means that one must also engage with the canonical works of French literature "in [a] dialogue with Racine and Voltaire, Proust and Descartes."[13]

In many ways, Vietnamese French author Linda Lê exemplifies this postcolonial female writer. Lê writes in French, conversing with French literature in a dual gesture to reassert and disrupt the canon. In her trilogy on madness, death, and loss—*Calomnies, Voix: Une crise*, and *Lettre Morte*—Lê reappropriates a Racinian leitmotif to describe and name herself, *le monstre*.[14] Like Racine's Phèdre, she expounds on her guilt and culpability within these three texts, which deal fatalistically with her having left *le Pays*, or the Country, as she generically calls Việt Nam. Incest, miscegenation, fatal pronouncements of silence and death, and loyalty to the nation are the anguished roots of tragedy for Lê's works in ways similar to the seeds of madness that strike Racine's heroine. Nonetheless, the funereal air permeating Racine's *Phèdre* is resituated in Lê's contemporary work as the legacy of French colonialism in Indochina. In Lê's texts the tragic irrevocability of one's roots is grounded in a colonial history and in the linguistic and psychological violence this history inflicts on the postcolonial subject in the metropole.

It is Lê's extensive engagement with French literature and her metaliterary style of writing that attracts literary critics to her work. Numerous French and US critics position her books as prominent examples of diasporic Vietnamese writing.[15] Outside of the academic community, Lê's writing also appeals to a mainstream French readership. The widely read newspapers *Le Monde* and *Le Figaro* often feature interviews with Lê and celebratory reviews of her texts. Further, one of the more notable publishing houses in Paris publishes her work. As noted on its website, Christian Bourgois Éditeurs has a distinct reputation for being highly selective in its endorsement of French and international writers.[16] Because of her prolific output and the acclaim she has garnered in the last decade, Lê presently holds an elite position as a literary critic in France, reviewing classic and contemporary French literature in her scholarly work.[17] Her aestheticized writing style—sometimes compared to that of Marguerite Duras, one of France's most beloved women writers of the twentieth century—partly explains her popularity in academic circles and with a literary French readership.[18]

Most pronounced in the academic reception of Lê's work is how scholars interpret her texts through the aesthetics of hybridity and analytics of psychoanalysis and deconstruction. Essays by Ching Selao and Martine Delvaux, for example, examine Lê's major text *Calomnies* with an eye to Derridian notions of lack and différance.[19] Indeed, Selao posits Lê's dual-voiced narrative as a staging of the theoretical suppositions of Foucault and Derrida.[20] Other critics also emphasize Lê's poststructuralist concerns with border-crossing.[21] In his seminal work on Vietnamese literature in French, literary critic Jack Yeager discusses how Lê's texts represent an apotheosis of this field. For Yeager, Lê's work most effectively complicates the binaries of "East" and "West" that striate earlier Vietnamese works in French during the colonial era; in so doing, her work allows for more nuanced understandings of a postcolonial gendered identity.[22] Centered on mostly hermeneutic analyses, these critical readings rightly highlight the ways a colonial history orders Lê's narratives of exile. Yet, this same scholarship also neglects the racial and class politics of French culture today, a milieu that certainly impacts Lê's thematic concerns about betrayal and how reading communities in the West receive her work.[23]

In contrast to this body of work, I make the case for the ways that literary production and the political economy of the French publishing industry must figure into studies of diasporic writing. Lê's work is situated within France's deeply splintered cultural and racial politics, which provides the crucial context for the kinds of betrayal that she writes about in her texts. Interrogating her texts through the problematic of writing-as-betrayal that postcolonial writers confront, I stress that critics' interpretations need to go beyond narratives of libidinal and colonial desire; rather, readings should also be tied to the material realities concerning the production of ethnic minority texts in the West, a site hegemonically defining the ways "Vietnam" is consumed. Equally important to consider is the marginalized position of ethnic women writers in the French literary and academic establishments. This section on Lê exposes the problems of betrayal and authenticity in the ways that readerships in France and beyond evaluate minority women's writing.

To trace how these conditions have been shaped, we begin with Vietnamese decolonization and post-1975 Vietnamese immigration. The American failure of the Vietnam War, as revisionists would have it in the United States, resulted from a lack of military power. In contrast, the 1954 battle at Điện Biên Phủ, a momentous French defeat at the hands of the northern Vietnamese army, symbolized a lost object of desire and lack of will on France's part by the middle of the twentieth century. The French understood Việt Nam's national independence as an "inevitable" stage in the country's progressive march toward self-determination. After the loss of France's "Pearl of the Orient," the government remembered soldiers and military officials as martyred heroes because, as Nicola Cooper argues, Điện Biên Phủ represented an idealized battle for the French.[24] By the end of the Vietnam War, France saw the Vietnamese as victims of US imperialism, a view leading the French government in 1975 to accept an unprecedented number of Indochinese refugees.[25]

As Alec Hargreaves notes, France's postcolonial relations with the formerly colonized constitute the visible evidence of a "civilizing mission that has come to fruition" today.[26] Embedded in Hargreaves's statement is a register of visibility and invisibility expressly resonant with how the Vietnamese French are imagined today. Colonial constructions of the "invisible" yet "industrious" Vietnamese immigrant prove rhetorically useful in a present-day milieu where the French are reappraising ethnic minorities for their ability or inability to integrate themselves into French national culture. Étienne Balibar has explained that the present-day gesture to assert the insurmountability of cultural differences in France formulates a "neo-racism." Neither based on biological determinism, nor on the postulation of "the superiority of certain groups or peoples in relation to others," this form of racism emphasizes "'only' the harmfulness of abolishing frontiers, the incompatibility of life-styles and traditions."[27]

During these intense debates about ethnic identity and national unity, Linda Lê's texts foreground a refusal to be culturally assimilated. Rejecting conformity to a majoritarian or minoritarian ideal, they continually stress the "monstrous" progeny created as a result of French colonialism: the colonial and linguistic hybrid. Most exactingly, her postcolonial critique targets the ways in which gender and ethnic difference becomes commodified in French national culture. Because of this rigorous and sustained critique, Lê is one of the most important women writers to have emerged in France in recent years. Lê's literary rise, as Rye and Worton note about women writers in the 1990s, dovetails with the "explosion in published writing by women that was the outcome both of feminist movements of the 1970s and of feminist archaeological work."[28] Exceptional and exceptionalized, Lê is an integral part of the conversations around French women's writing at the end of the century.

The context for the discourse on women's writing remains key to reading Lê's work, even though critics understand Lê primarily as an exilic writer, tethered to a racialized and exilic identity. Because French women's fiction and ethnic writings are marginalized in France, Lê's fixation on the nature of *female* treason lends her texts a disruptive visibility in national culture and allows her to capitalize on her marginalized position. In this way, Lê shares some commonalities with Hayslip; both women rework the cultural role they play in the French and American imaginations as gendered cultural mediators between East and West. More so than Hayslip, however, Lê explores the problem of writing for the ethnic female writer and critiques the demands that the French literary reading public have made upon her.

This literary reading public is particular to the ideology of French exceptionalism. Because of its originary narratives as a glorious republic, France looks to itself as a nation wherein immigrants are expected to incorporate themselves into the French polity, rather than perpetually remake the nation (as in the case of the United States).[29] Reflecting this, the parameters of what constitutes "good" literature in French are not beholden to the politics of difference for most of the French publishing *maisons*. In French literary production, a host of various players in the field work jointly: large and small publishers, book reviewers for popular newspapers like *Le Monde* and *Le Figaro*, book clubs like *France-Loisir*, as well as university academics. Some works are highlighted and celebrated at elaborate book festivals and contests for book prizes, sometimes sponsored by the publishing houses themselves.[30] Within this network, as William Cloonan argues, various components work together to produce changes in attitudes toward French literature.[31] Ironically, despite the investment in prestigious literary works, the demand for American works in translation remains high in France, leading to an anxiety about a lack of great French writers ("Les Grands Écrivains") representing France in the international literary scene at the end of the millennium.[32] To counter the tide of US cultural imperialism, many French publishing houses continue focusing on "French" literary productions in order to promote a national literature.

Within this field of production, the idea of a "French national literature" is pitched against the construct of "ethnic literature," a categorization reinforced by the government and its culture industries. Issues of categorization and valuation are also exacerbated when ethnic literature is largely perceived as sociohistorical, dealing exclusively with immigration and identity politics.[33] For those positioned outside of this national literature, such as minority writers, publishing opportunities are few, and they remain "marginalized by publishing, journalistic, and academic communities that act as gatekeepers to the wider public."[34] In a highly competitive market, these writers vie for placement in an elite French literary culture by strategically adhering to certain literary standards. Most notably, writers attempt to avoid the aesthetic of *misérabilisme*, defined as the "sentimental portrayal and moralistic denunciation of poverty and oppression."[35] Evading this form of sentimentalism, ethnic writers shun the stigmatization of being a writer who hails from a particular ethnic perspective, especially because the idea of particularism is pejoratively understood to be a "ghettoized" iteration of US multiculturalism.[36] In Alec Hargreaves's discussion of Beur writings and the strategy of ironizing distance, these writers "repeatedly make fun of their own misunderstandings and contradictions and laugh off material deprivations associated with an immigrant background."[37]

Countering this misérablist aesthetic, Lê's critical and creative works denounce the consumption of what Graham Huggan calls the "postcolonial exotic."[38] In *Calomnies* especially, the writerly narrator criticizes publishing demands for such works and the writer who gives in to these conditions. While other critics analyze the monstrous in Lê's texts as a colonial embodiment, in my analysis *le monstre* also signifies the burden of representation that minority women must carry. In *Calomnies*, Lê's female narrator is constantly menaced by the possibility that she might sell her autobiographical history for commercial reasons. That the female writer, a cipher for Lê herself, may be luridly documenting the refugee's story constitutes an unrelenting source of anxiety throughout the text. The anxieties of writing for a French readership resound throughout *Calomnies*. The next section analyzes the gendered metaphors of commerce that underlie her book. It looks at how Lê figures her self as a linguistic and cultural traitor to the countries in which she was born and in which she now writes: Việt Nam and France.

Linda Lê: The "Dirty Foreigner Writing in French"

In 1963, the year of Linda Lê's birth in Đà Lạt, Việt Nam, her family applied for and was granted French citizenship, making her, her three sisters, and her mother and grandmother "Frenchwomen" and "repatriates" when they left Việt Nam for France in 1977.[39] Lê eventually attended one of Paris's most elite universities, La Sorbonne, to pursue a doctoral degree in literature. During this time, however, she turned to creative writing, left academia, and published her first novel, *Un Si Tendre Vampire*, in 1987. Evidenced in her later writings especially, Lê's foray into education at a top French university was an estranging experience for a postcolonial subject. As Lê intimates, her French education, or *formation*, constitutes a *de*formation, dislocating her linguistic and cultural affiliation to both *la mère-patrie* as well as her birth country.[40]

Writing in French becomes the *idée fixe* of her book, *Calomnies* [*Slander*]. Slander is a defamatory speech act, a criminal offense committed against an individual or a collective. Acts of slander thread together the narrativizing perspectives of the young female protagonist and her insane uncle, both made deranged by the entanglements that yoke Việt Nam and France together. These entanglements have, in turn, spawned a monstrous postcolonial family, at the head of which is the monstrous matriarch. Both characters consequently betray the mother and mother country by expressing themselves in the colonizer's language. Lê's female narrator, however, commits a particular form of treason against two national cultures—those of France and Việt Nam—because of her writing. The female writer's condition is monstrous because she is unable to pledge allegiance to one country, identity, and language; *Calomnies* explores the psychological deformation and linguistic defamation resulting from such an irresolution.

Early in *Calomnies*, the protagonist, a writer, is given a list of demands by "the Counselor" about how she should write. He encourages her to indulge in a kind of sentimentalism that he believes is commercial and marketable. The Counselor is figured generically as her *éditeur*, her publisher and editor.[41] Fat and crass, he asks her to write about a journey to Việt Nam and to express the alienation from the homeland he assumes she feels. In a series of injunctions, he commands her to delve into her lost relationship with her past, embodied by "Vietnam."

> Écrivez des exercices de jubilation. Cessez vous calomnier, de *nous* calomnier. . . . Empocher l'argent et rentrer au Pays. . . . C'est une bonne aubaine. . . . En profiter pour revoir le Pays.

> [Write some exercises on jubilation. Stop slandering yourself, stop slandering *us*. . . . Take the money and return to the Country. . . . It's a nice windfall. . . . Use it go back to the Country.][42]

The Counselor is described throughout the text as a pugilistic man, one who eerily collects sculptures of human hands. Fixated with the writer's instruments of labor—her hands—he demands from the narrator a specific "product."[43] He advises her to dwell on her past for a film conspicuously entitled in English, *We can't go home again*, hinting at the consumption of US cultural productions in France as it references Nicholas Ray's experimental film (1976) of the same name.[44]

In contrast to the Counselor, Ricin is the narrator's companion, a character who serves as her self-negating conscience. Ricin accuses the narrator of claiming that she, like her seductress mother, wants to conform to the establishment's standards in being manufactured and becoming a "poupée du cordonnier," or a shoemaker's doll.[45] Throughout the novel, he attacks the female narrator for capitalizing on her own past for financial gain: "Tu utilises ton père pour ta publicité personnelle, comme une bonne sœur qui garde toujours sa robe la photo d'un orphelin qu'elle exhibe quand sa sincérité est mise en doute" [You're using your father for your own publicity, like a nun who always keeps a photo of an orphan under her robe to bring out whenever her sincerity is questioned] (23).[46] Ricin's voice, as well as those of the trio of white men who serve as her paternal mentors and lovers (the Counselor, Bellemort and Weideman), ventriloquize the writer's anxieties about the ways in which writing is both an aesthetic and commercial enterprise.[47] Despite trying to resist Ricin's nagging criticisms, the protagonist reveals that she is, in fact, seduced by commercialism. In the following passage, she speaks of herself in the third person as a way to mark the distance between writer and the spectacle of performance imagined to embody women's writing: "Il y a la marionnette avidé de succès, le morceau de chiffon qui voudrait être un oiseau bariole lissant ses plumes devant un public nombreux" [The puppet greedy for success, the piece of fluff that would like to be a gaudy bird preening its feathers for a large audience].[48]

For women, performing in this theater of display offers deadly consequences, psychically and physically. This is demonstrated when we are reintroduced to the Counselor and his authoritative presence later in the text. He reappears as his wife's killer. Lê writes of the Counselor's marriage to a woman whom he has made up in the image of Woman. In an echo of Ricin's words, the Counselor's wife is also a puppet, remade in the Counselor's hands. "Moronic" and parodic, she is presented as a heavily made-up blonde who wears a green suit symbolizing the color of money; her name, Mademoiselle Monnier, only affirms this.[49] Characterized as a prostitute, Mademoiselle Monnier acquiesces to her role in the Counselor's Pygmalion fantasy. The Counselor's wife, in this scenario, represents the woman writer molded and produced by the Counselor. In allegorical terms, the marriage between the commercial publisher and his "creation" ends in violence when the Counselor kills her and then himself. In this scene, the Counselor narrates his own death:

Le coup de feu à l'heure du café, se dit-il. La détonation le fit sur-
sauter. Puis la belle main blanche dirigea l'arme vers son ventre.
Le canon s'enfonça dans une masse de chair molle. Le Conseiller
pensa à un oreiller de plumes. Il ferma les yeux. C'était trop doux.[50]

[The shot rang out at coffee time, he said to himself. The detonation
made him jump. Then the beautiful white hand aimed the gun
at his stomach. The barrel sank into a mass of soft flesh. It made
the Counselor think of a down pillow. He shut his eyes. It was too
sweet.][51]

Implied in the horrific violence and brutal deaths of these two figures is
the prostitution of pathos and the threat menacing the woman writer as
an incarnation of the Counselor's "product." Through the violence of the
scene, Lê expresses the problematic relationships the female writer must
maintain with a male-dominated publishing industry and the demands
of the literary market. Representing a kind of grasping opportunism,
Mademoiselle Monnier is also reminiscent of other French women in the
book: the young women journalists who aggressively seek sensationalis-
tic stories like the narrator's own refugee story. In response, the narrator
renounces this model of womanhood because it reminds her too much
of her own mother.

Clearly the novel's most overt metaphor for crass capitalism is the
protagonist's mother, the uncle's sister. Described throughout the text
only as "Madamère," she is a hateful character who has sold herself to
those in power. In the same colorful and excessive ways Mademoiselle
Monnier is depicted, the Madamère serves as a *femme fatale* in the
uncle's imagination. The description of the Madamère below emphasizes
her callousness.

C'était une poupée tueuse à la peau douce, aux jambes longues, au
buste ferme, aux lèvres peintes d'un rouge violacé, elle avait des
beaux pieds—ils étaient fins, délicats, car *elle ne foulait jamais le
sol, elle ne marchait que sur la tête des humains.*[52]

[She was a killer doll, with soft skin, long legs, firm breasts, and lips
painted in purplish red. She had lovely feet—they were soft and del-
icate, because *she never touched the ground, she walked only on the
heads of human beings.*][53]

Portrayed as a decadent courtesan, the mother symbolizes a feminized Việt Nam during French colonialism. The mother's lovers are the

countries that have appropriated Việt Nam since the colonial era; the product of such profane relations is the colonial hybrid who remains disloyal to any nation or linguistic tradition. More succinctly, the mother embodies a colonial past, which has tainted her daughter's relationship with Việt Nam in the contemporary moment. The protagonist's mother is central to understanding why the uncle and female writer denounce the family. Both characters break their ties with the family through a renunciation of the mother and the mother tongue.

For the uncle, the only means of escape from the Vietnamese family and its traitorous past is to destroy his relations to the past and refuse to speak his native language. Emphatic about sequestering himself within the French language once he acquires it, he chooses to die by self-immolation in a library. Taught the language by a French monk, the uncle speaks of the salvific nature of literature. The fate he and his niece share is predicated on the redemption that literature holds for them. As refugees, one seeks political asylum after the war while the other is banished to France before the war ends; they both find refuge in the written word. He ruminates on the choices they made to renounce the family:

> Nous avons choisi . . . le même moyen pour rompre avec la tradition familiale: elle a fait son choix sous l'influence de son père . . . elle apprit à respirer, elle apprit à laisser entrer dans sa tête autre chose que des registres de comptes.[54]

> [She and I, we chose the same way of breaking with family tradition; she made her decision under the influence of her father . . . She learned to breathe, she learned to let other things into her head besides financial records.][55]

Tied by the symbolics of blood and language, the uncle and niece are conjoined, serving as gothic doubles anchoring the book as the text's perspective oscillates between them.

Through the niece's relationship with the uncle, readers trace the origins of her derangement. Obsessed with the past, the niece is maddened by the illegitimacy of her birth but also—and most damningly—by a family ruthlessly amoral in its dealings with the dominant regime. Exemplified by the maternal concubine and her actions, this family history consists of acts of collaboration, first with the French and the Americans (the "Foreigners"), and then, once the war ends, with the communists (the "men in black").[56] In addition to their shared, painful family past, marred by incest and insanity spanning generations, the uncle and female protagonist share a disdain for a *national* family of collaborators: those who collaborated with foreign powers to collude in the country's dissolution and destruction. As the writer/protagonist and the uncle attempt to disavow the family, they simultaneous disavow the Country, their break with their familial past rendered as a violent rupture with the homeland.

In the uncle's voice, Lê recalls this history of collaboration and collusion, claiming the (national) family in a passive sense yet denouncing them in the same breath: "Les miens ont toujours a été les porte-parole de l'oppresseur, les majordomes des bourreaux" [My relatives have always been the spokesmen of oppressors, the servants of butchers].[57] "Porte-parole" typographically implies a collision of two words, fusing discourse (*parole*) and the act of bearing or carrying (*porter*) this discourse. Situating speech within a politicized realm, Lê's use of the "spokesmen" as executioners signals her themes. She implicates the collaborator's complicity in speaking on behalf of the colonizer. Lê's doubled language refers to the protagonist/writer herself, who is also embedded in this colonial history of collaboration. Herein lies the monstrous burden of representation the postcolonial writer inherits from such a history. Underscoring the colonial ties between France and Việt Nam, Lê explicates how the act of speaking and writing for both the colonizer and the colonized positions her as "a *métèque,* a swarthy foreigner, writing in a language not her own."[58] For Lê, using the colonizer's language means slandering both Self and Other, an act ultimately involving a psychic destruction of the Self through linguistic means.

Nonetheless, through the French language, indeed through her position as a *métèque*, Lê slanders the hegemonic structures of French colonialism still operating in the postcolonial era. Placing the relations between France and Việt Nam within the recent past, Lê as narrator criticizes the ways France received Vietnamese refugees and adoptees, who the French media also exploited as victims of the war. Likening the refugees' escape to a grand filmic narrative, Lê's protagonist stresses how the media profited from the plight of the boat people and the image of victimhood (*yeux si doux si tristes*)[59] it perpetuated, "baptiz[ing] them as 'freedom fighters'"[60] in their journey from Việt Nam to France. She reserves her harshest criticism for French journalists, those pretty young women who, looking for the next narrative of victimhood, quickly moved on to the tragic plight of "Vietnamese extras,"[61] or those who were forcibly repatriated to Việt Nam and sent to reeducation camps. The narrator's disdain for the media's appropriation of victimhood, perpetrated by the *vedettes*, is matched only by her fear that she, too, will be co-opted by the literary establishment, a thematic strongly underwriting Lê's *Calomnies* and her other texts. Put together, her works are often cautionary tales about the psychic dangers minority writers face when they produce texts for a dominant readership.[62] Faced with these dangers, Lê's characters, once they renounce the imperative to sensationalize or sentimentalize experience, are plunged into madness and paranoia as a result.

Thematizing madness and betrayal in *Calomnies*, Lê shows that the word "asylum" connotes a terrifying state for the population of immigrants granted entry into France following 1975.[63] Yet, if the niece, as a recent immigrant, is living the French dream, the uncle, by contrast, has been living the French nightmare when he is exiled there early in the text.[64] The uncle describes life in the "asylum" where he is called "Chinétoque" and "Face-de-Singe," a habitus in which vomit, piss, and dirty linens line the walls.[65] With its history as an asylum-granting country (as *une terre d'asile*), France ironically becomes a ward housing a community made pathological by a colonial past (represented by the uncle) and a postcolonial present (represented by the niece). Marked by the gothic twinning of the uncle and niece, Lê's text asks, what happens when the secrets in the colonizer's house of horrors are unhoused?

But all is not lost by the novel's conclusion, particularly when the narrator recognizes that writing itself is a site of possibility. The narrative end for the writer functions as a regenerative beginning.[66] Turning away from the toxicity that Ricin represents (as signified by his name), she elects to keep her father's identity a secret, even after finally receiving the uncle's note about her paternity. Her leave-taking from Ricin is dramatized as a departure from a dominant patriarchal culture threatening to consume her: she walks away, stating simply: *"Je m'en vais."*[67] In this act, she moves away from the literary establishment's injunction to fetishize her identity. Premised upon a tenuous sense of optimism, these italicized words emphatically end the book. The ending alludes to Lê as author in the near future tense; in the texts following the publication of *Calomnies*, Lê continues exploring the themes of madness and loss in more autobiographical works such as *Voix: Une crise* and *Lettre Morte*. Beyond the book's framing, this homage to the writerly imagination also metafictionally relates to Lê's sustained role in the French imaginary as the profligate writer born of Franco-Vietnamese relations.

A French readership privileges Lê as one of the most significant authors writing about exile in the contemporary era, a reception of Lê's work that is mirrored in the United States. However, this US reception may partly be due to the ways the English-language version has been framed. The English version of *Calomnies* was published three years after the French original in 1996. This English edition features an afterword by translator Esther Allen, wherein she discusses Lê's prominence within the French literary scene as a "writer who remains at the margins," because she is not readily classifiable as French, Francophone, or Vietnamese.[68] As critical "paratext," defined by Gerard Genette as that which serves as an interpretive "threshold" for readers, this short text provides a formative context to the reading of Lê's book in English overall.[69] Expressed through an academic's perspective, this critical appendage enables readers and academics to understand Lê's text, first and foremost, as the work of a marginalized writer of postcolonialism. Mediating between the author and the reader, the translator and publisher's gesture to frame Lê in this way indicates the literary and academic audience to whom the English translation is directed. In turn, this audience is located within a specific moment in time—the moment when the field of postcolonial studies becomes even more "fashionable" and formative within the Western academy.[70] Allen's afterword points to the distinctions of class and high literacy that mark this readership. As Sarah Brouillette notes on the global marketplace, "postcolonial literature," especially as it relates to literatures translated or written in English, has only recently become marketed to a certain cosmopolitan demographic. On the centers of information and power located in the West, she writes, "a growing consensus holds that celebrated postcolonial writers are most often those who are literary in ways recognizable to cosmopolitan audiences."[71]

Ending this section on Lê, I underscore how specific historical contexts shape the production and reception of her work. Lê's writings tend to be dehistoricized and, ironically, even deracinated by her critics. While providing a thorough interpretation of Lê's writing, Marie-Magdeleine Chirol, for example, concludes that Lê rewrites the past in "a language so incisive that one forgets that she sends us to the inexpressible, an absence, the non-lived, the forgotten, in short, to a *paradise lost*: Việt Nam" (my translation).[72] Critics like Chirol elide how the aestheticization of this "lost paradise" is a highly refined, rhetorical strategy Lê employs to acquire prominence within an elite French literary culture. In her writing, Lê continually revisits the "fear and fascination"[73] a "phantasmatic Indochina"[74] holds for a French public. The effects of this strategy are material; Lê continues to accrue symbolic and material capital from the position of alterity that she privileges and the thematic of betrayal underlying her work.

In *Questions of Travel*, Caren Kaplan discusses the material and symbolic gains accorded to the postmodern writer who writes about exile. Kaplan argues that while migrants are often associated with labor and financial gains, a counterdiscourse about intellectuals and exiles is rooted in a discourse of displacement, one adhering to classical Western traditions of thought and a "modernist myth of authorship."[75] This myth draws upon "the redemptive power of writing (understood as specialized labor) and is assumed without investigating the conditions of production that often govern this craft."[76] My analyses of the conditions of production, which partly govern Lê's critical reception in both the United States and France, are grounded in Kaplan's formulations. Producing within a specific time and place—as postcolonial literature becomes most marketable at the same time that debates about race in France are erected around questions of "visible" difference—Lê's works are uniquely positioned to be celebrated as forms of "specialized labor" and as fetishized markers of postcolonialism. Centralizing a position of liminality in what Lê herself terms "littérature déplacée,"[77] or a literature of displacement, her creative and critical work nonetheless stands at the intersections of historical and aesthetic movements in France and beyond its borders. In contrast, Vietnamese American writer Le Ly Hayslip and her work are marked by questions of US imperial history and acts of coauthorship. The following analysis of Hayslip focuses upon issues of class and literacy in demonstrating how her writings are signs of both betrayal and accommodation, precisely because of the way her texts have been cowritten.

The Collaborative Impulse in the Autobiographies of Le Ly Hayslip

Le Ly Hayslip and her coauthored works show that literary labor and the accumulation of symbolic capital for Vietnamese American writers is manifestly different than it is for Vietnamese French authors like Lê. The two writers, how they write and how they have been received, cannot be more different. Hayslip is a Vietnamese American author who was producing autobiographies for an American audience still reeling from the traumas of the Vietnam War. Because of their autobiographical and legible style, Hayslip's coauthored writings are also not considered the products of auteurist or artisanal labor. Instead they signify the ways that Asian American women's autobiographies are highly commercial and commodified in the US literary marketplace. But her books and the feature film about her life have also given Hayslip a permanent place within US culture as well as in the literary scene. Translated into many different languages and used in multicultural classroom curricula, Hayslip's books confirm her status as one of the best-known Vietnamese American writers today. In this way, I argue Hayslip's texts deploy the genre of autobiography "as a coinage that purchases entry" into American culture.[78] Drawing on the commercial language cultural critic Laura Kang employs to describe women's autobiographies, my readings of Hayslip underscore the critical interplay between subject and writer, written text and historical context, to elucidate the "business" of writing with which Hayslip's collaborative work is thoroughly engaged.

Furthermore, unlike Lê's single-authored works, the reception of Hayslip's texts pivots on her cowriting acts, for example her collaboration with writer Jay Wurts on *When Heaven and Earth Changed Places* and with her son, James Hayslip, on *Child of War, Woman of Peace*. The collaborative and commercial aspects of her work have made her vulnerable to accusations of treason and mendacity by certain readerships, and yet for others, her courage and veracity may be unquestioned. Like Lê, Hayslip becomes especially open to accusations of "selling out" and of cultural betrayal as a result of her gendered identity.[79] More so than in Lê's work, however, Hayslip embodies the maternal prostitute herself, one whose sexual treachery is rooted in a colonial legacy. The association between cowriting and commerce also has overwhelmingly positive overtones for Hayslip. Equating writing with mothering and citizenship, she celebrates the labor pains that have given birth not only to her sons but also metaphorically to her books and organizations, all of which constitute for her the fulfillment of the American dream.

This book's focus on women's labor, collaboration, and commerce is especially foregrounded in respect to Hayslip's work. I have defined collaboration as mutual coaction and/or traitorous cooperation with the enemy. Hayslip's texts, more than any other work by a Vietnamese national or diasporic artist, embody these definitions simultaneously. Beyond collaborating with her cowriters, she has also collaborated with the "enemy": the northern Vietnamese and southern Republican armies, as well as the American GIs who were her lovers or the coproducers of her work. Additionally, Hayslip has cooperated with governmental agencies in Việt Nam and the United States, her former enemies and former Cold War foes, in order to establish her nonprofit organizations. Because her texts straddle these definitions and therefore seem to shuttle between the interstices of ideology, Hayslip's work becomes subject to as much criticism as celebration. Analyzing the reception of her work through collaboration only accentuates the term's inherent discursivity. The way the term is wielded depends upon who holds the power to define the terms of representation in both minority and majority cultures.

Focusing on the acts of collaboration in Hayslip's writing and in the creative exchanges preceding the writing event, I interrogate the relations amongst Hayslip, her cowriters, and her readers. This triangulation of actors points to a process of editing that marks autobiographical production as a heavily mediated and collective act, readily addressed to an ideal readership. Instead of analyzing what has been lost or excised from the process, however, the following analysis of Hayslip's texts concentrates on what is grafted together and how this is done. I neither attempt to recover Hayslip's original voice from the collaborative act, nor portray her as lacking, or as an "ethnographic dupe."[80] Rather, my readings stress the texts' rhetorical excess and the stylistic fullness with which they attempt to produce a coherent, legible autobiographical self with whom the American reader identifies. Read in this fashion, *When Heaven and Earth Changed Places* and *Child of War, Woman of Peace* are not just temporal and thematic extensions of one another. Juxtaposed, they dually reveal the writing processes engendering Hayslip's books and clear a space to read the form, structure, and literary conventions underlying them. The chapter presses for an intertextual reading of Hayslip's books, since in tandem, they offer a sustained understanding of the ways in which she is both a political, sexual collaborator during the American War and a maternal, literary collaborator in the writing of the self. Hayslip's double role as writer and traitor, encompassing the maternal and sexual, taps into great anxieties about gender, sexuality, and literariness within a post-Vietnam America.

"Allied Aliens" and Constructions of the Vietnamese Refugee

After the fall of Sài Gòn in April 1975, approximately 130,000 Vietnamese escaped Việt Nam to settle in the United States, constituting the "first wave" of Vietnamese refugees to come to the US.[81] This group consisted mainly of military and government people and their families. Participating in this mass exodus were former South Vietnamese soldiers, officials, farmers, nuns, teachers, and children. Crippled by a devastated economy, the Vietnamese government also faced border wars with Cambodia and China. Because the government continued to persecute the ethnic Chinese and former participants of the southern Vietnamese regime, such crises led to the flight of more Vietnamese, later called boat people, in successive waves during the late 1970s and early 1980s to the United States and other countries. Although Hayslip's history of immigration departs from these post-1975 immigration patterns, since she came to the United States as a war bride in 1970,[82] a discursive mapping of the ways the Vietnamese refugee was received, both by the government and in the popular imagination, provides the historical context for the ways in which Hayslip's texts are situated.

The migration of Southeast Asian refugees constituted one of the largest immigration influxes in US history. The reception of Southeast Asian refugees included provisions like social welfare programs that began once they left for refugee camps and then resettled in the United States. To mitigate tensions over jobs and the economy, the US government attempted to distribute Vietnamese refugees evenly throughout the country and provide them with training in terms of basic survival skills and language acquisition even before they arrived to the United States.[83] Accordingly, economics played a large role in the political and popular constructions of refugees as "emblematic victims,"[84] and then, as racial and class tensions increased in 1980s America, as "welfare recipients" and "model minorities."[85] Underlying these constructions is a particular notion of sponsorship that speaks to the ways Southeast Asian refugees entered the United States after the war ended.

Unlike other recent Asian immigrants, many of whom migrated after 1965, Southeast Asian refugees were reclassified as "allied aliens," whose urgent expulsion from the countries of Cambodia, Laos, and Việt Nam underlined their dependence on the US government. These refugees were defined as "foreign populations to whom a state extends protection approximating that of its own citizens," as opposed to "enemy aliens," or "those who [were] citizens of the state considered disloyal on behalf of ancestry, i.e., Japanese Americans during WWII."[86] During a severely weakened economy following the 1973 oil crisis, this redefinition permitted the US government to provide monetarily for the refugees and to continue its support for their staggered admission rates during the late 1970s and early 1980s. On the heels of America's first failed war, such a move further maintained the US's symbolic capital as a democratic savior to communist victims. While this reclassification accorded monetary aid to Southeast Asian refugees, it also stressed their hyper-visibility as "approximate" US citizens in need of rescue and reclamation and accented their exceptional difference among other minorities in the United States.

This era also saw the dramatic rise of the New Right coalition. As Lauren Berlant suggests, a "world of public intimacy" was created in the New Right's agenda to reterritorialize the national along the lines of exclusion and accountability, a formulation executed in affirmative rhetoric. Turned inward, nationality itself became "a zone of trauma that demand[ed] political therapy,"[87] especially needed after the iconic loss of "Vietnam." Within this "zone of trauma," the New Right ably constructed the failure of "Vietnam" as a failure of political will, or what was called the Vietnam Syndrome.[88] From this perspective, Vietnam War discourse recast the white male veteran as a victim of war, oppressed and used by the American government in its fight against communism. Cathecting the war as a symbolic wound became a vital national "pasttime,"[89] enabling an American body politic to heal from the loss and emasculation that lay in the wake of America's defeat by a third world country.

If, as Susan Jeffords argues, "the unspoken desire of Vietnam representation, and its primary cultural function, is to restage 'Nam' (read: gender) in America," Hayslip spectacularly draws from the gendered rhetoric of intimacy and victimization that redefined the American nation during Ronald Reagan's presidency and the revitalization of the New Right.[90] Crafting a subjectivity that embodies self-reliance and forgiveness, Hayslip remakes herself in the image of feminine healer to the wounded body of the American veteran and, by extension, the body of the nation. Within a conservative political climate, Hayslip's texts rely on an assimilationist form of politics, but they also demonstrate the careful orchestration of a highly politicized subject. She borrows from contemporary American political and cultural discourses to emphasize a productive identity, one that positions itself relevantly at the latter end of Reagan's politics of "demonology" and at the cusp of Bill Clinton's term in 1992 in a post–Cold War era.[91] In *When Heaven and Earth Changed Places*, Hayslip reuses Reagan's key terms like the "evil empire" to describe Vietnamese communism and orders the book under headings that address "multicultural" America. In *Child of War, Woman of Peace*, Hayslip's chapter titles include, "Stirring the Melting Pot" and "Pursuit of Happiness," to signal her act of claiming America, an important gesture as the United States and Việt Nam began the process of normalization in 1994.

In addition to her rhetoric of multiculturalism, Hayslip's autobiographies bear the marks of difference, especially in contrast to other Southeast Asian American testimonials, because of how they are written.

Situating itself within Vietnam War discourse, *When Heaven and Earth Changed Places* is a collage of autobiographical and melodramatic conventions, while her second book, *Child of War, Woman of Peace*, contains metaliterary references testifying to Hayslip's agentive acts of storytelling in renarrating the nation. These two volumes attest to Hayslip's exceptional production of a literary self that is both a US citizen and a writer, subject positions that not only bear productive meaning but are also integrally linked for Hayslip. The following sections closely examine Hayslip's literary strategies in light of the national context in which her books were conceived.

In Between Genres: *When Heaven and Earth Changed Places*

Hayslip's first collaborative efforts with Jay Wurts work in between the genres of autobiography and melodrama. Such a dynamic accounts for the book's legibility and commercial viability. The autobiographical style marking Hayslip's works focuses on the interiority of her perspective and the intimate object of her subjectivity. While referencing "the real," the impulse underwriting autobiography, Hayslip also writes within the melodramatic mode, referring to an internal self who is the measure of all things in a Manichean world. The dual emphases on autobiography (historically coded as a masculine genre)[92] and melodrama (historically coded as a feminine genre) delineate some of the literary flourishes in her writings and highlight the productive tensions at work in cultural texts that straddle these genres.[93] Interrogating how realism and melodrama operate jointly is relevant here because of the ways in which US filmic productions about "Vietnam" were themselves "highly encoded melodramas" that attempted to dramatize the "real" of history.[94] In particular, a reading of the melodramatic mode in Hayslip's autobiographical texts illuminates the sense of the literary underlying her work.

As Peter Brooks has discussed, melodrama's mode of aesthetics allows for an identification of and a contest between good and evil, the moralistic dialectic of which gives way to narrative tension and the elements of drama.[95] After American soldiers returned to the United States from Việt Nam, the need to reassert value, goodness, and righteousness in a US-centered moral universe was imperative, especially in light of the ways in which the Watergate scandal, Vietnam War protests, as well as the gay rights, civil rights, and women's movements, had severely eroded public confidence in the government's ability to govern with authority. Within this context, Hayslip's 1989 cowritten autobiography operates in the melodramatic mode. It works to ensure readers of her ability to transform from evil communist enemy to good American citizen. For Hayslip, however, the conflict between good and evil is not merely set in largely Manichean terms but also rendered in quotidian terms within the context of a brutal war. In her first book, she constructs a moral universe wherein American soldiers are not the enemy, but neither are the Việt Cộng; both are victims of the war and subject to the machinery of war.

Caught between political ideologies, Hayslip describes a "nobility of soul" that is modeled upon her self.[96] Hayslip narrates the war as both victim and heroine in *When Heaven and Earth Changed Places*. The oscillation between these two roles provides the emotional crescendos that structure this book. Personifying virtue, Hayslip conforms to autobiographical conventions by positing the autobiographical (traditionally masculine) subject as an exemplary model. Writing within the autobiographical mode allows Hayslip to celebrate the heroic individual of her narratives and the remarkable life at their center. As the heroine of her own texts, the "woman warrior" of her family's past, Hayslip brings together the individualistic imperative of American autobiography with Việt Nam's mythologized history of female anticolonialist fighters and attempts to inscribe herself into these metanarratives of self-strength and female fortitude.[97] Nonetheless her text is also inaugurated by the birth of a "puny" girl, an event that prompts villagers to want to kill her because she is so inconsequential and small. Referencing herself as a "puny little farm girl," "country girl," or "little Vietnamese girl" more than a dozen times in this volume, Hayslip is systematically subject to torture, rape, and patriarchal abuse as a young woman. Significantly, narrating these traumas as past victim, she later symbolically gives birth to the writer within a teleological charting of the self that culminates in not only citizenship but also motherhood.

In this alternation between victim and heroine, autobiography and melodrama, the true subject of Hayslip's work becomes her own "melodrama of consciousness."[98] We are privy to her consciousness at every moment of the text. Hayslip amplifies the drama of making decisions between oppositions that represent life or death. The negotiation of such difficult choices is typographically inscribed by a marked use of syntax and punctuation. Through this stylized form, we are afforded seemingly direct entrée to her feelings as if they are felt at the moment she feels them. For example, when she returns to visit her former lover, Anh, for the first time, Hayslip is apprehensive about being able to find his house as a *Việt Kiều* visitor. Driven by a cyclo driver she initially distrusts,

Hayslip fears they are lost in the city streets. At every turn, her thoughts signal her anxiety.

> Perhaps he—and they—have something more than robbery
> or murder on their minds —
> Stop it! I tell myself. You're losing your head—just like at the
> airport! Paranoid—that's what you are! It's this place—your
> memories—the ghosts![99]

Hayslip's emotions are cued through an abundant use of em dashes, which function to signal the spontaneity of her thoughts. Deployed as rhetorical embellishments, these typographical markings construct Hayslip's textual self as an impetuous subject whose impulsive thoughts are reproduced in written form. In the process, the reader's empathetic identification with her is also bolstered because Hayslip comes across as an innocent caught in the crosshairs of war.

At the same time, Hayslip as adult author is adamant about denaturing the patriarchal expectations binding women to traditional constructs like family and nation. In the middle of the book, she describes in detail the sexual economy of women's labor within the US military complex and condemns the exploitation of women in this milieu.[100] At another moment, as a young girl who tries to fulfill her filial and national duties as a Việt Cộng informant, she is tortured when captured by the Republican Army. She writes:

> I didn't mean any harm to anyone. I only wanted to see the
> play and have fun—
> The guard behind lifted me by my hair and I yelped and he
> kicked the small of my back —once, twice, three times—with
> his heavy boots. I now screamed as loud as I could—no act-
> ing!—but he kept me dangling.[101]

The brutality of the scenes is spiked by the use of long dashes and exclamation marks, which fuse internalized dialogue, as signaled by the lack of quotes, with external acts of violence. Because em dashes also index an informal way of speaking, Hayslip's childlike tone elicits sympathy for a young girl (essentially a Việt Cộng spy) who suffers the traumatic experiences of war instinctively and intuitively. Her instincts, in fact, enable her to survive the war. Tellingly, Oliver Stone's filmic representation of her childhood meticulously recreates these scenes of physical violence against women because of their sensational intensity. Ostensibly more adult in her perspective by the second book, this highly stylized manner of writing is still employed but not as pronounced. The mature voice—the "woman of peace" in the title of the second book—takes precedence without the reliance on such formalistic techniques.

For readers, the stylized swings in tone and subjectivity further contour an already dramatic narrative. There is both pleasure and horror as we endure pain and suffering alongside her. Commenting on the ways pleasure functions in the 1978 film, *Coma*, Christine Gledhill argues that the production of pleasure for women viewers is marked by the alternation between the portrayals of the protagonist as victim and heroine. Gledhill notes how the film appropriates the real-life context of the women's movement in constructing the figure of woman as an independent doctor and heroine. At other moments in the film, however, such identifications are overturned when the same protagonist is disempowered and functions as a sacrificial victim. The manipulation of spectatorial knowledge is key to this depiction and the anxious reactions the film elicits; the giving and withholding of knowledge is controlled to maintain the suspenseful structure of narrative events.[102]

Operating along the same lines, Hayslip's text shuttles between suspense and pathos throughout the book. Within the chapters, she and Wurts construct temporality as a tense juxtaposition between past and present, imbuing the shifts with dramatic force and cathartic release. As opposed to *Child of War, Woman of Peace*, which hews to a linear narrative, this first book is told in parallel narratives. One recounts her childhood in Kỳ La; the other documents her return to Việt Nam as an older woman with three children in America. The crosscutting of time and space is marked by intertitles that cut into the body of the chapter text, announcing parallels that invite the reader to see between past and present.

Suspending the narrative climaxes in a highly serialized manner, Hayslip and Wurts effectively heighten narrative tension by cutting off each chapter at opportune moments. In a chapter entitled "Open Wounds," Hayslip recounts how she is accused of leading the southern Vietnamese army into a hamlet, enabling the killing of Việt Cộng soldiers. For her crime, the Việt Cộng invite Hayslip to a meeting where she is raped by a soldier, then later raped again by his friend. Immediately following the double rape is a return to the present, wherein Hayslip, apprehensive about entering Việt Nam because of her past crimes as an informant, awaits approval by the communist officials at Tân Sơn Nhất airport in Hồ Chí Minh City. The message she receives from the Vietnamese official at the airport states: "*Moi chi di hop*," or please come to the meeting.[103]

As these invitations by soldiers and officials are frighteningly similar, the chapter ends with her fearing death. She recites a Vietnamese folk saying that foreshadows her treacherously emotional trip to Việt Nam. She explains portentously to her traveling companion, "The meat has been brought to the tiger."[104] A sense of pathos for the victimized heroine develops in this closing frame of the chapter because Hayslip symbolizes, of course, the "meat" of which she speaks.

Through this technique, the reader feels at once sympathy and anxiety for Hayslip, since she barely escapes from the pressures of each situation. Her text demonstrates how melodrama lays emphasis on temporality and the "rescue" that occurs at a specific moment in narrative time. As Mary Anne Doane argues, melodrama refers to the "irreversibility of time, its unrelenting linearity."[105] True to this tenet, Hayslip plays on the many times that she does not know the fate of her life and loses control of it. Yet, in the nick of time, Hayslip escapes from her perils, attributing her escapes to the notion of karmic returns and the timelessness of her spiritual beliefs, as embodied by her father. As Hayslip navigates through the horrors of war, there is a sense of dread and anxiety with each decision she makes. By the same token, an Aristotelian sense of catharsis is evoked when Hayslip finds her "safe" haven in America by the end of the first book and at the start of the second book.

Situated safely in the United States, Hayslip's second book more closely narrates her life away from the dangers that "Vietnam" epitomizes in the first book. However, addressing the reader in the same fashion as in the first book—sometimes through direct address and second-person narration—Hayslip stages the second book as a continuation of an intimate dialogue between author and reader. More importantly, she explores the process of becoming—both in terms of her becoming a productive citizen and becoming a productive writer. These two projects bookend the sequel and allow her to claim membership within US national culture. It is this claim to US cultural membership that fuels some of the controversy in the reception of her work. Analyzing the themes and reception of her second book, the next section extends my examination of Hayslip's rhetoric about belonging and citizenship in *Child of War, Woman of Peace*.

Child of War, Woman of Peace: Narrating Self, Narrating Nation

In *Child of War, Woman of Peace* Hayslip discusses the production of her textual self and the reclamation of her citizen-self as importantly twinned prerogatives. On her writing, she declares: "As a United States citizen of Asian descent I was as entitled to my spot in the United States melting point as any Caucasian, Hispanic or black woman, or any other race that made up the American soul."[106] While Hayslip claims an American soul, she also asserts that she remains "a daughter of Vietnam."[107] Emphasizing her binationality, she underlines how she is positioned between two cultures and two nations, and that "this is where she belong[s]."[108] As a result of Hayslip's position of in-between-ness, she can incisively critique the patriarchal nationalisms that arise from both cultures and both nations. At these moments Hayslip's rhetoric is at its most powerful. On a trip to Washington, DC, for example, she confronts the bounty of America but also its limits within this space of the national.

Reading popular culture's fascination with trips to the country's capital, Lauren Berlant contends, "As a borderland central to the nation, Washington tests the capacities of all who visit it: this test is a test of citizenship competence."[109] To pass the test would be to successfully "coordinate the multiple domains of time, space, sensations, exchange, knowledge, and power representing the scene of what we might call 'total' citizenship."[110] The act of failing this "test of citizenship" underlies Berlant's theorization of an infantile citizenship, which rests on the fundamental faith a child or childlike subject holds in the American system. Because of their idealism, this subject not only constitutes the ideal citizen but also holds the power to contest the hegemonic narrative of the nation, despite its mediated modes of interpellations at work in the nation's capital city. Such cultural narratives expose the "potential catastrophes of all visits to Washington."[111] Set against a backdrop in which subalternity ironically "bears the burden of representing *desire for the nation* generally," the story of citizenship can be reframed in this most symbolic of public spaces.[112]

Hayslip's visit to these sites represents a reframing of the story of citizenship. Describing herself earlier as an "apprentice American,"[113] she performs the rites of patriotism by following the tourist sites' narrative trajectories. However, she also undermines these pedagogical imperatives by critiquing—through an infantile voice—the arrogance of US military power. With the awed, childlike tone that marks the beginning of the second book—for example when she arrives in Yellowstone Park and finds that "America is magic"—Hayslip fashions a naive self open to the experiences of what it means to be fully American.[114] Later, when she goes to Washington, using this same voice, she notes in familial language: "I was especially impressed with the enormous statues of Thomas

Jefferson, and my favorite, Uncle Abe Lincoln, who stared down at me like Buddha, all-knowing, and a little bit sad because of what he knew."[115] What "Abe Lincoln knows" is that while men are heroes, "they [are] politicians, which [means] compromising and hurting some people in order to help others. From this perspective, religious statues [seem] much better, because the monumental size reflects the immenseness of the viewer's own spirit."[116] Finding the statues imposing and cold, Hayslip laments the ways that the statues' lack of warmth matches the visitors' lack of reflection about the acts of war that founded the nation. Her sublime pleasure in nature at Yellowstone is later replaced by elegiac sadness in visiting these monuments that praise the powers of men.

At the Vietnam Veterans Memorial, Hayslip's observations are even more critical about the US's material power to not only celebrate acts of war but also commemorate a nation's own war dead. Failing the "test of citizenship," she remembers those killed in the war on both sides, the "millions of Vietnamese, including civilian women and children,"[117] whose names, she notes, should also be included in the memorial. At this site, she wonders too about the soldiers who impregnated young girls and left their Amerasian children behind. On remarkable display, here, are Hayslip's trenchant critiques of nationalist masculinity and "patriotic prowess."[118] Constituting ambivalent reactions to the symbols of US national memory, Hayslip's pointed views reveal the complicated ways she understands her vexed relationship to her host nation as both an infantile and maternal subject-citizen. Concluding this passage, she defiantly writes from the position of a mother: "With such a terrible truth staring them in the face, no men born of women could ever again order their sons off to war."[119]

Rejecting and reclaiming America in this complex way affords Hayslip the ability to profess authorship to her life writings as well. Underscoring the relations between motherhood and citizenship, Hayslip reiterates how the act of writing is tied to these highly symbolic constructions. Writing is a laborious project akin to reproductive labor, like a "mouse giving birth to an elephant."[120] Yet she perseveres in this endeavor and means to exercise her right to write as a US citizen. In a chapter entitled, "Pursuit of Happiness," Hayslip aligns the performance of citizenship with writing and the notion of historical accountability: "Unless people took it upon themselves to share what they had learned, each country would never be anything more to another than colors on a map."[121] Extending this notion further, Hayslip delves into the process of writing that, in turn, alludes to audience and national identity. Speaking about her intended audience, she states, "What mattered was that my American brothers and sisters—people like Mom Munro and Erma and Dennis's sister and the cashier at Safeway and anybody else who could read—would now have access to a hidden safe of their own national experience."[122] To reach out to readers like Mom Munro, she stresses her "third-grade education" as well as a national experience that unites them all.[123] Because "ignorant farm girls don't write books,"[124] moreover, she imbues the act of writing as a spiritual enterprise in which she works with her son, James, who edits her first book and cowrites her second book. As a mother and son writing team, their collaboration "must be about [her] father's business."[125]

Certainly the "business" of publishing is well detailed in Hayslip's book, as she gestures toward the labor exerted in the writing and dissemination of her "American story," "written with a bamboo pen."[126] However, as "American" as her story is, Hayslip discusses the difficult processes she confronted in not only writing her first book but also in attempting to get it published. Several presses rejected the book because it was so foreign to them. As she writes, "Vietnam 'really wasn't [their] thing,'" or they responded negatively to the ways in which the "subject matter was based on the viewpoint of enemies."[127] In these instances, Hayslip reminds readers of the prejudicial publishing demands made upon her text as well as her pluck and self-determination in finally seeing the book to press. Only when Hayslip finds Jay Wurts, "a man about [her] age but with a very 'old soul'" is she able to publish her first autobiography.[128]

In these plentiful metacommentaries about her writing, Hayslip reveals how she is the producer of her own life-writing.[129] In her attempts to claim authorship, she remains conscious of her translating role as a mediator between two cultures, often anticipating the responses she knows she will elicit from her audience as a result of her storytelling. Outside of their diegetic function, these asides serve as testimonies to her fecund creativity and role as a productive citizen. She likens the production of her first book to manual labor, writing, "My paddy had become the printed page. I had sowed thoughts and feelings like rice and in return reaped words to nourish my readers' spirit."[130] As author to her life, she underscores that she alone has birthed her stories, the products of her imaginative labor. Despite the presence of two different authors' names on the covers of her cowritten books, she reasserts the "auto" in American autobiography, the empowered subject of which is an authorial one in the crafting and "graphing" of it.

contentious reception of Hayslip's autobiographical self
lly upon this question of authorship. Some readerships
works as authentic and true, while others decry her texts
ic and unreliable. Some of the animus in the charge that
Hay- cultural traitor may hinge upon her past relations with white
men, relations extending to the present. Aggravating the controversy
surrounding Hayslip's first autobiography is the presence of its cowriter,
Jay Wurts, whose authorizing signature of white male authority marks
its cover. As an autobiography, *When Heaven and Earth Changed Places*
purports to present readers with a faithful account of the war, deemed
more legitimate because of Wurts's involvement. His name on the book
signals Hayslip's lack of English literacy but also reassures readers that
the firsthand account of war within its covers conforms to literary standards. The pact of coauthorship for Hayslip and Wurts affirms the book's
access to the "real" because of the centralization of Hayslip's subjectivity.
Their collaboration also highlights that Hayslip's evidentiary experience
of war will be rendered familiar and domesticated for US readers.

Wurts's gender and his past experience as a war veteran also matter as further points of legitimacy or delegitimacy. Other Vietnamese
American women's autobiographies feature cowriters of the same
sex. Published in the same year as Hayslip's first text was Nguyễn Thị
Thu-Lâm's *Fallen Leaves* with Edith Kreisler and Sandra Christensson
(1989), and following that was Nguyễn's sister's book, *The Rubber Tree*,
by Nguyễn Thị Tuyết Mai and edited by Monique Senderowicz (1994).[131]
Published by smaller presses, these memoirs indicate the early academic
demand for Vietnamese American women's texts; at the same time, they
underscore a fraught division of labor that historically lies between white
women and women of color writers within nonfiction scholarly work.[132]
Out of these writers, however, only Hayslip, collaborating with a white
male writer, has become commercially successful. After the publication
of *When Heaven and Earth Changed Places*, she collaborated on the film
adaptation *Heaven and Earth* with another white male veteran, Oliver
Stone, whom she describes as a spiritual paternal figure in terms similar
to how she speaks of Wurts.[133] For reading and viewing audiences, such
extratextual collaborations replay a highly problematic scenario of the
white male savior and third-world female victim, stunningly portrayed
in the climax of *Heaven and Earth* and evidence of the enduring project
of Orientalism in the popular imagination.

But while Wurts's coauthorizing signature is comforting to a
dominant readership, for another reading community, such as that

of literary critics in Asian American studies, this collaboraᛏ Hayslip. Examining the oral histories of Vietnamese refugeᛏ the axes of power and labor, critic and writer Monique T.D. Tᛏ discusses the loss of agency marking the subjects' mode of storyteᛏ ᳵ in collaborative narratives produced in the 1980s. In her essay, "Vietnamese American Literature," she analyzes the aesthetics of noncollaborative Vietnamese American texts, which purport to rewrite the acts of appropriation scoring earlier works. Looking at single-authored texts like Nguyễn Quí Đức's *Where the Ashes Are* and Jade Ngọc Huỳnh's *South Wind Changing*, Trương contends, "Freed, at least on the surface, from the tension of co-authorship and the uneasiness of submerged textual collaboration and manipulation, these texts offer a much longed for and tempting invitation to engage with the poetics of two distinct Vietnamese American literary voices."[134] In addition to the problems of collaboration Trương highlights, which rest on classed issues of literariness and literacy, Hayslip also privileges white masculinity and exercises "feminine accommodation" to dominant structures of power.[135] Consequently, Asian Americanists and literary scholars seldom touch upon Hayslip's writings. Renny Christopher makes this same point in her 1995 book, *The Việt Nam War, The American War*.[136] The continued lack of discussion of Hayslip's writings in both academic and nonacademic contexts highlights how the genre of autobiography remains an extremely vexed subject in Asian American literature.[137] Because of a limited access to power and culture-making for a marginalized community, furthermore, it is without doubt that Hayslip's representativeness by either "consent or descent"[138] will be contested, if not elided altogether.[139]

Nonetheless, Hayslip's cowritten autobiographies are historically and aesthetically critical on several fronts. In terms of literary criticism, they manifest the fictive qualities of the autobiographical genre, the subject of much work on Western autobiography, and demonstrate the genre's strong "appeal" to readers, both in terms of rhetoric and taste. Through her alternations between "infantile subject" and maternal writer, Hayslip also provides readers with a stark critique of the United States as a war-making nation, especially when she accuses the US military-industrial complex of having made women into "war refugees" and prostitutes during the war.[140] Most of all, she effects a powerful subjectivity that foregrounds a gendered, working-class Vietnamese American perspective within one of the most conservative times in American cultural politics. Hayslip achieves all of this by elaborating on her gendered role as a cultural translator, a woman caught in between political ideologies, nations, and languages.

Both Le Ly Hayslip and Linda Lê powerfully underline their roles as mediators and translators in their work. They emphasize how their translations are unfaithful to an original narrative about both nationhood and womanhood. Such is the critical power that Lê and Hayslip exercise when they figure their textual selves as treasonous daughters to the national family. Through this metaliterary thematic, these women writers emphasize the binds tying women to both family and nation.

Maternal Concubines in the Works of Linda Lê and Le Ly Hayslip

The colonial threat of defilement for a patriarchal nation begins with the primacy of women's procreative bodies at the moment they engage in acts of translation and literary creation. Cherríe Moraga and Norma Alarcón have separately analyzed Chicana women's essential treachery. Their forceful analyses resonate with the discursive terms surrounding the work of Le Ly Hayslip and Linda Lê, for whom the (self-)indictments of betrayal are also deeply intertwined with translation, sexuality, and motherhood. In an essay linking these notions, Norma Alarcón writes that the historical figure of Malintzín, the forbearer of a mixed and illegitimate race, plays the dual role of translator and procreator, a doubling that signals the originary violence of colonial conquest itself.[141] Cherríe Moraga contends that La Malinche is the maternal "traitor who [begets] the traitor," who henceforth becomes "slandered as *la chingada*, the fucked one, or *la vendida*, a sell-out to the white race."[142] Along these lines, the consequences for Vietnamese women's treason manifest themselves in language, for example in the denouncements against them. Reminiscent of Alarcón's reading of Malintzín is the way in which these recriminations about the Vietnamese female traitor and collaborator converge upon a maternal figure who is further denounced for transgressing the boundaries of appropriate femininity and for transacting that elemental exchange of word and body.

Following Moraga's and Alarcón's analyses, my readings of Hayslip's and Lê's writings ultimately coalesce around the maternal concubine. In both cases, the mother is portrayed either as the *femme fatale* or the nurturing mother; she remains the hinge between two national cultures during the eras of colonialism and postcolonialism. Radically dissimilar in respect to tone, writing style, and the national contexts they address and from whence they come, the two women authors lay bare the history of colonialism from which the metaphorization of the maternal concubine is produced. In these women's writings, sexual collaborations that mark women's exchanges with men are embedded within a larger nexus of colonial and patriarchal power structures. Because acts of female treason are situated within a larger political economy, Hayslip's and Lê's self-referential representations of the traitor and collaborator critique the systems of (post)colonialism and patriarchy within which women subjects are caught. Kamala Visweswaran insightfully argues that if betrayal is a symptom of power inequities, then it is simultaneously a site of complicity and a source of agency for women.[143] The study of Lê and Hayslip in juxtaposition exposes the act of writing as a project marked by compromise and resistance. These vectors constitute women's writerly subjectivities and highlight how charges of betrayal against women are entrenched in colonial histories and the linguistic and sexual violence resulting from such histories.

Diasporic women authors are subject to nationalist patriarchies that also indict them for linguistic and literary treason. At stake here is not only that Lê and Hayslip are "triply-jeopardized"—as women, women writers, and women of color writers, as Trinh T. Minh-ha has explained— but also that their perilous situations point to an underlying problematic for Vietnamese women writers in the diaspora.[144] As writers, Lê and Hayslip are located within a complex web of ideological lineaments. Only within a transnational context that takes into account the histories of an internecine war, French colonialism, and US military involvement in Việt Nam can we fully investigate the charges of betrayal leveled against Lê and Hayslip, as well as the accusations of betrayal with which the women authors charge themselves. A transnational feminist method of analysis concentrates on the historical and political conditions framing their texts, as these conditions determine not only the ways the texts are produced and published but also how they are received. Continuing the book's inquiry into the politics of treason, the next chapter analyzes the ways that women traitors are treated in postwar Việt Nam.

3 / Heroes and Traitors: The Gendered Fictions of Đặng Nhật Minh and Dương Thư Hương

"Cô là người phản bội." In a Western-style café in Hà Nội, Dương Thu Hương tells me levelly that she *is* the country's traitor, a glint of mischief in her eyes. We talk for hours about her difficult relations with the state as the sounds of Vietnamese pop music play in the background.[1] Around the same time, I interview Việt Nam's most acclaimed director, Đặng Nhật Minh, in one of Hà Nội's myriad hotels near the Lake of Hoàn Kiếm. Seated on a spindly couch, Đặng tells me that in several moments in his films, he alludes to Nguyễn Du's epic poem, *The Tale of Kiều.* Đặng also asserts that Việt Nam is analogous to the protagonist Kiều and her travails in many ways, claiming that his country is a "young woman."[2] Even though these conversations took place at different moments, I juxtapose my interviews with one of Việt Nam's most infamous writers and one of its famous directors because they point to the ways these two cultural producers treat the question of women. While Dương Thu Hương calls herself a traitorous daughter of the national family, and the Communist Party has labeled her a "communist whore," Đặng Nhật Minh, the son of a former war hero, refers to the feminine paradigm of virtue—Kiều herself—to describe his country.[3]

These brief anecdotes demonstrate the ways that Đặng and Dương, two artists living and working in Hà Nội at the time of the interviews in 2003 and 2004, are important gendered personages positioned at opposite poles of legitimacy and illegitimacy from the perspective of the Vietnamese state. One is a male director who stands in for the nation, while the other is a female writer who is a traitor to the nation. Signaled by Dương's forceful quotation, the role of a traitor (*người phản bội*) is one Dương fully embraces; her knowing and well-known occupation of this role lends an aura of transgression to her work, especially since the state had stripped Dương of her ability to publish after her arrest for the 1988 publication of her book, *Những Thiên Đường Mù*, or *Paradise of the Blind*. The state also incarcerated her in 1991 for fomenting dissent against the Vietnamese government. After her release seven months later, Dương was closely monitored in Hà Nội and forced to send her manuscripts surreptitiously via fax to her collaborators in France. On other occasions, foreigners smuggled the texts out of the country for her. To this day, the government has banned her works, though translated, xeroxed copies of her books are readily available in Sài Gòn. Yet, in the United States and France, Dương's texts circulate freely in Vietnamese, English, and French. Due to the appalling conditions under which Dương writes and the state's persecution of her, the international community celebrates Dương as one of the most important voices of dissidence in contemporary Vietnamese literature. Since her highly visible and public expulsion from the Communist Party in 1990, she has also won international acclaim and lucrative awards outside of Việt Nam.[4]

Similarly, the discursive construction of Đặng Nhật Minh as a hero (*người anh hùng*) and male filmmaker affords him even more legitimacy within a male-dominated film industry. Because Đặng, a former National Assembly member and Head of the Cinema Department in Hà Nội, is understood by many to be a legitimate voice for the country, he is given some flexibility in working within and outside of it to promote his films. Nationally and internationally, he is embraced as Việt Nam's most significant director. Spanning a forty-five-year period, Đặng's body of work stresses the quietly heroic subjectivities of women, who represent the country as a place of honor and dignity in the postwar era.[5] Vietnamese film scholar Ngô Phương Lan characterizes Đặng's films and other works as "envoys of peace" for audiences in the United States and other countries.[6] The few US academic essays on Vietnamese cinema analyze Đặng's films mainly for their feminine address, poetic sensibility, and accessibility. Of all of the Vietnamese films available outside of the underground market in the United States, Đặng's films are often subtitled, featured at international film festivals, and screened on university campuses. Ironically, however, Đặng's films are rarely screened within Việt Nam because the postwar film audience has shown little interest in watching films about the country's past.[7]

In his essay on the "author function," Michel Foucault makes clear that the function of the author is not only historically contingent and discursively determined but also tied to a set of ideas about the production, consumption, and reception of texts. The author function is crucially related to state power and global institutions like the publishing industry. Demonstrating how author's names are vested with various authorial functions, Foucault writes, "Unlike a proper name . . . the name of the author remains at the contours of texts—separating one from the other, defining their form, and characterizing their mode of existence."[8] Foucault advances the idea that the function of the author serves an ideological role in a given historical period. His theory resonates with the ways that the state-endorsed classifications of "hero" and "traitor" effect a tremendous material impact upon Đặng's and Dương's ability to produce and circulate their works within the country. Outside the country, Đặng's and Dương's authorial identities are invested with immense symbolic power, serving a classificatory function that yields the benefits of notoriety and recognition. Drawing upon this system, this chapter seeks to answer the questions: Who is the collaborator in Vietnamese state politics, and how does the state deal with her?

Following Foucault's gesture to look at the different "contours of texts," this chapter explores the aura of infamy and acclaim surrounding Đặng's and Dương's works, a discourse including literary translations, reviews, and film scholarship. Within this discourse, Đặng and Dương are characterized, respectively, as heroic and treasonous, loyalist and collaborative—artists who must be publicly fêted and disciplined as such by the Vietnamese state. Đặng, in particular, is privileged as an important director for the state. The Communist Party, however, treats Dương as a traitor to the state and to the socialist family. But within the contexts of the United States and France, these same Vietnamese cultural producers are privileged because of their critiques of the state, especially since their work comes from inside the Party and within the country. For instance, because of Dương's personage as a collaborator and traitor, foreign readers herald her as a transgressive figure outside of the state's borders. This structure of classification and identification is integrally bound to the historical relations between Việt Nam, the United States, and France and speaks to the ways the West selectively screens and reads the works of those who originate from the global South.

The aura of transgression surrounding the reception of Đặng's film and Dương's book is bound to their representations of the female subject. My trans-Vietnamese feminist analysis centralizes the female body in my readings of Đặng's film, *Cô Gái Trên Sông* [*Woman on the Perfume River*] (1987), and Dương's 1988 book *Những Thiên Đường Mù*, or *Paradise of the Blind*. Dương's novel and its translations serve as one focus of this chapter, while the way Đặng's movie functions as a cultural translation of postwar Vietnamese society constitutes another. Both texts purport to translate the experiences of being a gendered subject in postwar Việt Nam. My close readings are guided by the Latin origins of the word *translate*: *trans+latus*, which means "to carry across." Studying "the site and sign of translation to see what is displaced, excluded or repressed," my inquiries point to the transnational way that "Vietnam" as a discourse has been translated in print and film.[9] This chapter examines the linguistic and filmic translations of "Vietnam" as forms of cultural knowledge that travel from the country to the West in the post-1975 era. Querying the meaning of translated works from a country that remains "unknowable" to reading and film-going publics in the United States and France, the chapter stresses how knowledge about "Vietnam" has been represented and disseminated to these publics.

In particular, the chapter concentrates on Dương's most important book to date, *Những Thiên Dương Mù*, as this book has catapulted her to fame and set a precedent for the ways in which she is perceived outside of the country. Dương's Vietnamese text is placed next to the translated versions of it. Reading across three languages, I expose the complex, multivalent tasks and collaborations undertaken by the French and US translators. In the latter part of the chapter, the prostitute in Đặng's film *Cô Gái Trên Sông* is examined. She undergoes sexual and psychological transformations of various kinds, even though the director is at pains to show her ultimate virtue. Comparable to the ways in which the translations of Dương's book stress the will to knowledge for American and French readerships, *Cô Gái Trên Sông* also delves into an epistemological search for Vietnamese female subjectivity, particularly in its focus upon two female characters, a prostitute and journalist. This chapter focuses on questions of literary and textual collaborations (as in Dương's book) as well as the representational politics of sexual collaboration (as in Đặng's film), all of which are pinned onto the figure of woman.

Finally, I emphasize a more nuanced understanding of Việt Nam's cultural history in particular and of the politics of distribution in general, as a certain political economy of cinema and literature essentially shapes how cultural productions originating from Việt Nam travel outward. Trans-Vietnamese feminism interrogates the circulation of those works selected to be translated and distributed outside of Việt Nam's borders, and at the same time explores those lesser-known works circulating along other circuits. This way of looking maps a different cartography of Việt Nam, one not dominated solely by the coordinates of war and trauma. Rather, an analytic reading strategy that considers the complex negotiations underlying cultural productions and their relation to the state allows us to complicate state rhetoric about art and politics. Most of all, this reading practice sets a different valence to how collaborative work is interpreted; here, collaboration is not only a thematic signpost for prostitution but also serves as a symbol for the material practices that underlie the production of contemporary Vietnamese literature and its distribution. Interrogating issues of knowledge production, the chapter highlights that literature and film are collaboratively produced and the effect of such collaborations is often a gendered narrative of "Vietnam."

Across Translations, Across Contexts: Dương Thu Hương and *Paradise of the Blind*

In the United States, a reader of Dương's novel *Paradise of the Blind* cannot help but know about her past. The book jackets for all of her English-language texts replicate the same biographical blurb regarding Dương's induction into the communist army to "sing louder than the bombs" during the American War, as well as her arrest for criticizing the Vietnamese communist government after the war. Similarly, the preface of the French version of Dương's book, *Les Paradis des Aveugles*, by writer and journalist Michèle Mançeaux, known for her interviews with dissident figures like Aung San Suu Kyi, highlights Dương's history as a communist cadre during the American War. Presumably lying outside of Dương's and the translators' control, these marketing strategies emphasize the political dissonance that resonates throughout her texts, marking her as one of Việt Nam's most notorious female dissenters. Dương's critical voice and its commodification reference what critic Sherry Simon calls the "paratextual elements of a translation," or the peripheral matter accompanying the texts of translations.[10]

Even before this moment of commodification, however, the move to quickly translate this text into two different languages attests to the faith that publishers and translators had in the symbolic value of the Vietnamese version. The gesture to translate Dương's book quickly contradicts the drawn-out and often-laborious negotiations that underpin a book and the publication of its translations. Lawrence Venuti observes that part of the "scandal of translation" is that translated texts usually take about five years to produce and are not profitable endeavors for major publishing presses.[11] Rather, translators are poorly paid, and translations represent potential risks, especially if the original texts are not already valued in the global literary marketplace and marked as "assimilable."[12] Dương's book and its translatability rest not on its literary merit alone but more on the novel's perceived ability to speak truth to power in a timely manner. The book's publication and its translations merge with historic world events. Translated in French in 1991 as *Les Paradis Aveugles* and then in English in 1993 as *Paradise of the Blind*, the translations coincide with the beginning of economic reforms for the Soviet Union and the official end of the Cold War. The death knell of the Soviet communist bloc reverberates within the Vietnamese original, particularly resounding because Dương's 1988 book may have signaled the moribund status of communism in Việt Nam as well.

Những Thiên Đường Mù was translated first into French and then English. Detailing that trajectory, my analysis of Dương's text maps out the editorial and translational decisions that necessarily speak to readerships in France and the United States. Certainly Vietnamese French translator Phan Huy Đường and American translator Nina McPherson perform an important cultural task in the work of translating Vietnamese texts. But I also show how the cultural, racial, and gender politics of the milieus in which their readerships are located have shaped their translation choices differently; accordingly, the effects of their translations reflect these differing ideologies. My readings of Dương's text and its translated "echoes" demonstrate the structure of compensations and displacements inherent in any translation.[13] Nonetheless, Dương's translators also further dramatize her critique of communism and patriarchy. In so doing, the translators engage in a linguistic and symbolic transformation of an already violent Vietnamese version, dramatizing a paradigmatic moment of violence involving a young girl in the novel. These mistranslations speak at once to the highly ideological nature of Dương's novel. At the same time, the English- and French-language texts are not evaluated here in terms of being either "faithful" or "unfaithful" to the Vietnamese original. As a number of critics have pointed out, such notions of fidelity and infidelity are used to denigrate the work of women translators and reinforce the traitorous relation between women and the word.[14] Rather, in looking at differences across the translations, my comparative study of Dương's text and its translations examines how all three are transmogrified across several national contexts. It also explores the effects of the work of translation that tries to render the Other more familiar.

Translated in French and English, Dương Thư Hương's *Những Thiên Đường Mù* manifests several moments of collaboration within an ideological and institutional framework. The original's translated iterations are complicated by a few turns. The French translation was published first by the feminist publishing press, *des Femmes*.[15] Two years later, Nina McPherson used the translated French text, rather than the Vietnamese original, as the basis for her English-language translation. McPherson also translated the book into English collaboratively, with the help of Phan Huy Đường and a host of other Vietnam scholars in the United States. Yet, despite this chain of seemingly fluid replications and reproductions of the original, key differences striating the three versions are apparent. My interpretations demonstrate how these fault lines fall on the question of gender and race and emphasize the ways in which translations are not just meaningful acts of interpretation of the text in question but also of readers' expectations of what "Vietnam" represents.

From the beginning of the three texts, gender difference pivots depending on the audience addressed. Dương's novel tells the story of three women, the main protagonist (Hằng), her mother (Quế), and her aunt (Tâm). All the women slavishly work to uphold a patrilineage that bestows honor for their family's name. The men, who hold dominion over the women's lives, are Uncle Chính and, in a more spiritual sense, Hằng's absent father. A true villain, Uncle Chính's character offers no redemption; he objects to his sister's marriage to a landowner and appropriates the land and wealth belonging to his brother-in-law. In contrast, Hằng's father is a kind teacher, one who finds himself caught in a power struggle with his wife's brother. With such characters, the stage is established for a narrative that involves polarizing characters situated in the most extreme situations, allowing the author to denounce notions of both filial and national pieties. A female-centered *bildungsroman*, the novel revolves around Hằng, who is, at the beginning of the novel, working in Russia after the end of the war. When she returns from Russia, she has a series of tense battles with several family members who, in their diverse ideologies, represent the national family. It is only when she buries her aunt at the end of the novel that she becomes free to choose her own fate. After Hằng buries the past, she can see clearly enough to escape from a "paradise of the blinded."

Evidenced by the narrative, the two most blinding ideologies for Dương are Confucianism and communism. The binding of the two together places women in an impossible situation whereby the female protagonists are pitted against one another in order to align themselves with patriarchy. A historical novel detailing the horrendous failures of the Land Reform Campaign of the 1950s and the export-worker program in the 1980s, *Những Thiên* launches a devastating critique of these ideologies. Indeed, Phan's and McPherson's adaptations emphasize the denunciation of communist and Confucianist patriarchy in their translations. However, they render this critique differently, especially manifested in the ways the translators interpret gender and racial difference for their French and American readers.

Early in the three narratives, Hằng's mother's words set the tone for the story. Hằng's mother recites a proverb that impresses upon Hằng the importance of enduring and weathering all that life offers. She states, "Làm người cốt nhất là không được thối chí. Chỉ một phút xuôi tay, mọi sự sẽ đổ nát. Gừng già gừng rụi, gừng cay, anh hùng càng cực càng dày nghĩa nhân" [To be human the most important thing is not to be discouraged. Just one moment of letting things drop, and everything will fall apart. The older and more ravaged the ginger, the more piquant it will be. The more hardship the hero endures, the more humanity they will acquire] (my translation).[16] As the expression goes in Vietnamese, one becomes a compassionate "hero" only when he/she accepts and overcomes life's misfortunes. Metaphorized as a gnarled and piquant ginger root, enduring hardships renders one more human. In this context, the mother's words reference a person and his/her destiny in general. Significantly, Dương uses the word *anh hùng*, or hero. *Anh hùng* in Vietnamese can refer to men explicitly but not definitively. As such, the term, *anh hùng*, retains an ambiguity in terms of its gender address. *Anh hùng* by itself defines gender in accordance to the context in which the term is used but also signifies through an additive gesture (*nữ*) that renders it a more specifically gendered subject. If one were to refer to heroines, the word *nữ*, which denotes the feminine, is usually added to the word, *anh hùng*, to make the compound word, *nữ anh hùng*. The semantic instability entrenched in the Vietnamese language lends itself to these rich ambiguities around gender, wherein part of meaning construction in this linguistic system depends greatly on contextual information.[17] Given the mother's predilection to submit to the will of patriarchy, she may be paying homage to a masculinized notion of agency, or it may also allude to Dương Thư Hương's own ironization of the term "hero." But the ways in which *anh hùng* is translated in French and English is rendered less ambiguously.

That the French and English versions interpret *anh hùng* differently speaks to the ways in which gender subjectivities operate variously within the French and English linguistic systems. The French version translates the mother's statement about heroism as such: "le malheur forge l'homme" [hardship forges the man][18] and thus consolidates "his" humanity. The French translation replaces the Vietnamese word, *anh hùng*, and the ambiguous connotations freighted with this term, with the word *l'homme*, or man. The subject of this sentence is unambiguously marked by the masculine pronoun, so that self-will is a sign of the masculine. Within *Les Paradis des Aveugles*, the use of the universal male subject is also linked to the ways that the French language is emphatically gendered. The masculine—even if the masculine subject is in the minority amongst other subjects—still becomes the norm in written and spoken form. As Sherry Simon notes, institutional power supports this gendered system of language, particularly since the "Académie Française insists on the rule that the masculine takes precedence over the feminine."[19]

However, the English version does not take for granted the presumption that the masculine subject stands in for the universal subject, with McPherson substituting "woman" for the French "man" and the Vietnamese "hero." Hence, Nina McPherson's text reads, "Unhappiness forges a *woman*, makes *her* selfless, compassionate" (my italics).[20] This adaptation—more so than the Vietnamese and French works—is especially invested in hailing women readers. Since McPherson translates from the French version, it would appear that her use of the feminine subject and possessive is a pointed and positive change to the masculinist form of the French language. The change also characterizes the translator's intention to speak to an audience attuned to a US-specific discourse about female literary subjectivities. This bears out in the reviews of the English-language text. US literary reviewers looked upon Dương's text as a distinctly feminist one; in a revealing moment of intertextuality, William Searle, for instance, draws upon US multicultural rhetoric in calling Dương a "woman warrior," referencing the body of knowledge specific to American readerships familiar with Maxine Hong Kingston's and Le Ly Hayslip's work.[21]

While the French and English versions may be different in the ways they manage gender address, these translations are nonetheless uniform in their condemnation of patriarchy throughout their texts. Both translations emphasize the ways that Confucianist forms of patriarchy subordinate women. The translations indeed draw upon Dương's overt critique of patriarchal domination and stylize Dương's text through the techniques of repetition and alliteration in a manner that is formally absent in the original. The translations are strikingly similar in their rhetorical attempts to translate the oppressed conditions of Vietnamese women. These translation strategies are evident in a crucial scene where Hằng remembers her homeland while on a train to Moscow; she reflects on both the geography of Việt Nam and the country's gender relations. At the same time that Việt Nam becomes a site of longing for Hằng, it is also a place of contradiction and ambivalence for the protagonist. She nostalgically recalls the noises and sights of the countryside:

Giữa vừng quê, nơi tiếng còi ô tô hoặc còi tàu hảo vẳng tôi như ảo giác. Nơi mà người đàn bà trẻ có thể chắp tay lạy đức ông chồng như nô tỳ lạy chủ nô, và gã có thể lấy đòn gánh phang vợ vì tội đã trái lời gã, dám cho người bà con vay dăm gánh thóc hoặc vai nghìn viên gạch. Và những điều đó xảy ra ngay trong thập kỉ tám mươi này.[22]

[In the middle of my village, the honking of cars or the whistling of trains reverberate in me as if in an illusion. It is a place where a young woman may be made to kowtow to her husband like a slave-servant to her master, where he can whip her because she has disobeyed his rules, for daring to lend some baskets of rice and bricks to relatives in need. And such things were happening in this decade, the 1980s.] (my translation)

Through the use of internal dialogue, Dương shows Hằng ruminating on men's abuse of women in the past as well as in the present. Employing colloquial terms to denote a "woman" (đàn bà instead of the more formal term, phụ nữ) and gã to refer to a "husband" instead of chồng, Dương attempts to retain a vernacular sense of the everyday and a classed familiarity in painting this portrait of Vietnamese rural women. Exemplified by this passage, Dương's writing throughout the novel is punctuated by the sounds and images of rural life, depicted as such in all of its unrefined beauty. In her nostalgic reverie, these onomatopoeic sounds and pastoral images are the emotional and sensory signals for Hằng's sense of longing for Việt Nam, particularly acute because she is an exile when she becomes an exported textile worker in the Soviet Union during the 1980s.

Dương's novel is full of these details of rural life, the aspects of which are mostly excised in the English version and more consistently registered in the French text.[23] The passage above clearly represents an underlying strain of romanticism that threads throughout Dương's book. However, I point to this excerpt in particular because it ends with the idea that such abuses were still happening in the present era. The implication here is that women's oppression is still present in everyday life, despite the proclamations of equality found within communist rhetoric. Conveying indignation, Hằng's thoughts can be literally translated as, "And such things were happening in this decade, the 1980s." Compare Dương's sentiment, then, with the French version of the same passage. Lost in translation is the sense that Hằng's observations are critiques against the communist society in which the protagonist presently lives. What remains in translation is the romanticization of the countryside that Dương alludes to in the original text.

> Un espace étrange où le klaxon des automobiles et le sifflement des trains avaient quelque chose d'insolite. Un espace où des jeunes femmes s'agenouillaient comme des esclaves devant leurs maris. Un espace où les hommes battaient leurs femmes à coups de fléau parce qu'elles avaient osé leur désobéir et avaient preté quelques paniers de grains ou quelques milliers de briques à des parents nécessiteux. Un morceau de terre des années quatre-vingt... [24]

The French text, from the beginning of this excerpt to the end, foregrounds the "foreignness" of Việt Nam, signified by the French terms, *étrange* (strange) and *insolite* (unusual). The use of such terms connotes an impression of the unfamiliar echoed throughout. The English-language version runs parallel. McPherson's translation, which repeatedly uses the words, "a place," also conjures the otherworldliness of Việt Nam for the US reader as well. Nina McPherson translates the passage in the following manner:

> ... a place where the honking of cars and the whistling of trains is something mysterious, exotic. A place where young women bend like slaves at their husbands' feet. A place where a man whips his wife with a flail if she dares lend a few baskets of grain or a few bricks to relatives in need. A strip of land somewhere in my country, in the 1980s... [25]

In their poetic and rhetorical qualities, the French- and English-language versions almost mirror one another in terms of language, sentence construction, and syntax. Both translators also shift between plural and singular subjects to refer to both men and women, which stand in contrast to Dương's consistent use of the singular subject in the same excerpt. Rather than demarcate a subject positioned in a clear time and space, the translators elect to unmoor the subject from the temporal and spatial specificity rooted in Dương's passage. The anaphoric rhythm in both of the translations aides in this effect: a lyrical repetitiveness runs throughout the passages not only in terms of a reverberating sound but also of meaning and emphasis. Most especially, Phan's and McPherson's translated paragraphs end on a neutral description of the "place" of "my country" in the 1980s, so that the last image remains fossilized: Việt Nam is "a strip of land in the 1980s." Absent from these last lines is a nuanced indication of how these practices of patriarchy were, in fact, still impacting women, a sentiment subtly relayed in Dương's version and signaled by the verb, *xảy ra*. This verb, which means to occur, always has pejorative connotations.

Positioning Việt Nam in its contemporary time, however, is the point of critique for Dương. She emphasizes Hằng's subjective thoughts regarding temporality—more specifically, the contemporaneity of Việt Nam as well as its forbidding future. Hằng not only critiques the Confucianist patriarchy that has marked the lives of women since feudalism but also the lack of socialist egalitarianism in Việt Nam's postwar era. The latter critique somewhat recedes in the French and English versions, even though Dương's book is thoroughly preoccupied with the passing of time, as it protests against the traditional structures of the past and the inability for Vietnamese society to move forward into the next century. In many passages, Vietnamese society is portrayed as backward in terms of its technology and industries, but especially regressive in its cultural customs regarding women. Dương maintains that for Vietnamese people to make progress, they must first be unshackled from the past, a point she underscores in the end when Hằng finally leaves the confines of her tradition-bound village.

To further stress this point, Dương situates in racialized terms notions of primitivism and progress along a teleological trajectory. For example, at a family dinner, a young Hằng raises a glass of red wine to her deceased father, narrating the story while using primitivist imagery. She refers to her family as "những bộ lạc da đỏ xưa" [ancient red-skinned tribes],[26] who perform sacred and secret rites. The French version renders Dương's racialized construction in more muted tones, describing the family as "des peuples primitifs d'antan" [ancient primitive peoples].[27] In marked contrast, the English-language text subtracts the image of the tribe from the passage altogether but maintains the image of rituals. The text reads: "I felt as if I were drinking to some solemn, merciless vow, some sacred, primitive rite."[28] Similar references to tribalism resurface in the Vietnamese original when Hằng describes the childhood activities of camping in the woods. Camping rituals for her and her friends are similar to partaking in the customs of a "bộ lạc man dại xưa" [wild tribe of the past].[29] Most notably, the French and English translations allude to a savage past but expunge its racist connotations and attempt to neutralize the passage. The French adaptation describes how the group of teens of which Hằng is a part romantically dreams of "une vie sauvage dans des temps recules" [a wild life in distant times].[30] McPherson's translation reflects this same sentiment when it alludes to how youths dream of and talk about "a life in the wild."[31]

Undoubtedly, the editing of Dương's primitivist language results from an acute understanding of how such politically loaded terms operate in the American and French cultural milieus. This gesture to detract from the racialized language, however, elides the ways in which Dương sets up a distinctly racialized hierarchy to thematize concepts of progress and civilization. In stark contrast to Dương's construction of primitive peoples of the past (as narrative elements, they are also anchored in Hằng's childhood past), the only people who Hằng understands to be advanced are the light-skinned, upper-class Japanese, who come from a post-capitalist Asian country located in a first-world economy. For instance, when Hằng observes a group of Japanese teenagers, she finds them fashionable, brimming with self-confidence, and endowed with a sense of modernity. She compares this group of young men and women to her own people, their lives marked by deprivation and misery. Dương's narrator reflects on the Japanese in this way: "Fate had blessed them. They had been reincarnated under a peaceful roof, marked by few storms and wind" (my translation).[32] The point of Hằng's comment about this group is to highlight the overwhelming distinctions between peoples from a superindustrialized Asian nation with those of the Vietnamese.

Reflective of the familial themes of the novel, Dương underscores how her cohort must compensate for the excesses of previous generations. Hằng pays for her family's spiritual debts because of a misplaced sense of filial piety and, by extension, a wrongheaded obligation to the national family. The terms Dương uses to configure the past and future of Việt Nam are highly racialized and stratified by class; problematic as this is, it remains critical to understanding the ways in which the novel's themes manifest. Despite this emphasis, both the English and French translations avoid the racialized essentialisms found in the original. Instead, both versions reference the issues of race and culture through extratextual devices.

The strategies by which French translator Phan Huy Đường assimilates cultural differences signal the milieu in which both translator and translation are found. As I discussed in the previous chapter, within a competitive French publishing market, the literary texts of ethnic minority writers in France are often marginalized and more routinely produced by small publishing presses, such as Actes Sudes and Éditions de l'Aube.[33] Translations of Asian texts in French belong in the same category of niche literary publishing and are most likely categorized in bookstores by the national countries from which the authors originally hail.[34] Given these conditions governing the French literary marketplace around ethnic texts, Phan's translation strategies try to emphasize the translation's value as a literary and ethnographic view into a foreign culture. Different from its English counterpart, the French-language adaptation stresses not only its lyrical qualities but also its accessibility to Vietnamese culture. Phan's version of Dương's novel offers numerous footnotes, explaining the cultural practices, exotic rituals, and literary and linguistic references found throughout the Vietnamese version. The footnotes also work in conjunction with the translator's insider perspective, especially since Phan is Vietnamese himself. This referent of continuity is further signed by the fact that Phan's name graces the cover of the book as well.

In contrast, as part of its critical apparatus, Nina McPherson's version draws more upon the personal history of Dương Thu Hương as it intersects with the country's political history. Along with Dương's stark black-and-white picture on the book's jacket flap, a picture taken after she had emerged from prison,[35] *Paradise of the Blind* features a historical preface on the failures of the communist programs in the latter half of the twentieth century, provides a short glossary of food and cultural terms, and concludes with a biographical "Note about the Author." This version emphasizes the political and historical context of the novel for a US readership for which the Vietnam War is more a part of Americans' recent memory. Part of the book's value for mainstream readers lies in filling the fissures of political knowledge about the country. One of the few books discussing Việt Nam from a Vietnamese perspective when it first came out in 1993, the English-language translation proffers itself to US readers as a means to understand a former, formidable enemy who defeated the United States in war. That the novel provides a woman's account of war is also imperative for the feminist framing of this version.

Translators Phan and McPherson employ key strategies to manage racial and gender differences. They do so primarily through supplementing or subtracting information, gestures that are intrinsic to any act of translating. But despite the differences in the ways that Phan and McPherson implement such strategies, they interpret an important rape scene identically—in ways that contrast to and align with Dương's writing of the same scene. Both adaptations sensationalize this climactic moment of the novel when a communist official sexually assaults a young girl, a scene meant to represent the cruelties of communism. The mentally challenged victim is fourteen years old in Dương's book; however, in the French and English versions, the translators write that she is only nine years old.[36] Perhaps these changes were inadvertent and allude to the publishers' demands for unambiguity about the immorality underpinning the scene, but the effects of such changes are undeniable. In rendering the rape victim a young girl, one who is more of a child than an adolescent, the translations emphasize the sexual perversion of the communist cadre in particular and the corruption of communism in general.[37]

While the translations change the girl's age, descriptions of the communist official in the Vietnamese version and their translated versions remain sexually explicit, associating the phallus with political domination. Dương's text describes the victimizer as "naked as a moth" [trần như nhộng] during the rape.[38] Using similar metaphorical language, the French version portrays the official as being "nu comme un ver" [naked as a worm] atop his victim.[39] The English-language text follows suit, utilizing the same figurative expression to describe his male member as being "worm"-like.[40] This portrayal of the cadre across all three texts encodes the idea that communism and feudal patriarchy are interpenetrating forces exercising a terrible prerogative against Vietnamese women. Viewed allegorically, this scene references the rape of a feminized Việt Nam in its sovereign infancy by a communist power.

In contrast to the rape victim, by the end of the novel Hằng is figured as the feminist subject. The lone survivor of the traumas of communist patriarchy, she envisions the future clearly and can thus leave "the paradise of the blind." Produced roughly during the same time of Dương's publication of *Những Thiên Dương Mù*, Đặng Nhật Minh's film *Cô Gái Trên Sông* contains similar women characters as well as corrupt male cadres. Interestingly, the US reception of Đặng's work moves along a related trajectory to Dương's. Both Dương's and Đặng's texts deal with an abject female subject pitched against a liberal feminist one who resists communist patriarchy. Analogous to the ways in which Dương's persona travels alongside her texts, Đặng's auteurist identity as Việt Nam's most renowned director also accompanies his filmic texts overseas. Đặng's construction of the heroic feminine is crucial to the critical reception his films have received.

Art of the State: Vietnamese Cinema and the Female Body

Released in 1987, Đặng Nhật Minh's film, *Cô Gái Trên Sông*, or *Woman on the Perfume River*, marked the beginnings of the historic transformation of Đổi Mới, Việt Nam's economic reforms. With these changes came the concomitant fear of the corrupting influences of the West and Việt Nam's Asian neighbors. Ever since the country's opening to world markets, the state has continued negotiating with foreign investors, while simultaneously attempting to balance the country's economic needs with its socialist ideals. By the same token, Đổi Mới has definitively transformed the Vietnamese cultural landscape. In the realm of film, the importation of international films offers Vietnamese film audiences more individual and consumer choices, particularly as more moviegoers frequent cineplexes than before. Evidence of a developing local film culture is the domestic hit film *Gái Nhảy* (2003), or *Bar Girls*.[41] As Việt Nam's first blockbuster film, since followed by many others like *Những Cô Gái Chân Dài* [*Long-Legged Girls*] (2004) and *Nụ Hôn Thần Chết* [*Kiss of Death*] (2008), Lê Hoàng's breakout film manifests the tastes of an emerging urban, middle-class population and represents a shift in the consumption practices of the country's movie audience.

Produced on the cusp of the economic reforms of Việt Nam, *Cô Gái Trên Sông* is historical, marking the moment before the flows of global capitalism transform the country's culture industry.[42] Moreover, it was one of the first Vietnamese films to be presented at international film festivals after the war officially ended in 1975.[43] The film's significance is mostly rooted in its thematic content: it recounts the travails of a prostitute, a character who ends up representing reconciliation in Việt Nam's postreconstruction era. As Vu Ngoc Quynh argues, though the film was controversial at home, when it was released abroad, international viewers regarded the film as a "symbol of renewal."[44] *Cô Gái* was also released at a particular moment in contemporary Vietnamese history, when Việt Nam opened its markets to the world but also simultaneously exhorted the return of Vietnamese women to the private realm following their public forays into war, politics, and the battlefields.[45] The film cinematically replicates a nationalistic sentiment about the role of women and their return to the home in postwar Việt Nam, especially in the ways in which Đặng narrativizes, shoots, and images the protagonist/prostitute in the film. I analyze the function of investigative journalism and the use of flashbacks in the film to reveal the cinematic mechanisms by which the figure of the prostitute is compromised, not only by the other characters in the film but also by the spectator's gaze.

Set in the present, *Cô Gái Trên Sông* begins with the narration of a prostitute's story. From her hospital bed, Nguyệt recalls to a female journalist (Liên) how she met a revolutionary soldier, whom she fell in love with and then saved when he fled from ARVN soldiers shortly before the war's end in 1975. Narrated subjectively, most of the film's flashbacks depict the tragic events structuring the prostitute's life: Nguyệt's work as a prostitute on the Perfume River; her relationship with Sơn, an ARVN soldier whose love she cannot return; her betrayal by the lover she saves; and her exploitation at the hands of male soldiers. The dramatic turn of the movie occurs when viewers learn that the journalist, Liên, is actually married to the revolutionary that Nguyệt rescued, a man named Thư who now serves as a high official in the post-1975 communist regime. We learn that Thư refuses to acknowledge his past love affair to either Nguyệt or Liên. A patriarchal and controlling figure, Thư also attempts to prevent Liên from learning the secret of his past and censors her story to avoid its publication in the state-controlled newspaper where she works. When Liên learns the truth, she leaves her husband and searches for Nguyệt. Liên finds Nguyệt with Sơn, Nguyệt's present lover. In order to give Nguyệt closure, Liên tells her a lie: her revolutionary "hero" has died. In the final frames of the film, Nguyệt imagines Thư heroically dying in battle, even though both the audience and Liên know the truth about him.

Because a prostitute—not a typical revolutionary hero—is the focus of the movie, historian Mark Bradley maintains that the film is commendable because the woman-centered narrative articulates a sharp commentary on the repressiveness of state ideology.[46] Importantly, Đặng's film features an agentive female voice in the reconstruction of popular memory, the production of which is clearly subjective and feminized within its frames. As film theorist Maureen Turim asserts in her study on the use of flashbacks as a narrative technique, flashbacks have the potential for positing subjective, individual memory over and against that of an established historical narrative. Since "[flashbacks] can take as their project the questioning of the reconstruction of the historical, the employment of subjective memory has a double sense of rendering history as subjective and the formation of the Subject in history, as the viewer of the film identifies with a fictional character's position in a fictive social reality."[47] As Turim details, a film's use of the past becomes a tool to voice what has historically been muted—the oppression of women in a patriarchal society. Flashbacks allow for a suturing of the past with the present, importantly presented through the voice and memories of the female speaking subject.

At the same time that flashbacks critique and naturalize subjectivization, however, the intense focus on the individual also works to distance viewers and discourage identification. For Turim, flashbacks, especially in noir films, "contain an element of philosophical fatalism. . . . This fatalism presents a cynical view of history [as] cyclical, guaranteed to repeat that which we have already seen."[48] This ambivalent mode of the flashback and the circular narration of history in films problematize the notion that a memory of the oppressed is subjectively presented. Turim argues that flashbacks can also nostalgically posit the past as a moral lesson. In the example with Đặng's film, flashbacks serve to construct an idealized memory about women's heroism and virtue. It demonstrates that the contested narratives of collective memory are ultimately marked by a patriarchal ideology about the suffering of women. Through its use of flashbacks, the film maintains that recurring tragedies are a necessary condition for female consciousness and lay out the conditions for female solidarity.

The positioning of women's powerlessness against men's seemingly absolute power in the film is critical, however, to its melodramatic address. Rather than understand the film primarily as a critique of state power as Bradley argues, I stress the film's endeavor to create moral legibility in its spectacular staging of the struggle against evil.[49] Đặng's melodramatic film clearly posits that the women characters are virtuous, while Thư, the main male character, is villainous. Exploring Thư's character, Bradley maintains that the film's subversive criticism rests on how the communist official is punished for his "lack of moral virtues," particularly as his behavior stands in contrast to the loyal prostitute's.[50] As Bradley explains, the "sympathy and quiet heroism accorded to the prostitute and the criticism of the cadre's postwar behavior overturn the state's most fundamental political assumptions."[51] However, to place the film within the generic codes of melodrama is to understand that Thư must function as the villain, as he manifestly reneges on his promise to find Nguyệt and take care of her after the war. Since this dialectical relationship between the powerful and powerless animates the melodramatic genre, Đặng's film deploys these characters to thematize the clear recognition of vice and virtue. Cast in this light, Thư does not represent the Vietnamese communist regime in total and cannot function to demonize communism in general, which stands in contrast to the characterization of the communist official as rapist in Dương's novel. While the figure of the revolutionary hero is overtly critiqued, the film does not necessarily conflate Thư's wrongdoing with the communist state's

vision of collective unity and progress. Instead the produ~ ~ctivity of laboring bodies, namely those of a southern Vietnamese soldier anu ~ a former and
prostitute by the end, conclusively attests to the state's beneficence ~
its ability to rehabilitate former traitors.

Addressing the contentiousness of Thư as a character, John Charlot's
essay, "Vietnamese Cinema: First Views," is illuminating. According
to Charlot, Đặng won a struggle for autonomy and to produce the film
because government officials did not want to be seen as defending the
"bad characteristics of any Vietnamese communist official."[52] Though
contentious, the film won a Silver Lotus Award via secret ballot that
year.[53] Albeit a difficult process, this official recognition of the film is in
keeping with the film's conclusion, which celebrates rather than critiques
communist officialdom. For the ending proposes that a new, cohesive
social body can be constructed by those who come from the lower rungs
of Vietnamese society, including two former enemies of the state: the
ARVN soldier and the prostitute. As Charlot and Bradley separately
note, the prostitute further enables a sense of resolution and rapproche-
ment in the film's conclusion. However, neither critic employs a feminist
critique to delve into the ways in which this figure must be doubly re-
formed in the final images of the film.

M. Jacqui Alexander discusses the forms of "erotic autonomy" that
prostitutes and lesbians possess, and which the neocolonial state tries
to deny them; their unruly sexuality alludes to a nonprocreative form of
sexuality that must be reharnessed for national reconstruction. In this
configuration, "loyalty to the nation as citizen is perennially colonized
within reproduction and heterosexuality, so that erotic autonomy brings
with it the potential of undoing the nation entirely, a possible charge of
irresponsible citizenship or no citizenship at all."[54] To demonstrate the
ways in which nationalist logics of loyalty are placed upon the female
body, the last sequence of images must be carefully examined here: the
journalist, Liên, finds Nguyệt to tell her that Nguyệt's hero is dead. This
lie is preceded by images of Nguyệt, who, having reunited with a past
lover, Sơn, works side-by-side on building a sampan for their new life
together. They represent the new socialized unit successfully reeducated
by the communist regime and ideology. As a prostitute and a southern
Vietnamese soldier during the war, Nguyệt and Sơn once represented
corruption and treason, but in the film's final images, these two characters are re-formed as productive citizens in a new era. Most crucially,
they are also the heterosexualized subject-citizens deemed necessary for

FIGURE 3.1. Rehabilitating the former prostitute and ARVN soldier. From the film *Cô Gái Trên Sông* (*Woman on the Perfume River*) © 1987. Vietnam Feature Film Studio.

the reproduction of the country's ideals and its inhabitants in the era of national reconstruction (see Fig. 3–1).

Of the two re-formed subjects in the end, however, Nguyệt is more of an unknowing subject than Sơn. Nguyệt is constrained by her lack of agency and knowledge in the construction of her own narrative throughout the film. While central to the diegesis, Nguyệt's subjectivity is mainly a vessel the director uses to address women's conditions. Even so, cultural critic Kathryn McMahon views Đặng's films as oppositional and resistant because of their feminist liberatory premises. Đặng's films create what she calls a paradoxical space, where "one occupies inside and outside, center and margin simultaneously so as to critique the master subject."[55] However, as I show, the film orchestrates the prostitute's betrayal through the enlistment of the spectator's participation in Nguyệt's exploitation, a process that renders impossible the creation of an oppositional and feminist subject position.

In several instances, an objectifying camera gaze constructs a spectatorial position that partakes in the disciplining of the prostitute and her body. Even though Nguyệt may narrate the film, Đặng's camera over-takes his speaking subject's narration several times. In one of the earlier flashbacks, upon meeting Nguyệt for the first time, Thư induces her to speak about her past. Quickly thereafter, Thư recites to Nguyệt a passage from *The Tale of Kiều*. Afterward, an inconsolable Nguyệt cries because at this point she understands her fate so decisively; she embodies Kiều and her tragic destiny as a virtuous prostitute. In this scene, while Nguyệt narrativizes her life, she is paradigmatically defined as lack; the signifi-cations of her life are ordered by a stranger (Thư), an act later replicated by Liên when she pieces Nguyệt's story together. To emphasize Nguyệt's lack of control over her own story, the camera gaze moves away from her speaking voice and body to the exterior of the sampan, her home and the site where she has sex with her clients. The camera movement marks the director's distillation of Nguyệt's suffering into an objective correlative; the small boat floating unsteadily on the Perfume River is a leitmotif, a metaphor for the waywardness of Nguyệt's life as a prostitute on the river. This technique indicates a directorial flourish that extradiegeti-cally signals the director's power over Nguyệt's act of narration.

Another instance of the director's intervention occurs when Nguyệt awaits Thư outside of his office. Nguyệt stands in front of the security kiosk; slowly, the camera tracks away from her, emphasizing her alien-ation and humiliation because the security guard finds out that she was a wartime prostitute (see Fig. 3–2). Later she is turned away because Thư refuses to speak to her. Clearly Thư means to avoid confronting his past relationship with a prostitute. The next faraway shot pronounces Nguyệt's despair, but then the camera pulls back further to reveal, only to the audience, that Thư himself is watching Nguyệt through a window. In this sense, we are not presented with Nguyệt's story as she tells it, since she evidently does not know that he knows who she is. Rather, Đặng's direction dominates Nguyệt's story and allows spectators to experi-ence the first in a series of astonishing revelations that supplement our own spectatorial knowledge about Nguyệt. Spectators are thus placed in a privileged position, privy to what the main protagonist does not know and will never know. Finally, in a strange twist, the spectator is also allowed access to Nguyệt's body. The film forces spectators to adopt the position of one of her clients through a camera gaze that reenacts the surging back and forth movements of heterosexual sex. In essence, the camera moves on top of her body, aligned with this camera perspec-tive; spectators find themselves simulating a "dominant" sexual role. Of course, these cinematic efforts emphasize Nguyệt's victimhood and

FIGURE 3.2. Nguyệt as an unknowing subject. From the film *Cô Gái Trên Sông* (*Woman on the Perfume River*) © 1987. Vietnam Feature Film Studio.

tragic sensibility, but they do so in a highly stylized manner, rendering her body an abject site of exploitation by several characters in the film as well as by the spectators.

The journalist in the film, Liên, is the only character who does not exploit Nguyệt's body. However, Liên's power over the amnesiac patient is exercised through the withholding of information regarding Nguyệt's past. The reconstruction of Nguyệt's narrative is performed primarily because of Liên's gentle and sisterly insistence for Nguyệt to "tell all," a central gesture within the genre of melodrama.[56] As a journalist, Liên remains crucial because she also represents the desire for truth and justice within a repressive society. As the story unfolds, her desires for truth are represented in her acts of investigating Nguyệt's story and publishing it. Defined by her profession and her "will to know," Liên's pursuit of truth represents the spectator's own desire for knowledge. Through Liên's mediation of Nguyệt's narration and her own investigative discoveries, viewers understand Nguyệt's story as one that is about women's victimization. Playing the role of investigator-as-analyst, Liên sifts through and interprets Nguyệt's past. Instead of speaking out "truthfully," however,

Liên's lie to Nguyệt in the end is premised upon a class-based prerogative; as an educated woman who knows what is best for Nguyệt, she
manipulates the story about Nguyệt's revolutionary hero so that Nguyệt
can forget the past and lead a more productive life.

In spite of this lie, and in contrast to the abject figure of the prostitute, Liên serves as an important locus of spectatorial identification,
particularly for the non-Vietnamese viewer. Throughout the film, Liên is
strongly figured as the educated, strong, and liberal modern subject, one
who resists patriarchy. Spectators are encouraged to feel allied with this
ideal and whole subject of the film, especially because Nguyệt's exploited
body does not offer a viable subject position for the feminist viewer. The
figure of the journalist may be especially resonant for American viewers
for whom, as Matthew Ehrlich has noted, the theme of journalism in
American films embodies the ideas of freedom founded in a democratic
society.[57] Liên, though a reporter hailing from a socialist country, reinforces these liberal notions of freedom and expression because she alone
struggles to have her voice heard within the context of a patriarchal and
authoritarian society.

Liên's character prompts me to further explore the position of the US
critic and her desire to understand Vietnamese cinema through the lens
of war and the figures of women. Precisely because Đặng's films hinge
on aesthetic refinement and questions of historical memory, they impel
the critic to probe the poetics and politics of his films, often framed
around the images of resistant women such as Liên. Against a corpus
of hypermasculine images found in Vietnam War films, for example,
Gina Marchetti argues that the Vietnamese concept of suffering—as
it is rooted in *Tale of Kiều*—makes Vietnamese melodramas an especially enabling genre for Vietnamese directors. However, as Marchetti
contends, the same concept of suffering becomes an obstacle for the liberation of Vietnamese women in recent Vietnamese melodramas. She
writes that women in such films "remain trapped in a world in-between,
without any feminist consciousness of their plights as women and only
a resignation of their fate."[58] In this way, Marchetti obliquely positions
"feminist consciousness" as that which is defined by Western feminist
notions of agency.

While foundational to the emergent field of Vietnamese cinema, these
critical works on Vietnamese filmmaking have not taken into account
the historical context of the Vietnamese film industry, or the fact that
Đặng holds a distinct position within the film industry as a former
head of the Cinema Department. The fact that male filmmakers have

historically dominated these positions, as Charlot has argued, allows the same filmmakers some flexibility in defining the aesthetic parameters of a national cinema and in negotiating with the censorship authorities about their films' production.[59] The son of a former war hero, Đặng Nhật Minh also served in the National Assembly and made a celebratory film about Hồ Chí Minh, *Hà Nội: Mùa Đông 1946* [*Hanoi-Winter 1946*] (1997). That Đặng has a considerable amount of state power behind him does not inherently make his films representative of official products of the Vietnamese state, but within this highly regulated industry, it must be noted that his work has been allowed to be produced and circulated outside of the country with great regularity and visibility since the start of *Đổi Mới*, or "Renovation."

Permitted to take part in numerous international film festivals as Việt Nam's most important director, Đặng has cultivated an international following who appreciates that his films are artistic, aesthetic, and at times, critical of the communist regime. Winning several awards and garnering critical acclaim throughout Asia, Europe, and the United States, Đặng has worked as a second-unit film director in Philip Noyce's *The Quiet American* (2002). Since then, Đặng has toured his films throughout the United States, Asia, and Europe. Most recently, he released his film *Đừng Đốt* [*Don't Burn*] (2010), based on the best-selling memoir, *The Diaries of Đặng Thùy Trâm* and a project into which the state invested heavily: US$687,500 when the average budget for a film is usually only US$60,000.[60]

However, it is debatable whether Đặng holds much sway among non-elite film-going audiences in Việt Nam. Only a small minority of the Vietnamese population has access to Đặng's films.[61] This problem of access speaks to the strapped financial situation of the Vietnamese film industry, producing state-sponsored films that do not reach domestic movie theaters because they lack commercial appeal. The disinterest in "high" art films in Việt Nam indicate a profound lack of concern on the part of filmgoers about issues of collective mourning, loss, and recovering the national past, themes that make up the country's most celebrated films. Caught between the desires to develop the industry domestically while propagating the idea of a Vietnamese national cinema internationally, the state must negotiate with local and global audiences in regulating the country's filmic output and filmic exports.

The paucity of Vietnamese films available for US film critics to watch—as well as what gets selectively chosen to be subtitled, translated, and disseminated—should alert us to the problems of the uneven cultural exchanges in the consumption of global South texts within the global North. Vietnamese "high"-art films produced in northern Việt Nam are also distributed more frequently outside of the country's borders than "low"-art southern Vietnamese films, a situation speaking to the regional biases in the promotion of Hà Nội-produced Vietnamese texts and the critical dismissal of films originating from Sài Gòn. In addition, the process of subtitling "high"-art works is a costly endeavor, and for an impoverished film industry, this means that film-production companies often have to consider carefully which films are translated, subtitled, and exported. Issued by the state, subtitled films are extremely important in instructing foreign audiences on what film expert Ngô Phương Lan argues is the benevolent "humanism" of the Vietnamese people.[62]

As much as Đặng's body of work is celebrated as the country's best, US film critics ironically argue that his films subvert official narratives. As these critics contend, the representations of his heroic women characters are used to denunciate the repressiveness of communist regimes, especially in respect to the issue of free speech and the value of artistic expression. Feminist critics also try to point out that moments of opposition and resistance reside in the figure of woman and her transgressive acts against the state. This hermeneutic gesture of looking for resistance in this figure, however, only works to reproduce the ontological absence of Vietnamese women entrenched in nationalist narratives. Cô Gái Trên Sông parallels contemporary state discourses that use images of women to commemorate women's labor and valor. As evidenced by the film's conclusion, the film reflects the postwar nationalistic sentiment that Vietnamese women should retreat to the home. At the same time, they are also asked to serve a primary role in the economy. In today's economic context, Vietnamese women are conscripted as industrious worker and nurturing mother. As other critics have noted, such constructions can be found in popular discourses as well as in state-sponsored representations of Vietnamese women.[63] I draw from this social context of the film and place it with my reading of Đặng because crucial attention to the "institution of cinema" in Việt Nam and how it "occupies a historically variable space within a social formation" is lacking from the scholarship on Vietnamese cinema.[64] The connective relations between social context and cinematic representation need to be mapped out; as Michael Renov has cogently argued, "the apparatuses of representation . . . must be examined together, for these forms constitute the overlapping currents of public imagery."[65]

Renov's notion of examining the "overlapping currents of public imagery" is crucial to my concluding arguments about Đặng's film. Specifically, the "public imagery" I refer to are two museum spaces in Hà Nội. The imagery contained within these museums correlate with Đặng's films about the nation. In the current era, the Vietnamese government has authorized a particular form of official feminism, sponsoring, for example, a wing devoted to "Heroic Mothers" at the Revolutionary Museum. Some accounts of the "Heroic Mothers" detail horrific stories of Vietnamese women losing more than three sons as well as countless family members due to the wars with France, the United States, and other countries. Narrated visually through black-and-white close-up shots, these women's stories are pictured on a wall; their faces are old, grizzled, and grief-stricken. The portraits are testimonials to their past roles in the war as mothers. Many streets away, the Women's Museum in the same city also privileges women's past valor, renarrating the women's resistance movement, their history of combat, and their close political ties with Hồ Chí Minh.

However, in the foyer of the Women's Museum also stands a glorious and enormous golden statuette of a young Vietnamese woman holding her child on her shoulders. It serves as a reminder that a woman's heterosexualized role, especially important in times of national reconstruction, is to reproduce and to mother. Such images speak to the conflicting demands placed on women's labor and their bodies in a postwar society and neoliberal economy. On this recent dynamic, Thu-Hương Nguyễn-Võ asserts, "The state no longer tries to produce women who can subsume themselves into obsolete categories of masculinized proletarian subjects. Rather it must somehow manage women as feminized libidinal subjects who at the same time must work to produce what the local or transnational market demands."[66] Rewriting the history of Vietnamese women's resistance movement, state feminism sentimentally celebrates the valor of women in the past but also manages their subjecthood according to the needs of its new economy.

Đặng's films participate in this political discourse about women's roles in an era of reconstruction. In eliding the issue of access and availability so pertinent to the ways cultural productions in Việt Nam circulate, film critics inadvertently elide the prudent management of "high"-art films and their circulation in the West. An increasing number of Vietnamese films are now showing at film festivals, especially since an international viewing community recognizes the historical and cultural importance of films produced in Việt Nam. The Vietnamese state's participation in film festivals and award competitions must be seen as a sound venture for the government; through such collaborations, the state acquires the value of prestige for what it labels as artistic films and further develops a national Vietnamese cinema within the international arena.

Juxtaposing the works of Dương and Đặng, this chapter exposes the relations of power structuring the politics of reading and receiving Vietnamese works more than three decades after the American War has ended. In doing so, this chapter also maps out the epistemic effects resulting from the contemporary circulation of knowledge on Việt Nam, focusing mostly on those highly visible and lauded works that travel within the United States and France. The manner in which Đặng is heralded as a heroic filmmaker and an important personage in Việt Nam is similar to how Dương Thu Hương has been privileged as the feminist voice of opposition in the West. The same institutional structures that bolster the platform upon which Đặng speaks are the ones that condition Dương's authoritative speaking voice in an international context. Given these structures of power, a more complex reading of the ties between the Vietnamese artist and state in the contemporary moment is imperative. Once we situate the Vietnamese state within a larger geopolitical context in which it aspires to achieve political power and presence, we move away from the subject positions of victor and victim rooted in the West's discourse about "Vietnam." We recognize the processes of negotiation marking the lived realities of artists and the ways in which they produce and circulate their works. Speaking to these processes, I conclude with a closer look at the symbolic act of Việt Nam's expulsion of its most notorious female traitor.

The Woman Question and the Nationalist Imperative

Dương's public arrest and ousting from the Communist Party continue the Vietnamese state's history of censorship and repression. Here I am referring to an ignominious event in Vietnamese history, the Nhân Văn-Giai Phẩm Affair. In 1956, a group of dissenters voiced their discontent with the state of art, publishing their works in journals like *Nhân Văn* and *Giai Phẩm*. For a short duration, these publications were tolerated "in keeping with trends in the communist world such as Kruschev's de-Stalinization speech and Lu Ding Yi's '100 Flowers' speech."[67] However, party hardliners also made the decision to enact a two-pronged response soon after: "a crackdown on dissidents and a vigorous literary campaign led by intellectuals who remained loyal to the party and the dictates of socialist regime."[68] The regime then began an intraparty purge of writers and artists deemed ideologically unacceptable. From the late 1950s to 1960s, several writers and editors who protested against the Party's dictatorial control over cultural output were prosecuted. Hundreds of intellectuals were sent to prison or labor reform camps as a result. Since then the state has kept a stranglehold on the creative freedom of expression.[69]

With Đổi Mới, the relation between state and art changed—but only slightly and for a short amount of time. In the spirit of Đổi Mới's economic reforms, the Politburo of the Central Committee issued Resolution No. 5, which stipulated, "Freedom of creativity is a vital condition for creating true values in culture, literature and the arts."[70] In all realms of culture, including those of film and literature, censorship policies appeared to relax. Critical works by Nguyễn Huy Thiệp, Bảo Ninh, and Dương Thu Hương that previously had been banned by the state were more freely published and circulated within the country than ever before.[71] Đổi Mới was thus crucial for the revitalization of overtly political Vietnamese cultural output. However, this cultural renaissance was brief. By August 1989, Politburo members reigned in these cultural expressions and prohibited any critiques against the state from appearing in print. The crackdowns against writers and journalists persist to the present day.

The parallels between the persecution of dissidents in the early 1990s and the Nhân Vân-Giai Phẩm purge are indeed arresting. As Zachary Abuza argues, dissidents of the 1950s and 1990s advocated for the same issues: "intellectual freedom, freedom of the press, democratization, greater transparency and implementation of the rule of law for everyone, including the party."[72] However, the differences between the two events are also telling. During the middle of the century, the socialist state's Leninist-style tactic in controlling dissent was not about repression per se, but, as Thu-Hương Nguyễn-Võ maintains, a "rejection of an imagined social realm separate from the state."[73] Nguyễn-Võ historicizes this moment as "a crisis in party-expert relations at a moment when expertise was crucial to the party's initiation of socialist transformation."[74] Similarly, I contend that the discursive manner in which we frame the debates around artistic expression is key. Given the geopolitics of the current era, we must closely examine the historical differences between the two events for what they infer about state rhetoric and state objectives.

In its postwar era, Việt Nam has emerged as a victor, if not economically, then politically, having won an arduous and protracted war against French colonialism and American imperialism. As a result, the state has acquired symbolic capital, which it wields to enter into the arena of international politics. The kinds of associations and memberships that the state now wants to take part in—after years of economic deprivation—suggest a complex portrait of the collaborative relations that the state wants to enact with its foreign Others and its diaspora. Dương Thư Hương's persona and the ways in which her texts are disseminated in conjunction with her authorial identity are tied to such economic and political developments.

For Dương, public denunciation, social ostracization, incarceration, house arrest, and police surveillance marked her post-Đổi Mới years. After her novel Những Thiên Dương Mù was published, the state quickly removed it from bookstores, though the novel was highly popular, selling sixty thousand copies before being pulled.[75] Soon after, all productions of this text were stopped. As a result, Dương's second novel, Tiểu Thuyết Vô Đề [Novel Without a Name], had to be faxed to her translators, Phan Huy Đường and Nina McPherson, both of whom live in France. Once Party officials discovered the telecommunications between Dương and her translators regarding Novel, the Party swiftly denounced her texts and revoked her passport. In April 1991, the state arrested Dương and imprisoned her for seven months for sending her manuscripts outside of the country. She was released through the help of the French president François Mitterrand and his wife, who petitioned for her discharge. After her release, Dương's phones were tapped and she lived in social isolation, prohibited from leaving the country. Nonetheless, Dương managed to send her work out to be translated and published, however illegally and clandestinely. Since the publication of Novel Without a Name, French and English translations of her works have been published steadily: Au-delà des illusions (1996); Myosotis (1998); Memories of a Pure Spring (2000); Beyond Illusions (2002); and most recently, No Man's Land (2005). The publications of her work in different languages attest to its power to speak to audiences outside of Việt Nam, including an overseas Vietnamese community that protests against the repressiveness of the homeland regime and takes inspiration from her books. As a testament to this, her Vietnamese-language texts are found in community enclaves and local bookstores, such as those in Northern and Southern California where the largest concentrations of Vietnamese Americans reside.

Worth underlining is that the successive publications of old and new books by Dương signal a changing political climate since Paradise first appeared in French and English. While Dương lived in Việt Nam and before she eventually left for France in 2006, her prolific output and their translations indicate that the relations of power between Dương and the state remained tense and tenuous but were also transformed in the post-*Đổi Mới* era. Certainly the state can rupture the relationships between the writer and her translators, as the history of reeducation camps, gulags, and purges in the *Nhân Vân-Giai Phẩm* Affair amply demonstrate. But while they continue to strictly monitor Dương and her translators in France, the state does not incarcerate her indefinitely. This is not to say that state control of political expression has attenuated; political expression in the post-Renovation era is still "permitted dissent," to use Kim Ninh's words.[76] More recently, however, there is also a pronounced awareness of how much governmental power can be exerted and exercised. As a member of the ASEAN (Association of Southeast Asian Nations) trade bloc, and more recently, the WTO (World Trade Organization) and the UN Security Council, the country has certainly acquired a more prominent presence in the Southeast Asian region. Keenly attentive to how they appear on the global stage in terms of human rights, especially as economic trade relations pivot on this issue among others, Vietnamese authorities tolerated Dương's limited mobility within the country during the time she lived in Việt Nam, but they disallowed the circulation of her works domestically. This maneuver points to the ways in which the state uses the tactics of accommodation.

In the post-*Đổi Mới* era, government officials have also had to collaborate with foreign economic powers like the United States and Japan in order to revitalize the economy. At the same time, the state must navigate through Việt Nam's own fractured domestic politics, marked by racial and religious tensions as well as a major transformation in the country's population: 60 percent of eighty million Vietnamese are under the age of thirty and have no concrete memory of the wars that dominated Việt Nam's past. This renovated government tries to manage the thorny issues of religious, ethnic, and artistic freedom in a highly nuanced manner. Between market demands and authoritarian control there is a small provision for Dương's texts to circulate outside and inside the country. In such spaces, contestations of power do exist, as different classes and ethnic groups resist totalitarian forms of control in various ways.[77] This limited space for a negotiated form of power between Dương and the Vietnamese state is rendered more complicated due to the fact that Dương openly embraces her role as the country's traitor.[78]

Dương's release from prison and, later on, from state borders signals an innovative, "flexible strategy" in dealing with its former "communist whore."[79] This act represents a highly symbolic execution of state power: the public expulsion of one of its own female members, its own daughter of the nation, can also be read as a promise of punishment for those who would fall outside of a new gendered order. Dương's high visibility in state discourses evidences its need to draw on the gendered figures of "hero" and "traitor" to strengthen its cultural borders and national territories in the context of globalization. According to Leslie Bow, this move is in keeping with how the representation of Asian American women traitors usually functions in the national imagination.[80] Seen in this light, as a woman engaged in *realpolitik*, Dương is the paradigmatic enemy whom the state can continually persecute but not prosecute indefinitely. Such actions represent a productive compromise for the state.

In reading the relations between art and the state, feminist critics should note that these refurbished deployments of state power displace the idea that "Vietnam" discourse is a continual contest of resistance between the powerful and the powerless in the realm of art and politics. The complex and evolving relationship between the artist and the state is especially lost in translation when the artists' works are transported overseas and notions of resistance and subversion are not thoroughly contextualized. As Lila Abu-Lughod argues, rather than look for resistance, we should see "resistance as a diagnostic of power."[81] She insists that instead of taking these acts of resistance as "signs of human freedom, we must use them strategically to tell us more about forms of power and how people are caught up in them."[82] Abu-Lughod's premise becomes a powerful impetus to look at "Vietnam" through a different formulation of power and resistance, particularly because the idea of resistance itself can be appropriated by the state.

To understand both resistance and sporadic forms of patriarchal domination, trans-Vietnamese feminists should take into account not only the country's history but also the new alignments forged by former enemies like Việt Nam and the United States. This new configuration of power colludes with global capitalism and necessitates a different perspective when we analyze Vietnamese culture. The global transnational family that the Vietnamese state imagines itself to be clearly operates on the management of gender and sexuality. Within this paradigm, Đặng Nhật Minh and Dương Thu Hương function as the nation's exemplary models of heroism and treason; these artists serve as boundary markers for the country's cultural borders. The recent reformations of state governance require that we reconsider the ways that expressions of power and resistance are read and translated across multiple regions. This chapter has stressed such a reading practice, one I call trans-Vietnamese feminism, which investigates how films and literature are not only produced but also circulate inside and outside of Việt Nam. The next chapter uses this reading practice to trace the circuits of meaning and textual production in the works of Trinh T. Minh-ha.

4 / Traitors and Translators: Reframing Trinh T. Minh-ha's *Surname Viet Given Name Nam* and *A Tale of Love*

As a Vietnamese woman declares in Trinh T. Minh-ha's *Surname Viet Given Name Nam*, "heroism is monstrous." In the film, she was speaking as part of a generation of Vietnamese women who live in postsocialist Việt Nam and for whom conditions have not changed much in the wake of national revolutions. If the opposite of heroism is treason, as Trinh's film shows, then being a traitor is also monstrous. The dialectic of heroism and treason that traditionally characterizes Vietnamese womanhood underlies Trinh's films on Vietnamese women. In these films, Vietnamese women in the homeland and diaspora commit acts of linguistic and cultural treason against community and nation, especially in their function as linguistic or cultural translators. Being both a female traitor and translator is a dynamic that plays out in Trinh's work as well, whereby the woman translator (Trinh herself) performs as a traitor to the content and form of her own film and to the national family. In framing her texts along these nodes of analysis, I conflate the terms of traitor, translator, and collaborator in order to ask: Who is the traitor, and whom or what is she betraying? Parallel with Trinh's critique of heteropatriarchal discourses in the homeland and the diaspora, in this chapter I give female collaborators—or those deemed by the powerful as traitors to the family and nation—a positive valence in order to cast the work of Vietnamese and Vietnamese diasporic cultural producers in a different light.

Trinh has made two important films about Vietnamese women as they figure in the folds of the national family: *Surname Viet Given Name Nam* (1989) and *A Tale of Love* (2003). Expounding on the idea of feminine betrayal through acts of collaboration, *Surname Viet* exposes how translation and treason are tied to the female body, especially when placed against nationalist contexts. The first part of the film features women actors reenacting the personae of Vietnamese women. Later on, these same women speak of themselves in the first person, narrating their experiences as diasporic women situated in the United States. From the film's beginning, Trinh betrays the notion of feminine authenticity by rendering incomprehensible the women's heavily accented speeches; even though there are subtitles, they elucidate little about what the women are actually saying. Subtitles are a translational operation that typically tries to effect a "cultural affinity" between West and East, Self and Other. Trinh, however, problematizes the idea that translations and subtitles serve as "visualized speech," rejecting how translation guarantees access to the female Other.[1]

While other critics look at Trinh's *Surname Viet* as a theoretical exercise for the auteur, I reorient a critical gaze back onto the speech and bodies of the women in the film and contextualize how these women engage in not only acts of translation but also the performance of memory within and outside the film.[2] For collaborative acts constitute the film's spine. The text comes from a book of interviews called *Vietnam: un peuple, des voix*, collected in Vietnamese and translated into French by Mai Thu Vân. Some of the interviews were then translated into English by Trinh and reinterpreted by the Vietnamese American women actors in the film. These translations-upon-translations reference a colonial and imperial legacy in which some of the interviewees deliberately situate themselves. Through manifold acts of translation, the film posits that the "original text" does not bear originary meaning, nor does an originary bearer of meaning—the third world woman—affix it. In relation to film as translation, Rey Chow argues in a different context that Trinh's film shows "a process of 'literalness' that displays the way the original itself was put together, that is, in its violence."[3] In the second half of the film especially, Trinh demonstrates the fragmented ways Vietnamese woman has been composed in nationalist discourse.[4] The stories the immigrant women narrate point to the possibility of a feminist understanding of difference and the creation of alliances between women in Việt Nam and the diaspora. As film scholar Glen Mimura puts it, *Surname Viet* "illuminates the cultural circuits along which these stories have traveled and the marks that these displacements have inscribed on the original texts."[5]

This chapter investigates further the displacement of meaning located in the "original" and its translated versions; at the same time, it locates meaning in the exchanges among the women actors involved in both the book and film projects. In this, I do not characterize these women actors as "sisters in struggle," as Amy Lawrence has argued; rather, I foreground their stories to show how they comprise a partial archive that pivots on affective ties among women and stands collectively opposed to the masculinist narratives in national and community discourses.[6] Trinh addresses this masculinism in the ways that she reappropriates the famous words of anticolonial resistance leader Phan Bội Châu in the film's title. Trinh critiques a form of heteropatriarchal nationalism requiring women subjects to defend the national home against foreign invaders and to reproduce the nation during a time of nation building. In parallel fashion, Trinh takes aim at a diasporic community that favors male-dominated discourses of wartime soldiering and postwar suffering while censuring Vietnamese American women for speaking out against such narratives.[7] My reframing of Trinh's film details the extent to which Trinh, as translator of and traitor to the production of knowledge about women, critiques the ways the terms traitor and translator circulate around the Vietnamese female body.

Such terms also structure Trinh's feature film, A Tale of Love. In light of the self-referentiality of this text, we must historicize Trinh's work and recognize its inherent intertextuality. Trinh's two films integrally inform each other, especially as they both fundamentally draw on Nguyễn Du's classic, The Tale of Kiều, and radically depart from it. The acts of mediation marking Surname Viet are further concretized in A Tale of Love, in which meaning-making is again displaced onto the subjects making up Trinh's core focalization. These subjects are the many women who identify as Kiều. A faithless adaptation of the original, Trinh's film offers a loving "haiku"of feeling based upon women's experiences rather than providing a transliteration of Nguyễn's poem.[8] With this gesture, Trinh stresses how translation, essentially an interpretative and appropriative practice, proliferates in women's everyday acts in the ways that they reappropriate Kiều for themselves. A Tale of Love thus makes visible the interstitial spaces Vietnamese diasporic women occupy in culture, community, and nation. Viewed from another perspective, her reclamation of Kiều in the film reflects Trinh's position as a diasporic female artist, one who betrays the Vietnamese community's expectations of a visual rendering of the beloved poem.[9] I analyze Trinh's cinematic, subjective treatment of Kiều within a larger context of other diasporic reworkings of Việt Nam's most famous prostitute. This contextualization of her work emphasizes the ways that Trinh's film does not stand in isolation, as her work is usually understood to do; rather, *A Tale of Love* takes part in a broader conversation about Kiều's meanings in the diasporic context.

In the final analysis, this chapter underlines the ways that women's acts of translation and collaboration constitute the political grounds for a trans-Vietnamese feminism. Reading *Surname Viet Given Name Nam* and *A Tale of Love* jointly shows that translation is not merely an interpretative act: it generates meaningful exchange, a signal passing that is politically charged and creatively engaged between agents and actors. To analyze Trinh's texts and their intertextual address, we need a reading practice that takes into account not only form and content, but also how films travel as material artifacts. Centered on this reading practice, the chapter animates other meanings circulating within Trinh's movies and beyond their filmic frames. Most of all, in centralizing Trinh's work with women and women's peformative acts, the chapter's objective is to further define the contours of a trans-Vietnamese feminism, one that is both collaborative and transnational.

Collaborative Acts and the Displacement of Authorship and Meaning

As critics like Hamid Naficy have noted, *Surname Viet Given Name Nam* is multilayered and aurally dense.[10] The film interweaves dialogue, music, and graphic text to critique the strictures of documentary, anthropology, and Western feminism, all of which purport to know and represent the Other truthfully. Yet, if the film deconstructs Western modes of analysis, it also targets Vietnamese nationalism. The film's title is based on the words of anticolonial French resistance leader Phan Bội Châu and his charge that a single woman must proclaim her union with the nation when responding to heterosexual courtship. In replying to a young man's inquiries into her marital status and family name, she would need to say, "My surname is Việt, given name is Nam." Taking Phan's dictum for the film's title, Trinh reveals how the Vietnamese female subject is not only caught in the heteronormative binds of the family and the nation but also that she holds no singular identity.

Critical of how nationalist discourses appropriate women's stories, Trinh demonstrates the "radical multiplicity" that women represent in order to resist the reductive, monolithic representations produced by these discourses.[11] Trinh cites and reframes an assemblage of heroines from Vietnamese folk and literary history; this includes Lady Triệu, Hai Bà Trưng, and Kiều, a character from Việt Nam's most beloved literary masterpiece, *The Tale of Kiều*. With these references, Trinh establishes the ways nationalist patriarchy mythologizes Vietnamese women, constructing them via masculinist acts of appropriation and translation. Foregrounding the issue of translation, Trinh discusses the multiple ways in which the state has appropriated the character of Kiều during the country's most tumultuous time periods.[12] Consequently, Trinh's use of Nguyễn's text represents a doubled appropriation. She alludes to the ways Vietnamese male authors like Phan and Nguyễn deploy a woman's voice to advance national liberation or to agitate for social change. Secondly, because Kiều has been interpreted as either a dangerous collaborator or paragon of filial piety, Trinh recites the ways that women's subjectivity often hinges upon the dualism of treachery or heroism. She shows that women are often caught in an impossible dialectic of loyalty and disloyalty to family and nation.

The film's formal structure reflects its thematic concerns. The first part of the movie stages Vietnamese American women performing the translated interviews of women who live in postwar Việt Nam. The second portion of the film then focuses on the actors' lives themselves in order to reveal the structural threads holding the film together: acts of translation and collaboration. With these two parts, Trinh frustrates the Western spectator's will to knowledge through translation. Throughout the first half of the film, Trinh occupies the role of translator and traitor, willfully mistranslating and misrepresenting the Vietnamese female subject in ways that render her unintelligible and illegible as an object of Western inquiry. At the start of the film, the women's halting tones and awkward intonations of spoken English mark their voice-over narrations.

Addressing the problem of either translating by "ear or by eye," Trinh contends, "translation seeks faithfulness and accuracy and ends up always betraying either the letter of the text, its spirit, or its aesthetics."[13] Trinh superimposes multiple voice-overs while the subject speaks and fills the screen with subtitles of parts of the women's speech at various moments in the film. However, sometimes the subtitles are cut off on the screen, or what the "talking head" says does not always match the words on the screen. To this end, Trinh's film betrays the documentary mode and audience expectations, demonstrating the ways in which the female subject is unrepresentable and unknowable, an idea the film underlines from beginning to end. Deploying a variety of formal techniques, particularly vis-à-vis text and sound, Trinh incites viewers to read, hear, and see in a fractured fashion.

To further rupture viewers' access to meaning, Trinh intersperses the women's staged monologues with Vietnamese songs and folk sayings, heard in the background and sometimes overpowering their speeches. The songs' lyrics and sayings are often subtitled, thematically emphasizing the popular understandings of Vietnamese gender roles: "She who is married is like a dragon with wings/She who has no husband is like a rice-mill with a broken axle." At the same time, Trinh subverts the meaning of these lyrics by placing them adjacent to quotations from several women poets of the eighteenth and nineteenth centuries and from writers who have protested against Vietnamese patriarchy. As an example of this, she cites feminist poet Hồ Xuân Hương, famous for integrating double entendres into her poetry: "To marry and have a child, how banal! But to be pregnant without the help of a husband, what merit!" Underlying this reference to literary foremothers like Hồ Xuân Hương is Trinh's remapping of a feminist genealogy rooted in women's oral and folk culture. This remapping represents an important move for Trinh in establishing the agentive power found in women's storytelling, especially in the second half of the film where the pleasurable act of telling stories is most apparent.

Juxtaposed with these recitations of poetry are the objectified images of Vietnamese women. The film interweaves the sounds and text as part of Trinh's practice of reframing Vietnamese women, whose bodies have been visually captured during the French and American wars and within Vietnamese cultural history. Trinh's technique launches a critique against the scopic regime that has appropriated the idea of womanhood within a patriarchal imagination.[14] For example, the film begins and ends with women's bodies swaying in traditional costumes as they perform on a brightly lit stage, the spectacle of which is shot in full color, up close, and in slow motion (see Fig. 4–1). During the interviews of the women, Trinh also frames them in extreme close-ups while they speak; at the same time, she directs the camera in a seemingly wandering manner to catch the subtle movements of their hands, feet, and heads. Refusing to assign meaning to these bodies, however, she relays the problem of how nationalist causes have reinterpreted women. She challenges viewers to apprehend the objectifying manner in which visual imagery reifies woman-as-nation. However, if she critiques the spectacle that is "Vietnam," she also gives viewers a glimpse into what the women subjects take pleasure in seeing and realizes the moments when they themselves enjoy being seen. Trinh's practice of reframing and the "re-photography"

FIGURE 4.1. Women dancing for the nation. From the film *Surname Viet Given Name Nam* © 1989. Women Make Movies.

of women's bodies does not simply obliterate truth: it also points to a regeneration of meaning and import within the diaspora.[15]

The second half of the film, which features "real" interviews of Vietnamese immigrant women in the United States, further troubles the notion of veracity in documentaries and critiques the genre's overreliance on voice-giving claims. Here, Trinh emphasizes the inadequacy of translation and "the problematic of translating experience onto film."[16] This latter portion of the film accents Trinh's positioning of herself as collaborator in the filmmaking and interviewing process, one faithless to the ethnographic imperative. An off-screen narrator (the voice of a second-generation Vietnamese American, Lan Trinh) "interviews" Trinh on the reasons why she chose to make the film, which stories she wanted to retell, and how many interviewees were picked. Trinh states, "Interview: an antiquated device of documentary. Truth is selected, renewed, displaced, and speech is always tactical."

At this point, Trinh stresses her performing self as an integral part of the interviewing process. In effect, she becomes the "framer" who is "framed" within this collaborative project. She writes, "Because of the film, I am constantly questioned in who I am, as its making also transforms the way I see the world around me."[17] Viewers thus realize that she confronts the problem of having to revise her own practices in representing the Other. We also learn that Trinh inhabits the subject of her own film; she is both a translator and traitor as a result of the collaborative act. As Trinh retells it, the problem of being "framed" had actually been sutured into the fabric of the film from its inception, a point Trinh emphasizes repeatedly in her film. At the crux of the film is a demystification of the collaborative processes of filmmaking and storytelling.

Relaying faulty translations and subtitles, Trinh especially demonstrates the problematic of translating Mai Thu Vân's five-year research project from Vietnamese into French and then into accented English. Even so, critics understand Mai's work on Vietnamese women, *Vietnam: un peuple, des voix*, as ancillary to Trinh's project. Such scholarship, which perceives Trinh as the sole author of the film, relies on a Eurocentric idea of the auteur. In actuality, within the film and the theoretical writings that complement it, Trinh frequently discusses how authorship is continually displaced in the making of the film. She underscores the act of collaboration threaded throughout the film and thus, the film's "unsewing" of image and meaning, sound and text.[18]

When critics privilege Trinh's film over and above *Vietnam: un peuple, des voix*, then, they miss the critical textures that both Mai Thu Vân and Trinh weave into their works. Fundamental to Mai's collection of interviews is her postcolonial critique of a Western idealization of revolutionary socialism. Overwhelmingly, her female subjects narrate lived experiences marked by deprivation within socialist Việt Nam. As a Marxist, Mai felt compelled to change her views on socialism because the women's narratives shook her preconceptions of its effects on Vietnamese women. In conjunction with Mai's book and her participation, Trinh redoubles her critiques against the structures of knowing embedded in Western feminism. In the second half of the film, Trinh enunciates the difficulty Mai Thu Vân faced when she tried to get her book published by major presses in France without an accompanying preface by French feminist Simone De Beauvoir. Mai critiques a hegemonic French feminism that disallows a feminist voice divergent from its own. On the book's negative reception, Trinh reads Mai's letter in the film: "Dear Minh-ha, Since the publication of the book, I felt like having lost a part of myself. At least in France where, in spite of the Mouvement de Liberation de la Femme, maternalism remains the cornerstone of the dominant ideology."

Moreover, to read through the women's narratives making up *Vietnam: un peuple, des voix* is to understand the process of negotiation by which Mai herself had to transcribe, translate, and edit in order to craft a text for a predominantly Western audience. Published in 1983 by Pierre Horay, the book is organized into several distinct sections: an autobiographical preface, ethnographic details about post-1975 Vietnamese society, the testimonials, and then finally, Mai's scholarly work on family, socialism, and women's conditions. Like Trinh, Mai is careful to select women from different class strata, regions, and occupations to render a composite sketch of contemporary Vietnamese society. Although less self-reflexive than Trinh, and therefore less invested in deconstructing an authorial voice, Mai Thu Vân is aware of her privileged position in the book. Prefacing her interviews, she writes that her encounters with Vietnamese women in the late 1970s were initially predicated on mistrust because she was a foreigner to them, a *Việt Kiều Pháp* (overseas Vietnamese from France) as they called her.[19]

Where the text and the film converge is in their sharp, shared critique of the expropriation of women's labor and the commodification of their bodies. Mai's book focuses on how the women's narratives object to the socialist state and its failures to address their needs in the postwar era. Trinh's film does not merely reiterate this critique; *Surname Viet* extends it to speak against a gendered nationalism founded in the diaspora as well. Juxtapositions of beauty contestants and intertitles that detail feminine virtues (beauty, speech, charity, and labor) reference the continuity with which patriarchal norms, supposedly rooted in homeland traditions, seek to discipline women in the diaspora. At this point of convergence, I draw the women's self-narrations in Mai's book together with those of the immigrant women featured in the second half of Trinh's film. Like the immigrant women's life stories in *Surname Viet*, the Vietnamese women's narratives in the text have also been effectively rehearsed, dramatized, and staged. The women featured in the film cannot therefore be merely passive players in the execution of Trinh's theories; rather, an active collaboration between women—the ethnographer (Mai), documentarian (Trinh), and storytelling subject (women in Việt Nam and the diaspora)—emphasizes a pact of the imagination, one laying the groundwork for the "staging of action."[20]

In the dialogues between Mai and her various interviewees, there are many instances of performing and punning that speak to the women's awareness of their roles as informants. During several interviews, the women subjects preempt Mai's inquiries with their own questions.[21] Early in their meeting, for example, Liên, a thirty-two–year-old artist, asks Mai, "Pensez-vous qu'il est intéressant de parler de tous ces problèmes de femmes?" [Do you think it is interesting to speak about all these problems concerning women?][22] Constantly underpinning the interviews is a self-reflexive mode of performativity on the part of the women subjects. In another instance, Mai writes that before the interviews, some women, including an official representative from the Women's Union, served tea and biscuits to facilitate conversations and maintain "good" relations between subject and researcher.[23] Some of the interviewees also challenge a Western feminist articulation of women's equality; they argue for a form of gender equality that involves the rights and participation of men within any feminist project in Việt Nam.[24]

At play in Mai's book are illustrations of humor in the women's deployment of language and self-inscription as well. In an interview with Thu Vân, a young health technician, she recounts how an engineering or medical diploma offers little value in Vietnamese society; a diploma (*bằng*) does not make one *bằng lòng* (satisfied).[25] The pun only works in Vietnamese and the French translation must be accompanied by Mai's explanatory footnote. Thu Vân's clever rewording in Vietnamese makes an astute point about postwar Việt Nam: having a diploma does not make one content in a society struggling with the traumas of war and postwar economy. It is at once a criticism of both the state and society. A mocking parody of official sentiment is also rooted in the women's refashioning of themselves as subject-citizens. The southerner women speak of having to craft politically correct curriculum vitae to avoid being sent to prison after the North's liberation of the South. A woman, Cát Tiên, describes how she tricked the cadres by simply retranscribing a previously submitted resume.[26] What these details reveal is the women's recognition that their political identities must be fluid, fictionalized, and performed in the public space.

A keen awareness of postwar Việt Nam's position on the global stage and the women's positions as critics of the state further marks the narratives. Playing such roles, the women are alternately ferocious in their critiques or apprehensive about what they are saying, depending on their class and regional location. One woman, in particular, embraces the stance of a critic wholeheartedly. A sixty–year-old musician, An Thư explains that she is committed to building national and international coalitions as a way of countering the state's acts of war-making against Cambodia and China so soon after the American War ended in 1975. An Thư claims, "Hier nous étions tous frères ... Nous jurions fidélité comme les cinq doigts de la main . . . Aujourd'hui, nous devenons ennemis . . . Toute notre histoire est une histoire de trahison" [Yesterday we were all brothers . . . We pledged our loyalty to one another like the five fingers of a hand . . . Today we have become enemies. Our entire history is a history of treason].[27] This proclamation speaks to the problem of women's treason and fidelity so fundamental to this book. More than this, An Thư's words represent an ironic and critical reframing of Hồ Chí Minh's own words about the national family. Hồ Chí Minh's famous slogan, akin to Phan Bội Châu's famous saying that serves as the title of *Surname Viet Given Name Nam*, refers to the cohesion and unity of the Vietnamese that connects people together like the five fingers that are "unequal in length" but "united [as a] hand." As the women's narratives collectively show in *Vietnam: un peuple, des voix*, their storytelling is not only highlighted by Mai's acts of collation and organization but also underlined by the women's rhetorical power of imagery and figuration. In this is not the production of truth per se but rather the workings of the imagination as a "social practice,"[28] a theme translated in Trinh's re-presentation of women's stories and their storytelling practices in *Surname Viet*.

Nevertheless, in the film's feminist critical discourse, Mai's voice and the voices contained in the collection are referents for a traumatic "real." Despite Mai's self-positioning in her work and sense of discomfort while writing the book ("It is very difficult for a Vietnamese woman to write about Vietnamese women"),[29] one critic has mainly looked at Mai's scholarly work as autobiographical in purpose. Katherine Gracki writes, "[Her] ethnographic project is framed by and seen through the prism of an autobiographical quest for origins and self-knowledge."[30] Gracki goes on to claim, "Like Mai's interviewees, who are asked to take the risk of speaking out against a corrupt regime, Trinh T. Minh-ha wishes to take a risk in revealing the abuses of power and silencing of Vietnamese women in ethnographic representation and documentary practices."[31] While it may be true that the women in Việt Nam took a risk in speaking out against the state, Gracki's statement conflates all Vietnamese women, collapsing Vietnamese and Vietnamese diasporic women as well as the author, Mai Thu Vân, and filmmaker, Trinh T. Minh-ha.

Similarly, Amy Lawrence's essay on women's voices in "third world" cinema underlines a homogenous construction of women. Feminist critics like Lawrence neglect the fact that Trinh's project was a collective effort, not only produced in the global North but also distributed by a major US-based feminist distributor of independent films, Women

Make Movies.[32] Such critical work tends to ignore the relations of power structuring the collaborative efforts in the making of Trinh's film, while also dismissing the web of access that references the ways such texts are circulated. What we must take into account is how Trinh's filmic and critical texts circulate widely within many contexts. Having accrued intellectual capital since her first film and publication, Trinh has access to make and disseminate culture; her long-term relationship with Women Make Movies attests to this. A prominent feminist academic, director, and critic, Trinh's positionality is thus markedly different from that of the women subjects in the film. Any conflation of the women involved in this project homogenizes these key differences of class, capital, and status.

By the same token, however, because Mai's book is bound in a collection and published by a major French publisher, the women's voices contained therein are unquestioned as authentic representations of political and patriarchal repression. In contrast to the Vietnamese women's stories of subordination, which are *recognizable* scripts of "third world" oppression, the oral testimonials of the Vietnamese American women are little studied, since their narratives are cast in more conventional settings. Consequently, viewers see the immigrant women as living subjects in the film whose biographies are recounted through their stories and photographs. Hewing to naturalized filmic techniques and the tenets of US immigrant narratives, the women's stories in the second half of *Surname Viet* are understood as being less forceful in terms of their rhetorical power. Linda Peckham notes that such techniques allow us to see the actresses in more "natural" settings: in their homes, with children, and at work. But while Peckham recognizes the inherent differences between these two communities of women found in the film, she also delineates how the halves of the film ultimately serve a methodological purpose. In effect, the immigrant women's bodies and speech are reflexive elements in Trinh's assault on epistemology. On the reenactments, Peckham observes, "the speaker is an actress, a substitute, a 'fake,' [so] that the interview style becomes subversive . . . the artificial subject points to the absence of a 'real' speaker, an absence that suggests internment, kinship, and death, as well as the survival of a witness, a record—a history."[33]

Without anchoring a "totalizing quest for meaning" to the women's words and their bodies, I flesh out what Peckham calls "a record—a history" and examine the actresses' narratives as part of a meaningful history.[34] I propose that we recenter rather than decenter these women's stories as performative acts in the reenactment of the history of southern and central Vietnamese refugees as survivors. In doing so, what we will hear if we listen "nearby" is the notion that the women actively cooperated in the film for various reasons—to partake in a dialogue, to see themselves on-screen, to be a star.[35] Most resoundingly, the immigrant women indicate that they wanted to participate in a project that addresses their conditions as diasporic women, desires consonant with the needs of marginalized peoples to be recognized as imaginative agents in dominant cultures. I take into account the ways in which the four women's testimonials speak of the problems of adjusting to American life after the war as well as life under the oppressive regime of communism. The topics they touch on are not assimilationist in nature; rather, the women address how they have had to negotiate with inhabiting a Vietnamese female subjectivity in the United States.

It is to the latter half of the film that my analysis now turns, particularly because other critics have looked at this second half as more of a theoretical exercise for the filmmaker than as an expression of meaning. There is a curious lack of critical engagement with this portion of the film, perhaps because of its stylistic plainness and gestures toward sentimentality. Rather than ask if there is anything "real" about the film, given its subversion of truth, the following sections interrogate the structures of looking and speaking with which the actors are engaged. Unlike Bill Nichols, who argues that Trinh simply flattens out women's subordination under a "monolithic construction of patriarchy,"[36] I cite the ways in which Trinh and the actresses' collaboration hinge upon a shared sense of purpose and clear a space for an apprehension of difference among women. The collaborative project that defines the film lies at the meaning of a trans-Vietnamese feminism, which attempts to sharpen transnational solidarities enacted between subjects in multiple spaces.

Accenting the Archive: Structures of Looking in *Surname Viet Given Name Nam*

In the film, *The Fact of Asian Women* (2003), Celine Parreñas-Shimizu works with Asian American actresses who reenact the personae of Anna May Wong, Nancy Kwan, and Lucy Liu. Theorist and filmmaker Parreñas-Shimizu argues that the interaction between filmmaker and actress alludes to a "metaprocess . . . that not only dramatizes the relationship between actor, filmmaker, and spectator but also dramatizes the idea of authorship itself as a contested issue."[37] Parreñas-Shimizu deemphasizes the fact that Asian American stereotypes proliferate in popular films; instead, she reinvests energy and import in the creative interplay between director and actor. Similarly, *Surname Viet*'s productivity rather than its negative critique is accented here.[38] I underscore Trinh's divestment of authority to demonstrate how power can be redirected back into the voices and bodies of the women, shown to perform multiple roles in the film: as women in socialist Việt Nam, as women in the diaspora, and as women subjects interpellated by both nation and community. Through this way of looking, women are not only screen actors but also *social* actors, integrally involved in acts of looking and looking back in the second portion of the film.

Surname Viet Given Name Nam constitutes an archive of images and stories accessible through film. Framed in this way, the film becomes a performative process, enacted by a collective of women and underlined by the pleasures of storytelling. As Diana Taylor argues in another context, "performance carries the possibility of challenge, even self-challenge, within it. As a term simultaneously connoting a process, praxis, an episteme, a mode of transmission, an accomplishment, and a means of intervening in the world, it exceeds the possibilities of these other words offered in its place."[39] In the ellipses of the narratives—placed variously between the musical segments, voice-overs, and voice-offs—are the performances of women that encompass these connotations of performance that Taylor outlines. Most of all, their performances underline the power they wield in the telling of their stories. Brian Wallis also notes the storytelling modes that underpin Trinh's documentary work. Wallis contends that the use of stories "acknowledge[s] the craft of construction and delivery, the pleasures of interchange, the biases of the teller and the moral or lesson unmistakably transmitted."[40]

True to Wallis's words is a certain pleasure in the sharing of stories between women in the film. An actress by the name of Khiến Lai, who plays the role of "Thu Vân" ("a thirty-five–year-old technical cadre from Việt Nam"), animatedly shares the account of her interrogation by a Vietnamese soldier after the war. Narrating in English, she proclaims to the cadre that she loves her country and does not plan to escape. She pleads with him, "Please, don't shoot me." Khiến Lai's testimonial tells of the traumas afflicting southern Vietnamese women after the war but also stresses a strategy of speaking in camouflage at the moment when she emphasizes her patriotism to save herself. In another recounting, spoken in Vietnamese but not subtitled in English, she narrates how her hair caught on fire at work, jokingly comparing her burnt hair to crispy fried noodles.[41] She relays that after the trauma of war, the physical injury does nothing to her psychically. Like An Thư's words resignifying Hồ Chí Minh's propagandistic slogan about the national family that is like a hand, this story points to how Khiến Lai's embellishment—in the form of figurative language—is an imaginative act, translating horror into humor. Captured on film, the pleasure of storytelling underlies how the "gift of storytelling" brings people together.[42] While this move opens Trinh up to a critique of her reification of women's experiences,[43] as well as of her idealization of the Other,[44] I see it as part of a deconstructive undertaking that enables a broader critique of the masculinist structures of power that silence women's stories and obscure female bonds in both Việt Nam and the diaspora.

Essentially, the pleasure of telling stories coincides with the pleasures of looking. The viewing that the four actresses (besides Lan Trinh) enact is key within the film because they are caught gazing at and speculating upon several spectacles: dogs on tightropes, performing dancers, and concert singers during a Tết festival and at other community events. Trinh's camera not only demonstrates how the women look at spectacles but also reveals their pleasure in being spectacles themselves. In one sequence, a woman by the name of Hiền, who earlier played the role of Cát Tiên, performs the role of cultural interpreter when she talks about the Vietnamese national costume, the *áo dài*, in front of a group of young students, while wearing an *áo dài* herself. The scene ends with two white children wearing *áo dài* in turn. Especially meaningful is Hiền's orchestration of this sequence of show-and-tell, reversing the Western gaze and displacing the ethnic spectacle onto the Western body as Other. On this issue, Trinh describes how the women's clothing was a point of contention for her.[45] Though wanting to resist commodifying ethnicity, she assents to the women's desires to promote their identity through sartorial display.

Trinh employs the metaphors of veiling and costuming to fashion a film about women's relationship to the national costume, especially since sewing is considered feminine labor.[46] Nhi Lieu argues that the *áo dài* is a figuration for the nation, a piece of clothing for women cathected with affect, pride, and nationalism, especially pronounced within diasporic beauty pageants.[47] Given the symbolic importance of the national costume for women, choosing to wear an *áo dài* is a political act for diasporic women. Trinh gestures to such a sentiment, maintaining that women's choice of fashion in the film "constitute[s] one of the critical threads woven through the entire texture of the work."[48] For Trinh, the repositioning of Vietnamese American women as agents of the look appears to be just as important as peeling back the sedimented layers of meaning that have constituted "woman."

Furthermore, the second half of the film firmly alludes to the role the women play prior to the metafictional development of filming. They are creative participants in the processes of self-representation, positioning themselves in the settings they chose to be filmed against. Trinh's interviews with the women point out that they had imagined themselves on the screen prior to the film's recording, placing themselves in particular scenarios in order to be filmed. Khiến Lai asks to be placed near a "fish pond" where she can be aestheticized against a natural and beautiful backdrop. Because of their collaborative exchange, the film features scenes of Khiến Lai looking at koi in a Japanese garden and drinking tea in a teahouse. For Khiến Lai, these sites are meaningful, serving as places of peaceful meditation.[49]

As a material product, the film is, finally, a significant part of a Vietnamese feminist repertoire. The film archives images and narratives invariably inflected by postwar trauma, but also archives the spectacles of a Tết festival, music concerts, and beauty pageants for an emergent diasporic Vietnamese population after their emigration to the United States. Produced in 1989, *Surname Viet* was one of the first films to encapsulate the cultural practices dominating the theater of diasporic Vietnamese community life during this time. Three years prior, the Vietnamese state opened itself to market capitalism, thus dramatically changing how the government has done business with its foreign others and the diaspora from that time onward. From this perspective, the film composes one historical document within what Ann Cvetkovich calls an "archive of feelings." As Cvetkovich describes, an "archive of feelings is an exploration of cultural texts as repositories of feelings and emotions, encoded not only in content but the practices that surround their production and reception."[50]

Cvetkovich's analysis of this archive focuses mostly on lesbian public cultures and trauma; however, her work on trauma's expressivity in ephemeral and elliptical sites is deeply relevant to my understanding of Trinh's film, since much of the film's second half dwells on the traumas as well as the joys of diasporic women. Cvetkovich's work is useful because it provides a lexicon of affect with which to study the sentiment interwoven with the women's words and photographs. To emphasize this point, when the women actors speak of their lives in the United States, Trinh's camera pans across the women's photos, reframing these images in ways that force viewers to focus on the highly personal portraits. Representative of an affective archive, the poignant images making up the women's past and present are mostly black-and-white photographs of their lives as young girls. The pictures are invested with meaning and sentiment on the screen because they narrate a meaningful story about the women's religions, families, pasts, and occupations. Accompanied by the women's spoken narratives, these still images compose a partial but moving history of southern and central Vietnamese female refugees.

The archive provides the basis for a trans-Vietnamese feminism, one committed to seeing differences as well as similarities between Việt Nam and the diaspora. Yen Le Espiritu alludes to this feminist way of looking when she argues for a critical transnational perspective. Espiritu makes clear that a structural analysis of war, interrogating the impacts of war for Vietnamese women in multiple sites, is necessary for exploring Vietnamese women's lives in a comprehensive way. For "racialization and the racial formation of Vietnamese women does not begin in the United States but rather in the 'homeland' already affected by United States economic, social, cultural and military influences."[51] Through an understanding of the dynamics of war, we delineate how war is a "subject-making project—fashioning both Americans and the 'enemies' in ways that were and continue to be mutually implicated in each other."[52] Along with Trinh, Espiritu offers a positioning that takes into account the forces of war and neocolonialism that continue to configure men's and women's lives. Such a mode of analysis comprises a vital aspect of a trans-Vietnamese feminism, one that looks at the larger structures of power that bring postwar national and diasporic subjects into being but also queries the acts of agency and resistance marking women's everyday lives. This line of inquiry also allows us to see the twinned disciplinary systems by which nationalism is gendered and gender is nationalized in the Vietnamese and Vietnamese diasporic contexts. In its pointed references to Phan Bội Châu and Nguyễn Du, Trinh's film makes us aware of this dualism, which takes place on the site of women's bodies, countering this patriarchal discourse by privileging women's collaborative acts and collective sense of agency.

As much as Trinh invites us to be suspect of the speaking subject in her documentaries, the historical narrative nonetheless shapes a class and community of women in the diaspora. Despite its claims to decenter master narratives, the film creates a space for the exchange of women's remembrances about the narrative of war. More than this, the film houses these women's stories and photographs, which bear witness to history and contradict the male-centered American versions of "Vietnam." The remembrance of this regional aspect of Vietnamese history is especially critical when we consider Thu-Hương Nguyễn-Võ's assertion that Vietnamese Americans, many of whom were southerners prior to coming to the United States, "mourn the dead as a way to accuse the living."[53] As Nguyễn-Võ relates, particularly expressive are the stories within US borders that attest to the failures of American imperialism. Nonetheless, feminists need to further claim this archive in speaking of this history from women's perspectives. On this point, Nathalie Nguyen contends that diasporic "women's stories are still largely unknown and undocumented,"[54] so that when women's memories are narrated, they "redress the perceived 'silence' of women in the wider Vietnamese diaspora."[55] Viewed in this way, the film becomes even more emphatically an "embodied practice," countering the ways male patriots and their narratives dominate a Vietnamese American political public.[56] Southern and central Vietnamese women's traumas are rarely encoded as part of the traumatic history that a southern Vietnamese regime experienced during the war and under communism in the war's aftermath. Part of Trinh's powerful critique of nationalisms is a criticism of a form of cultural nationalism—as an extension of patriarchal power—that takes root in the diaspora as well.

To this end, the framing of *Surname Viet* is telling, even as Trinh returns us to the images and mechanisms of spectacle that doggedly constitute "Vietnam." Since the final frames of the film repeat images of woman-as-nation, there appears to be a cyclical return to the film's beginning—yet, with a difference.[57] If the film begins with the theatricality of war and the spectacle of womanhood, *Surname Viet* also shows how the actresses are bound up in this same system of image-making but simultaneously attempt to resist it. Interviews with the Vietnamese American actresses conclude with Trần Thị Bích Yến within a sequence pointing to the film's thematic of women's solidarity. Looking toward a setting sun, she speaks in a regional accent and claims a sense of commonality with Vietnamese women, identifying herself as a woman originally from the central region of Việt Nam, an area notorious for having been battered by the battles between North and South. Articulated as such by Trần, this space of communality gets lost amid the celebrations and critiques of Trinh as a deconstructive auteur. As Trinh argues in respect to the emotive ways the film speaks to spectators, including Vietnamese viewers, "The question of rendering visible the manipulations [in the second half of the film] or not is not so much the point, as that something

different is happening which would provoke awareness and reflection."[58]
A contemplative moment pointing to "something different," Trần words
enunciate a transnational feminist politics that becomes a generative
point of convergence between the diaspora and homeland.

These concluding remarks about *Surname Viet* sharpen the radical
edge of Trinh's film, since it dispatches several critiques but also archives
Vietnamese American women's roles and realities on film. The film
stands as a material product reforming documentary practices and the
viewing of ethnographic films. More importantly, however, it remains
a recorded document of postwar Vietnamese American women's performances of memory. In this fashion, *Surname Viet* encompasses "a
membrane that brings its audience into contact with material forms
of memory," underpinning what Laura U. Marks names "intercultural
cinema."[59] *Surname Viet* alludes meaningfully to the felt experiences of
diasporic women. At the same time, I emphasize that we must contextualize cultural productions to avoid dismissing the relations of power
operating within a powerful discourse like "Vietnam" in the Western
imagination. This includes critically looking at and historicizing Trinh's
work, in effect, seeing her self-reflexive texts as interlinked with her own
body of work and the work of others. Reframing her films, we recognize
the ways that her films speak to forms of pleasures specific to women and
their imagination. Such is the impulse of a trans-Vietnamese feminism
that looks at how women narrate their stories and pleasures in different
places. Illustrative of such pleasures, *A Tale of Love* cinematically realizes
diasporic women's loving sentiments toward Nguyễn Du's epic poem.

Translation Effects: Refraction, Rhythm, and Reflexivity in *A Tale of Love*

If *Surname Viet Given Name Nam* delves into the problems of translation, Trinh's next film, *A Tale of Love*, explores these same issues, but is
accented by a different set of tools Trinh uses to examine the themes of
heroism, female sacrifice, and betrayal. Realized as a feature film that
pushes the boundaries of realism and fantasy, Trinh's *Tale of Love* is,
in her words, a "scenography of love," which abounds with passion and
color.[60] It also betrays Nguyễn Du's original text in significant ways.
Instead of hewing to a singular construct of the feminine, the film cinematically translates women's multiple desires and identifications as
they relate to Nguyễn Du's protagonist. As Trinh notes, Kiều embodies
not a character in a story but "a mirror that reflects other mirrors."[61]

Consequently, the many displacements marking the film's use of sound and image serve to "[break] loose from the dualistic relation between translator and originator."[62]

Unfaithful to any single interpretation of the poem or of the character Kiều, the film demonstrates that Nguyễn's work creates a spiraling effect of meaning across time and space for Vietnamese women. The term "spiraling" references the ways Trinh evocatively theorizes the processes of both translating and looking. She writes:

> You, as the onlooker, position yourself differently according to different contexts and circumstances, but so does the "other" whom you are looking at. Each constitutes a site of subjectivities whose movement is neither simply linear nor circular. In the spiraling movement, you never come back to the same, and when two spirals move together in a space, there are moments when they meet and others when they do not. Trying to find a trajectory that allows the two movements to meet as much as possible without subsuming one to the other is also how I see the process of translation.[63]

Trinh employs the image of two spiraling movements to describe the work of translation. This image speaks to the ways that *Surname Viet* and *A Tale of Love* can be viewed: as dual, moving arrangements of film, that is, being in motion and marked by emotion. Juxtaposing these two works enables us to see the ways they produce meaning and sensation, as they touch upon similar images and themes. Like *Surname Viet*, *A Tale of Love* creates a displacing effect through its striking images and sounds, which come together at times poetically and at times discordantly, in order to form the filaments of its narrative. The analyses of Trinh's *A Tale of Love* stress that this ever-reflexive film is simultaneously a reverberation of *Surname Viet* as well as a refracted translation of *The Tale of Kiều*. However, if Trinh's films resonate with each other in some ways, the two films do not synchronize at other moments; the latter film was made in a later moment in Trinh's career as a filmmaker and therefore is shaped by a different set of aesthetic concerns.

In *A Tale of Love*, the elemental aspects of the storyline centralize the diasporic figure of Kiều. At the start of the film, Kiều is a model who also conducts research, as a writer, on the impact of *The Tale of Kiều* within the diaspora. The film implies that she may be entangled in heterosexual relationships with Alikan, her photographer, or Minh, a man whose wife is soon coming from Việt Nam to the United States. Yet, outside of these relations with men, the most important relationships rest on Kiều's loving ties with women: her mother in Việt Nam, her aunt, and her friend and boss, Juliet. Comparable to *Surname Viet*, the conversations between women stand in for the meaningful dialogues about women occurring outside of a masculinist and nationalist frame. We continually return to the images and sounds that matter most: the staged conversations between Juliet and Kiều and between Kiều and her aunt, and Kiều's aural and visual memories of girlhood (see Fig. 4–2). We are afforded a recurring soundtrack of Kiều's exchanges with Julie and her aunt about Nguyễn Du's Kiều. Through a voice-off, we hear Kiều's mother calling out her name periodically throughout the film, and we glimpse into dreamlike moments when Kiều, as a young child, plays near a lake. And yet, Kiều is neither defined by her past nor infantilized as a female subject. In a crucial sequence, Kiều is—literally—a streetwalker, as Trinh's fluid camera follows her as she walks the city streets at night. In this moment of movement Kiều is a modern-day flâneuse, a figuration that reflects how Trinh views Nguyễn's protagonist as not only mobile but also forging her own path in choosing love.

Remaking *The Tale of Kiều* as a sensual tale of love, Trinh creates a hall of mirrors, whereby the central female subject's identifications with Nguyễn's Kiều are evocative of her own memories and refractive of other women's lives and loves as well. Articulated through the filmic Kiều, diasporic women's reclamation of the *literary* Kiều becomes visualized in cinematic form and narrated in a subjective manner. One instance in the film speaks to this idea especially. Discussing with Julie the affective power the poem holds for women, Kiều retells a story of a Vietnamese American woman who understands herself as an incarnation of Nguyễn Du's character. Sutured to Kiều's voice-over is a poetic image of a woman's back as she walks along a sidewalk. The faceless woman wears an *áo dài*. Her long, dark hair almost brushes the ground upon which she walks. While Kiều relays the story, Trinh's camera stays focused on the woman's back and hair. Splicing together the visual and aural registers of cinema, this sequence underlines how the storytelling acts of women function as a major force in the film, founding the stage upon which the fantasy of identification is reenacted.

Through a rhythmic fusion of sound with image, Trinh reveals the enduring effect that Nguyễn Du's work has on generations of Vietnamese women. Off-camera, a woman's voice sings verses from the poem for diegetic effect; however, her singing also lends distinct shape to the formal qualities of the film and its sound design. Through the singer's and others' voices, Trinh focuses on the rhythms of sound and women's conversation

"she'll live an artist's life,
a life of pain"

FIGURE 4.2. Reimagining Kiều in childhood. From the film *A Tale of Love* ©
1995, Moongift Films.

as a soundtrack making up everyday life for Vietnamese American women.
In using some lines from the 3,254–verse poem, Trinh stresses the orality
of Vietnamese folk culture and of women's work in transmitting this culture. With its emphasis on women's oral discourses, the film underlines
how women in the diaspora translate the archetypal figure of Kiều in their
own ways, authoring and performing scripts of Kiều that counter the masculinist, nationalist narratives about her. As previously demonstrated in
Surname Viet, these acts of translation and oral transmission by women
lay the foundation for Trinh's formulation of a feminism that renarrates
the story of Vietnamese nationalism as it has been told through Kiều. *A
Tale of Love* illuminates the ways in which translations are not only hermeneutic but also agentive acts between women.

As a faithless filmic translation of the national poem, *A Tale of Love*
metacinematically manifests the ways that Nguyễn Du's text translates
multivalently in the lives of women. In the film, the act of retranslating
Kiều becomes politically empowering, premised on the ways diasporic
women reclaim a literary figure that has engendered a seemingly timeless construction of womanhood and nationhood. Staging these recla-
mations, *A Tale of Love* underscores that Vietnamese women's attachments to Kiều are layered with connotations, what Sarah Ahmed calls the
"sticky" effect of affect. Through repeated circulations, as Ahmed writes,
"objects become sticky, or saturated with affect, as sites of personal and

social tension."[64] Trinh's film ruminates precisely on this circulation of affect for women, particularly because the poem has accumulated such a surplus of emotion through its widespread dissemination. The film's mode of self-reflexivity prompts us to reflect upon the circuitries of excess emotion produced by the poem. The storyline fuels this impulse. Kiều, the main protagonist of the film, occupies multiple roles: she is a lover, model, writer, and researcher, but also a daughter who sends remittances to Việt Nam to support her mother. Inhabiting all of these roles, she represents a metonymic figure for diasporic women and their storytelling agency. In concentric fashion, we revisit the kernel of feminist autonomy structuring *Surname Viet* as well. We also spiral back to Trinh's positionality within the film, as it represents her own imaginative reappropriation of Kiều herself. In her version of Kiều, Trinh clearly privileges Kiều's resistance and her penchant for love.

To read *A Tale of Love* is to read into Trinh's self-reflexive position in the making of the film. By the time she made *A Tale of Love*, Trinh's stature as a woman filmmaker was firmly established. Because of her critical work and films, Trinh remains an eminent force in postcolonial feminism and film theory. The institutional acclaim Trinh garnered since making *Surname Viet* and other films gave her better access to funding that allowed her to experiment with the film's narrative structure and form. While there is repetition in some aspects of Trinh's filmmaking process here, for example in working with longtime collaborator and partner, Jean-Paul Boudier, a point of difference is also present in the making of her first narrative feature. This film is set apart from *Surname Viet*; she collaborated with a larger crew and, consequently, is not afforded as much leeway for improvisation.[65] However, because the film is in narrative form, her actors in *A Tale of Love* perform as scripted characters and thus enunciate more clearly the themes underlying *Surname Viet*. In a dialogue between Kiều and her aunt, the two women discuss the possibilities that Nguyễn's character, Kiều, holds for women in the diaspora. While for the older aunt, Kiều symbolizes the woe and beauty of Việt Nam, she nevertheless remains a figure of misfortune and a symbol of prostitution. For the younger Kiều, the literary Kiều represents not adversity but resistance. Echoing the concerns in *Surname Viet*, the discourse between Kiều and her aunt shows how generations of diasporic women are unified through a reconceptualization of solidarity in difference, concretized within the frames of the film as a literal conversation between women.

A Tale of Love also differs from *Surname Viet* in shot composition. While *Surname Viet* was shot in 16 mm, *A Tale of Love* was shot in 35mm with camera equipment donated by Panavision. In order to counter the depth of field that the camera affords her, Trinh renders the images as experientially sensorial and flatly as possible. Eschewing the notion of depth, for example, her camera captures objects and bodies in a way that emphasizes not only the surface of things but also the relations between things and people.[66] She also decentralizes the body in the ways she tracks figures inside and outside of the frames of her film. At other times, an array of objects (gauzy netting, plastic toys, and soft sculptures) foregrounds the images of bodies, forming a tactile border around the characters as they speak or traverse the profilmic space. Whether executed through a still camera or a steadicam, the camera apparatus depicts the two-dimensionality of bodies, images, and objects—sometimes partially, sometimes wholly. This technique lends itself well to her metacommentary on how filmic knowledge about the Other in narrative filmmaking—as in the case for documentary film—is an incomplete assemblage. This practice also enables Trinh to extend her critique, rooted in *Surname Viet*, of the ways in which we gaze upon the female Other and are complicit in the objectification of women and, by extension, "Vietnam." This film's self-conscious gestures of voyeurism, however, highlight more specifically Trinh's objective of illustrating that "power must be seen at its limits."[67]

While her work represents most acutely the meaning and relations of power in the discursive constructions of Kiều, Trinh is, at the same time, not the only critic or diasporic artist to investigate and appropriate the figure of Kiều in their work. Translator and scholar Huỳnh Sanh Thông argues that the predominant understanding of Kiều for the exiled Vietnamese diaspora is that the "*Kiều*" in *Viet Kiều* comes from the character of Kiều in Nguyễn Du's text. According to Thông, since the literary Kiều is always looking homeward to be reunited with family, "*Kiều*" defines an existential state for an overseas community that longs for reunification with the homeland. Thông's conflation of the character of Kiều with the designation of *Viet Kiều* can be read as a political act, informed by the Vietnamese state's designation of the term *Viet Kiều* as a way to denigrate the overseas community as traitors after the war ended. Only recently has the state put a more positive twist on the term.

In critical essays on diasporic literature and filmmaking, Kiều is interpreted through various prisms, exemplifying the extent to which she resonates with the diaspora as a figure to be wrested from the nation's institutional memory. Writing on Francophone women writers, scholar Nathalie Nguyen explains that Kiều as a literary trope can be found in the contemporary work of French Vietnamese writer Ly Thu Ho in a political novel called *Printemps Inachevé*.[68] Scholars Mariam Beevi and Viet Nguyen argue separately that Vietnamese American writer Hayslip appropriates Kiều's narrative of sacrifice and virtue for the advancement of Hayslip's political causes.[69] Within the realm of cinema, Vietnamese diasporic filmmakers also use Kiều as inspiration for their work. In 2006, Vietnamese American Vũ Thu Hà directed a short film on Kiều set in present-day San Francisco, California. Called *Kiều*, Vũ's film features a modern-day prostitute laboring to send money home for her family in Việt Nam. On the other end of the spectrum, *Saigon Eclipse* (2007), a feature film by Vietnamese French director Othello Khanh, is a campy, contemporary updating of the poem, featuring metafilmic references to Kiều as an actress who prostitutes herself for fame. Shot in Sài Gòn, it showcases the talents of Vietnamese American and Vietnamese actors in a transnationally funded film project.

Given the many ways Kiều reproduces meaning in diasporic cultural productions, one way of reading *A Tale of Love* is to contextualize Trinh's films with and against those in the diaspora who reimagine the figure of Kiều in their work. Doing this allows us to read Trinh's work not in its discrete singularity, but in its complementarity, as she herself encourages viewers and readers to do when she publishes theoretical texts and interviews that serve as mirrored supplements to her films. In contrast to other diasporic texts on Kiều, however, Trinh's feminist rendering of Kiều is distinct, since the Kiều in her films remains exceedingly open to being interpreted and translated many times. Within her films, Kiều embodies a narrative system of excess, signifying an inexhaustible production of meaning and affect for and by women. In this, Trinh points toward a trans-Vietnamese feminism, one that contravenes in nationalistic reinterpretations of Kiều.

Precisely because of this system of excess that Kiều represents, I venture further than Trinh in probing the ways that diasporic subjects across the genders claim Kiều, an issue Trinh foregrounds but does not address completely. On Nguyễn Du's text, Trinh writes, "What is exceptional to me is that the national poem of Viet Nam is a love poem rather than an epic poem, and that the figure her people persistently choose to represent their collective self is that of a woman."[70] Trinh seems to ask: What does it mean for a national and diasporic community to identify with a woman who is a sex worker, albeit one marked by filial piety? Trinh implies that it may be exceptional that masculine subjects want to identify with Kiều, but such a claim needs further complication. For the tale of Kiều represents not only an allegory for the country of Việt Nam, as Trinh states in her texts and films, but also, as understood by many in Việt Nam and the diaspora, a stand-in for the author, one beholden to declare fealty to the new king in his lifetime.

As George Boudarel argues, author Nguyễn Du serves as a figure of treason himself.[71] His biography and the controversial reception of his text are part of the work's provocative aura. Nguyễn played the role of mandarin to transitioning dynasties marking the eighteenth and nineteenth centuries. The poem, with its subtle political critiques and allusions to Chinese literature, manifests Nguyễn's betrayal of loyalty to the new ruler. Viewing Nguyễn as a quintessentially *male* artist, consigned to produce for a new culturally dominant and political regime, shows how men can also appropriate Kiều and her story as their own. More specifically, male subjects perhaps identify with Nguyễn Du as a transgressive collaborator and heroic traitor to the politics and literature of his era. As Chapter 1 demonstrated, diasporic male artists like Bui and Tran undergo a similar crisis of allegiance about art and politics in the marketplace. Through the figure of the male artist and the articulation of his alienation, Bui and Tran demonstrate a kinship to Nguyễn Du in expressing their masculinist anxieties about the production and reception of their artistic labors.

My foray into Vietnamese literary history does not concretize meaning for the poem and provide historical depth to the film, an explanatory move that Trinh wants to avoid as a filmmaker. Rather, this historical footnote broadens the politicized notions of traitor and collaborator that prove so enduring to the figuration of Kiều. Ultimately the many incarnations of Kiều in the diaspora signify her ability to produce mobile identifications that cross the boundaries of class, generation, and gender, as well as geography and temporality. The feminization of nationalist sentiment that Trinh queries indicates the extent to which identification and desire are truly complicated processes for both men and women at home and abroad, especially as such sentiments are related to the tale of Kiều. If feminine virtue is often tied to the nation, the final chapter of the book examines alternative scripts of gender that can be found in Vietnamese popular culture.

5 / Betraying Feminine Virtue: Collaborative Effects and the Transnational Circuits of Vietnamese Popular Culture

On a balmy summer evening in 2004, the crowds for Vũ Ngọc Đãng's *Những Cô Gái Chân Dài*, or *Long-Legged Girls*, at the Korean-owned Diamond Plaza in Hồ Chí Minh City were enormous. Sleek motorbikes were parked in rows around the mall; animated throngs of young, fashionable people congregated for drinks before they watched the new film. The mall is flanked by tall business towers and lies adjacent to the Notre Dame Cathedral and a national park that is, by night, a notorious meeting place for lovers and for prostitutes and their clients. Diamond Plaza offers foreigners and a flourishing Vietnamese middle class an air-conditioned respite from the heat during the summer months. It remains a place of leisure for a well-heeled generation of Vietnamese youth, called the "@ generation." Comprised of four levels, Diamond Plaza is devoted to various consumerist pleasures that include the latest in domestic and foreign movies, screened in the plush cinema on the top floor.

Diamond Plaza is not, however, the only theater in Hồ Chí Minh City. The other cineplex is located at the outskirts of downtown, near a famous ice cream parlor and the infamous Backpacker's Alley. Run-down and cavernous, the theater offers cheap tickets priced at less than $2.00. At the Vinh Quang Cinema, among an audience of mostly young couples, I saw a murky, videotaped version of Ang Lee's *Crouching Tiger, Hidden Dragon* (2000). Featuring painted movie posters along its exterior walls, the theater provides creaky seats that are large enough for two, accommodating those who want a covert sexual tryst. In fact, movie theaters in Việt Nam provide the few dark spaces for people's sexual encounters, since distinctions between private and public spaces are blurred. The domain of the home often includes both close and extended family members, while liaisons can occur in places like the park outside of Diamond Plaza. These cinema-going experiences at Diamond Plaza and Vinh Quang—their stark contrasts and unevenness in terms of projection and sound quality, atmosphere and space—are reflections of the country's economic trajectory that have wrought scattered transformations since Đổi Mới. A quick look at these two spaces, where the semipublic expressions of sexuality, youth culture, consumerism, and technology all converge, frames my interrogation of the vibrant context of Vietnamese popular culture.

This chapter asserts the importance of reading Vietnamese popular culture and the collaborations that underlie it. In particular, I explore male filmmakers' parody of feminine virtue in "low" cultural texts like *Long-Legged Girls* and Nguyễn Quang Dũng's *Hồn Trương Ba Da Hàng Thịt* [*Souls on Swings*] (2006). In using the term "low" to describe commercial popular culture, I suggest that films deemed "market-oriented" (*thị trường*) stand in opposition to those productions that are "artistic" (*nghệ thuật*) in ways similar to Western academic classifications of "low" and "high" cultures, with their connotations of gender and class.[1] As cultural critics have demonstrated, such cultures are often pitched against the other; "high" culture is usually associated with the masculine and the elite, while "low" culture is most often associated with the feminine and the masses. These classificatory terms, while historically situated within capitalist and industrial societies, resonate in the neoliberal economies of Việt Nam and diasporic communities. Even as I recognize that the divide between "high" and "low" cultures is highly relational and culturally specific, I employ these distinctions here because they are useful in delineating how Vietnamese culture flows between homeland and diaspora.

Cultural elites in both the homeland and the diaspora understand Vietnamese popular cultural items to be "lowbrow," apolitical, and shallow—and thus not consistently worthy of censorship by the Vietnamese state or deserving of protest by the Vietnamese diaspora. In this way, the films' classification as popular entertainment ensures their mobility across political and national borders. Through the transnational collaboration of Vietnamese production and distribution companies, such films travel without the taint of communist politics as they circulate within Việt Nam and from Việt Nam to the diaspora. In contrast, films with more overtly political themes by auteurist directors like Đặng Nhật

Minh have been met with protest in the Vietnamese American community.[2] This chapter contends that Vietnamese "lowbrow" films do carry the charge of the political, particularly when they explore the politics of youth culture, consumption, and sexuality as Vũ's and Nguyễn's films do. Vũ's and Nguyễn's films also contest notions of feminine virtue as they have been defined in Vietnamese highbrow culture, exemplified in works like Nguyễn Du's *The Tale of Kiều*. More exactingly, the two films betray the desire for alternative scripts for both men and women, ironizing the affective, collective sentiment surrounding constructs of gender, family, and nation. This last chapter is a rejoinder to my first chapter on Tony Bui and Tran Anh Hung, whose works exalt the female body in masculinist terms. These diasporic Vietnamese films also deploy symbols of wretchedness, as signified by the prostitute's body and the cyclo, in order to critique communism and capitalism in the country's epicenter of commerce, Sài Gòn. In contrast to diasporic Vietnamese fears about the corruption of a prior, purer Việt Nam, the two films by Vũ and Nguyễn showcase a thriving Sài Gòn that is the site of agentive forms of looking, consumerist pleasure, and queer desire.

One of the first films to be collaboratively produced and subtitled by Thiên Ngân [Galaxy] Production Company, *Long-Legged Girls* is a distinctively transnational product; from its inception it sought to find investors and markets at home and abroad.[3] Part of the film's allure lies in the way it makes visible the circuits of consumerist and sexual desire found in Vietnamese youth culture. Certainly the highly sexualized images of young men and women accommodate popular tastes and lend the film a more commercial appeal. Vũ Ngọc Đãng's "blockbuster" movie employs objectifying images of both men and women.[4] Nonetheless, the film's objectification of the body produces queer points of identification particularly potent within a state trying to regulate desire and urge the youth to appreciate the wartime sacrifices of older generations.[5] Ironizing the notion of feminine virtue against the backdrop of the fashion industry, *Long-Legged Girls* visualizes an array of subjectivities and activates forms of looking rarely found in either Vietnamese or Vietnamese diasporic cinemas. Producing "self-images and subject positions for [both] makers and viewers," the film effectively tests the boundaries of gendered behaviors and sexual norms in both the homeland and diaspora.[6]

Similarly, *Souls on Swings* constructs multiple subject positions in its narrative framing and its travels at home and abroad. Having collaborated with director/friend Vũ Ngọc Đãng on the music for *Long-Legged*

Girls (they also cameo in each other's films), Nguyễn Quang Dũng's first feature centers on the theme of body switching. Sold in Vietnamese and Vietnamese American DVD shops, *Souls on Swings* features the same casting choices as Vũ's *Long-Legged Girls* (model-turned actress Anh Thư plays the lead in both films) and a similar, colorful aesthetic that dominates the film's set design and costuming. Like *Long-Legged Girls*, the film heralds an exciting vision of post-*Đổi Mới* Việt Nam, namely of Hồ Chí Minh City. What makes this film distinct from Vũ's film, however, is the Vietnamese American star who plays the gay lead, Johnny Trí Nguyễn. In his first collaboration with a Vietnamese director, the film indeed showcases Nguyễn's looks and talent. Extratextually, *Souls* marks the beginning of the actor's collaboration with Vietnamese filmmakers in several transnationally produced Vietnamese works that follow.[7] Moreover, *Souls* reflects the increasingly transnational elements of funding and talent that structure southern Vietnamese filmmaking today.[8]

Placed together, *Long-Legged Girls* and *Souls on Swings* illustrate the ways a young generation of Vietnamese male filmmakers deals with identity and hybridity, the themes of which are formally aestheticized in their filmic techniques. In so doing these directors betray the nationalistic impetus that Vietnamese cinema is supposed to be premised upon. Reflecting the urban, youthful audience who make up the majority of filmgoers today, these films instead deploy an MTV-style aesthetic to narrate their stories, which often revolve around the styling of identity and the fracturing of the national family. This final chapter extends my proposal for a trans-Vietnamese feminist media practice by looking at gender and sexuality vis-à-vis the registers of popular culture, which serves as a battleground for the contestation of values in contemporary Việt Nam. Based on this emergent "mediascape,"[9] I emphasize the productivity of popular cultural works and their pleasures for viewers. Given the historical juncture in which the country and the diaspora are situated, emerging studies of Vietnamese and Vietnamese diasporic culture must consider the influences of youth culture and the shifting notions of gender and sexuality marking social relations in the country and outside of its borders today.

Sexing the City: Urbanity and Modernity in *Long-Legged Girls*

After its cinematic release in Việt Nam in 2004, Vũ Ngọc Đãng's *Long-Legged Girls* circulated in the United States as one of the few contemporary Vietnamese films subtitled in English. From an opening mini-video sequence to the DVD release's "Behind the Scenes" featurette, the film emphasizes its narrative legibility and accessibility. Beyond these marketing strategies,[10] the film also signifies the tremendous changes in the Vietnamese film industry since the 1986 economic reforms instituted in Việt Nam. In 2002, "Decision 38 of the Ministry of Culture and Information . . . sanctioned the operation of private film studios and the opening of Vietnamese movie screens to foreign imports."[11] *Long-Legged Girls* is one of the first major film coproductions to be transnationally distributed by the private production company, Thiên Ngân, or Galaxy. Thus, the film makes a compelling case for the analysis of the transformations wrought within the spheres of state policy and popular culture. It also exemplifies the development of a practice of commercial filmmaking that now plays a significant role in this film industry.

In the same year that *Long-Legged Girls* was released, *Ký Ức Điện Biên Phủ* [*Memories of Dien Bien Phu*] was also shown in theaters in Việt Nam. A lavish movie commemorating the nation's victory against the French in 1954, *Ký Ức* cost about US$900,000 to make but performed poorly at the box office. Nguyễn Văn Nam, head of the Việt Nam Feature Film Company, consequently lamented the loss of money invested in this film and the corrupting influence of commercial demands on the aesthetic value of Việt Nam's cinema.[12] As Nguyễn Thanh Vân, director of *Đời Cát* [*Lives of Sand*], puts it, "For me, movies are art. Making films is not a game or a business."[13] In fact, Nguyễn's criticism echoes much of the critical reception in Việt Nam surrounding commercial films.

Vietnamese viewers, however, offer a different story. Box-office receipts for commercial films suggest a desire for films to reflect the tastes and trends of a growing community of urban moviegoers. Letters and commentaries in Vietnamese online and print magazines manifest an active and responsive imaginary underlying youth culture. On glossy forums singularly devoted to Vietnamese youths' growing preoccupation with cinema, the articles and blurbs about Việt Nam's film industry reveal an intense curiosity in filmmaking, international cinema, and the star system.[14] In this context, clear divisions are drawn between artistic and commercial films, separating out socialist aesthetics and mass commercialism. Exacerbating this problem is the issue of rampant piracy: products flow illicitly throughout Việt Nam, with Hollywood and Asian cinematic imports remaining popular because these films are more accessible than indigenous ones. Films like *Đời Cát* [*Lives of Sand*] are not readily available for purchase; instead, highly regarded, artistic films by Nguyễn Thanh Vân and Đặng Nhật Minh are housed at private film studios and archives. The lack of popular interest in artistic films lies partially in the state's inability to enforce legal sanctions regarding piracy and its own tight hold on the country's cultural products. As Thomas and Heng point out, the question of the popular in Việt Nam is therefore not merely situational but results from structural political and economic changes that have been wrought throughout the postwar years. The restructuring of Vietnamese media in post-*Đổi Mới* Việt Nam has contributed to the development of both a popular and populist culture. Writing on the formation of celebrity culture in the country, Thomas and Heng observe, "Việt Nam is on the brink of becoming a fully-fledged media culture in which popular narratives and cultural icons are reshaping political views, constructing tastes and values, and crystallizing the market economy."[15]

Dovetailing with these developments, *Long-Legged Girls* is a commercial film that had massive appeal at the box office in Việt Nam and acquired some currency at home and abroad when it was released in DVD format. In the United States, the film's mobility and accessibility attest to changes in US-Việt Nam relations. Since the lifting of the trade embargo between the United States and Việt Nam, the movement of capital, culture, and people has increased exponentially. Accompanying this increase in traffic between Việt Nam and the Vietnamese American community, the vociferousness with which the diasporic community once denounced Vietnamese cultural productions as communist propaganda has lessened, depending on the nature and classification of the imported works. As media texts, filmed popular cultural events, including fashion shows, theatrical comedies, and beauty pageants, circulate in Việt Nam and the diaspora more freely than ever before.

Long-Legged Girls is marked by a sense of movement and transgression in other ways, as it contains queer and female desires that set it apart from contemporary Vietnamese films. Most notably, the film projects images of looking between same-sex subjects. Unlike other works that construct an essential "Vietnam," *Long-Legged Girls* depicts the contemporaneity of Việt Nam and draws upon a notion of present time that runs counter to the ways Vietnamese nationalist discourses reify Việt Nam as a country with a tragic but glorious past. In contrast to other filmic commemorations of the past, the film proclaims Hồ Chí Minh City's modernity and thus promotes an exciting urbanity not only to the Vietnamese but also the diaspora. To local and diasporic audiences, the film shows a modern city made over by *Đổi Mới*, one that appears contemporaneous with those in the Pacific Rim and in the West.

As part of a transnational consumption of popular culture, Vũ's film defines a particular mode of cultural politics for its youthful consumers by celebrating the public fantasies of youth culture in Việt Nam in terms of both content and structure. *Long-Legged Girls* fetishistically reproduces contemporary images from television, photography, film, and cellular phone technology in a manner that elides the question of war and history altogether. The conspicuous absence of flashbacks, a predominant feature of the Vietnamese films preceding it, also testifies to *Long-Legged Girls'* intent to be situated in the present moment.[16] This elision of Việt Nam's struggles with foreign invaders speaks to the country's overwhelmingly young generation, a population with little memory of the wars that mark recent Vietnamese history and for whom cultural contact with foreigners is a sign of cosmopolitanism, rather than betrayal. A self-conscious catalogue of consumptive acts, *Long-Legged Girls* expresses a critical desire for modernity for and by Việt Nam's youth. In the film, one of the main characters drives a lemon-yellow Vespa, an antique Italian-imported motorbike that is fetishized on screen as a nostalgic commodity. Unlike the cyclo that serves as a signifier for wretchedness, the motorbike in this film is imbued with both postmodern elements of "style" and pastiche,[17] running as a comic gag because it falters and breaks down throughout the film.

Expressions of modernity appear not only in the characters' consumerist desires, but also in the urban milieu in which the film takes place and in the film's techniques. *Long-Legged Girls'* mobile camera movements, swooping angles, and MTV-style editing show a knowing sensibility, as well as a gendered way of seeing and experiencing Hồ Chí Minh City in the Đổi Mới era.[18] The main story deals with the rise and fall of a fashion model, Thúy, whose values are called into question on the road to success. The narrative is familiar: a country girl migrates to the city and realizes she has lost herself in the pursuit of fame. In the process, Thúy also alienates her boyfriend and destroys her relationship with her older sister. True to the tenets of the romantic comedy, the movie has a happy ending: the protagonist returns to her sister's house and reconciles with her boyfriend, Hoàng. The flashy finale celebrates family reunification and heterosexual coupledom, but only ironically so.

While appearing to instruct audiences about female virtue, *Long-Legged Girls* ultimately shows how the characters attempt to acquire a "cosmopolitan aura."[19] The youthful, stylishly clothed characters desire differently than the generations before them. The cast of characters surrounding Thúy comprises what Chris Berry calls a "post-Confucian family," living outside of traditional family relations.[20] As the film nar-rates, this new post-*Đổi Mới* family consists of young, attractive singles finding their place in a modern world. The women in *Long-Legged Girls* may be bound by familial expectations, but their attitudes toward the family dispel the notion that they are *only* interpellated by the family and, by extension, the nation. Rather, situated in a neoliberal economy, they pursue their dreams and careers ruthlessly alongside other driven women. This is keenly exemplified by Thúy, who tries to make it to the top of the fashion industry as a model.

In spite of its cheerful ending, the final sequences of the film dem-onstrate great ambivalence about Thúy's ambitions in her trajectory of going from "model to model citizen."[21] In the film's climax, Thúy makes a tearful speech praising the values of happiness and "true beauty" during the beauty pageant. The director then cuts to a scene wherein she sleeps with her sister in the same bed. With a stationary camera above the bed, we witness the tender embrace of the two women, which signifies not only the reunion of the sisters but also the resolution between tradition and modernity. The elder sister represents the paradigm of traditional virtue; childless and husbandless, she is nonetheless a comic figure, lam-pooned because of her absurd tendencies to demand order and discipline in a youthful and changing context. In opposition, Thúy serves as the young "new woman," one who negotiates with the forces of change in a transformed world. However, this coming together of the two sisters is not without its complications: on the bed, Thúy drapes a scantily clad leg over her sister in a tableau complicating the return to tradition. They embrace, but not without a final shot for viewers of Thúy's objectified body. After this sequence, we are transported to the concluding scenes of the film—the reunion of Thúy and Hoàng. With such a quick cut, there is no emphatic conclusion to her modeling career or pursuit of success within the fashion industry. In actuality, the image of her leg is a final and fetishistic reminder of the protagonist's main commodity within a patriarchal and capitalistic industry.

On a diegetic level, the film outwardly embraces traditional and rural values, but Vũ's images and soundtrack compromise the film's own the-matic concerns. Following the reunion of the two sisters, the conclusion takes place in an empty kiln in the countryside from where Thúy originally hails. Ostensibly a celebratory return to an ideal space, this scene features Thúy and Hoàng reuniting and kissing in a repeat of an earlier scene. The ending, however, is markedly excessive, overflowing with poppy music and flashy 360-degree camera angles. Most remarkably, while the two lovers passionately embrace, Khoa, the gay housemate who longs for Thúy's boy-friend, sits outside of the kiln. The final shots of the film are of a forlorn Khoa as he waits for his friend to reconcile with Thúy. Until the end, Khoa functions as a reminder of the failure and artificiality of the heterosexual romance genre, even while the film struggles to normalize heterosexual coupling. Unlike other films that attempt to privilege originary narratives, the return to one's roots in this film is framed as pure, romantic fantasy.

Gender, Sexuality, and the Pleasures of Looking

If heterosexuality is artificial in the film's conclusion, in contrast, there is a certain authenticity about Khoa's queer devotion to his roommate. In fact, Khoa's presence in the film's love triangle functions to upstage the generic tenets of the romantic comedic formula about heterosexuality. His charac-ter centrally frames the film, as it not only ends with his melancholia but also begins with his fantasies. Setting up the film's irreverent tone toward sexuality, the beginning opens with a music video sequence establishing the relationship between the three characters: Khoa, Hoàng, and Thúy. First, we see Thúy in a rural setting, atop a haystack as she hunts her pet pig. Abruptly, the camera cuts to a shot of two seminaked men sleeping together in a closed room, one embracing the other. This intimate image of the two roommates, Khoa and Hoàng, is repeated throughout the film, which insists on trou-bling the relationship between the two heterosexual leads.

Overlaying such shots is the catchy tune called "Giấc Mơ" ["Dream"] that becomes central in reading the queer-identified sequence. These scenes are accented by the song's lyrics, subtitled in English. Sung in Vietnamese by a male singer named Aikia (his name, *ai kìa*, can be translated as, Who is that there?), the words revolve around love, sex, and romance regarding a long-legged lover whose gender is never named ("Like the long legs/I had dreamed of coming to see/For me to love").[22] The lyrics bring a dynamic coherency to the queer images, visualizing a moment of pleasure for the gay character, Khoa. As he is the only fig-ure on screen, the lyrics enunciate his fantasy (see Fig. 5–1). Image and sound cohere because of how Khoa's face conveys pleasure throughout this sequence. Serene in sleep, this character's smiling face is intercut with shots of his roommate's dancing legs, buttocks, and body in the shower. One shot shows Hoàng's gyrating nude body; then immediately after, another shot presents us with Khoa sleeping restfully. During these quick juxtapositions, the sexually explicit lyrics intoned are, "These long legs that came here many times/even if only in my dreams/I thank you

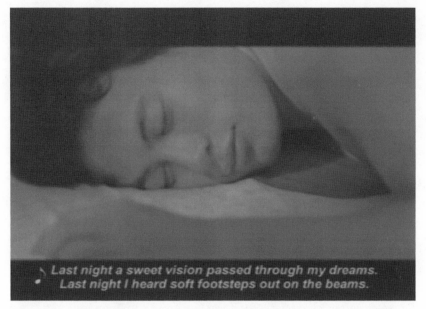

Last night a sweet vision passed through my dreams.
Last night I heard soft footsteps out on the beams.

FIGURE 5.1. Khoa's fantasies on screen. From the film *Những Cô Gái Chân Dài* (*Long-Legged Girls*) © 2004. Thiên Ngân Film Studio.

for coming."[23] Brightly lit and filling the screen for long moments of time, Khoa's expressions register the erotic desire in the song's words.

The opening sequence becomes endowed with meaning not merely because of the simultaneous emphases on the visual and aural registers underlying the shots but also because of the allusions to sexual dreams and fantasies that the shots provide.[24] Drawing on the work of Freud and Metz, Teresa de Lauretis contends that popular culture narratives hold great emotive value for spectators and thus serve as "public fantasies," since they "perform at the societal level and in the public sphere, a function similar to that of the private fantasies, daydreams, and reveries by which individual subjects imagine their erotic, ambitious, or destructive aspirations."[25] Whether asleep or awake, Khoa's private fantasies are made public when they are projected on-screen. These instances give way to a rare moment in Vietnamese film history: a depiction of homosexual desire that rivals the heterosexualized romance between the two lead actors. In the film, this sequence and others like it establish the play of and on sexual identities underlying the narrative.[26] The subjective queer male fantasies of Khoa, a key player in the film who constitutes the third but crucial vector of a love triangle, are thus briefly indulged on screen.

In the same way that he visualizes Khoa's desires, filmmaker Vũ also renders women's pleasures in looking, but he presents this circuitry of gazes in a more conventional manner. At the center of the film is the spectacle of women's bodies and specifically their legs, which are often fetishistically imaged on film. Because the film revolves around the fashion industry, it often presents images of photography and film equipment in the mise-en-scène to signal the milieu within which the film takes place. These images comment metacinematically on feminine performance and spectacle as well. Vis-à-vis the camera, we are afforded voyeuristic views of models undressing and titillating shots of women's legs, shots that stress a masculinist, heterosexual way of looking. This is most evident when the character of Đồng Hải, a top photographer, looks at a model and her body. Through his point-of-view, accompanied by an eyeline match, we see the woman's long legs and witness her smile of delight in being noticed.

Nevertheless, the camera also highlights women's gazes at each other. Various forms of high technology enable the looking relations instigated between women characters like Xuân Lan and Thúy. Thoroughly engaged as well as implicated in the politics of looking, both women project contradictory and ambivalent desires. Soon after she arrives in the city, Thúy happens upon a photo shoot in the street. Instantly, the *vedette* of the fashion world, Xuân Lan, captivates Thúy. Shot in slow motion, the scene is marked by upbeat, cheerful music, the same music that will later be used to herald Thúy as a rising star. Centralized in the shots, Xuân Lan is dressed as the quintessential woman in red; her movements are slowed down as she poses seductively for the photographer's/director's/spectator's gaze. The centerfold-type poses the model strikes are tinged with an ironic performativity, as spectators witness the framing and objectification of a clichéd "Oriental" beauty. Emphatically framed as the "woman-as-spectacle,"[27] the model paradoxically contains these notions of femininity by contradicting the conventions of Vietnamese female beauty with her dominatrix-like attributes (see Fig. 5–2). Intercut with these shots of parodic femininity are shots of Thúy's covetous looks of desire and appreciation.

Though coded as envy and admiration for Xuân Lan's status as object-of-the-look, Thúy's looking contains a frisson of female-to-female desire that runs concurrently, especially given the queer-identified sequence preceding it. Much like the musical video sequence beginning the film, these scenes are excessive to the diegetic narrative. Framed as a (hetero) sexual object of desire, Xuân Lan nonetheless poses (homo)erotically

FIGURE 5.2. Desiring women and the spectacle of womanhood. From the film *Những Cô Gái Chân Dài (Long-Legged Girls)* © 2004. Thiên Ngân Film Studio.

for Thúy's female gaze as well as for the audience. Most conspicuously, "when the woman looks"[28] in this film, as our heroine does often, her look is usually framed in a homosocial, yet eroticized, gaze directed at other women and their body parts. When Thúy looks with fascination upon a fashion show, for example, her looks of ecstasy and wonderment are accentuated by a sequence that cuts back and forth between the show and her apparent pleasures in beholding the spectacle of women's bodies. Zooming in on the women's bodies on stage and then intercutting these zooms with close-ups of Thúy's rapturous face, the editing relays how women's scopophilic pleasures are tied to visuality and consumption. Beyond this homoerotic subtext, Thúy's looking signifies a longing for status, one that consolidates class and access within a nexus of power relations reflecting how women are situated in a visual culture that objectifies their bodies. When Xuân Lan returns the look, for instance, her gaze incriminates Thúy and effects a form of punishment for Thúy's queer, excessive identification with her. In a scene that takes place in an underground nightclub, Xuân Lan uses her Nokia cellular phone to humiliate Thúy by recording her performance in an illegal modeling show. However, the final look executed between Xuân Lan and Thúy near the end of the film also shows a mutual understanding that indexes the competitive and exploitative milieu in which the models are uncertainly positioned.

In comparison to other filmic representations of femininity, the exchange between women in *Long-Legged Girls* becomes an imperative move. In contrast to how national and diasporic films often use native women to represent anteriority and fixity, *Long-Legged Girls* shows Vietnamese women as thoroughly modern in their mobile gazes as well as in their manipulation of technology. Highly respected films like *Thương Nhớ Đồng Quê* [*Nostalgia for the Countryside*] (1995) by Đặng Nhật Minh also have centralized female characters. Yet, in Đặng's film, women serve as ciphers for a male subject, who alone possesses the capacity to narrate stories and capture images with his gaze. As the first chapter of this book established, we see such timeless and feminized constructions of Việt Nam in films like *Three Seasons* and *Scent of Green Papaya*. The diasporic imaginings of the country, produced by an overseas male elite, feature the homeland as a battleground for the struggles between tradition and modernity, socialism and capitalism. Such battles are often played out on native women's bodies, marked as authentic signifiers for the homeland. The complicit looks between the women in *Long-Legged Girls* differ from the gendered looking in Vietnamese and Vietnamese diasporic films that utilize "woman" as a naturalized repository of tradition. In such films, she does not and cannot look back.

Souls on Swings: Swapping Bodies and Sexuality in Hồ Chí Minh City

Long-Legged Girls ironizes the notion of feminine virtue, featuring a female lead who is neither a collaborator nor a traitor to the national family. Rather than labor for this national family, Thúy is a modern woman who strives for a higher-class status; her desires for fame and wealth are what propel the narrative. Along the way, Vũ's film shows women doing their own looking and deconstructs high culture's notions of Vietnamese femininity. In contrast, Nguyễn Quang Dũng's Vietnamese comedy, *Souls on Swings*, plays on the constructs of gender roles and heterosexuality. In this film, both men and women, straight and gay, betray the nationalist injunction to reproduce the nation. The national family in the film is displaced onto a fraternity of overweight butchers who are ordered about by a childless matriarch. Indeed, *Souls* depicts an anarchic fantasy about subjects who engage in role-play and identity swapping. They upend class and gender hierarchies as a result. Like *Long-Legged Girls*, this film constructs a circuit of gazes between male and female subjects that stress a highly charged, eroticized way of looking. While *Long-Legged Girls* features homoerotic gazes between women, *Souls on Swings* deals more with the appearance, or "look" of the Vietnamese

American male actor, Johnny Trí Nguyễn, and the scopophilic pleasures his body offers to spectators.

Known for his Hollywood and Asian roles as an action star, Nguyễn is central to reading diasporic "masculinity as spectacle."[29] The film traffics in his movie-star good looks and references the intertextual quality of his star persona. A Vietnamese American actor, Nguyễn currently lives in Việt Nam in order to make films. His image and his popularity in Vietnamese films reflect his ability to straddle two languages (Vietnamese and English) and two types of audiences (local and diasporic). Extending my queries into the queer images and gazes characteristic of several Vietnamese comedies, I interpret *Souls* as a carnivalesque film about male corporeality and homosexuality. Hewing to Bakhtin's formulation of carnival and the "lower bodily stratum," my analysis hinges upon a configuration of the male body that is at once a metaphor for the malleability of sexual identity in today's Việt Nam and an extratextual signifier of diasporic cosmopolitanism. My study focuses not only on the cosmopolitan setting of Hồ Chí Minh City but also on the bawdy semiotics of Johnny Trí Nguyễn's body, one that gestures and performs as a sign of desire.

The beginning of *Souls* lays out its madcap premise, which deals with the act of switching bodies between Sang, a working-class butcher played by the film's coproducer Phước Sang, and Trương Ba, a suave lothario played by Johnny Trí Nguyễn. The film parodies a well-known folk story and derives some of its satirical shape from a 1984 play of the same name and written by popular playwright Lưu Quang Vũ. The opening also alludes to the film's use of the occult, a theme that will also be threaded into Nguyễn Quang Dũng's later films, highly popular movies like *Nụ Hôn Thần Chết* [*Kiss of Death*] (2008), and its sequel, *Giải Cứu Thần Chết* [*The Rescue of Death*] (2009). A diminutive sorcerer, Đế Thích, loses a chess match to Trương Ba and then takes revenge by switching Trương Ba's body with that of a homely butcher, Sang. After the swap, the men spend the rest of the film trying to find their rightful bodies.

Films like *Souls on Swings* use Hồ Chí Minh City as a backdrop.[30] Urban comedies that have been produced by a young generation of filmmakers based in this southern city weave the themes of sexual reproduction, body swapping, and mistaken identities. Hồ Chí Minh City not only serves as the staging for carnivalesque comedy, it is also the site of a burgeoning film culture, one that revolves around the business of filmmaking. Images of contemporary Hồ Chí Minh City in Vietnamese films point to a cosmopolitan identity built into the city's historical image as the country's capital of commerce and the site of foreign influences. Understood to be the decadent "sister" city in comparison to Việt Nam's more austere capital, Hà Nội, in northern discourses, Sài Gòn has often been troped in communist discourse as the breeding grounds for vice, corruption, and greed.[31] Historically, Sài Gòn was territorialized and controlled both by the French (who ruled Indochina mainly from Cochin China) and Americans (who based their occupation in Sài Gòn) during French colonialism and the American War. Film production in the South reflects this history. Films produced in the South have historically differed from those produced in the North in terms of funding and reception. A regional bias also continues to view Hà Nội as the cultural center of the country rather than Hồ Chí Minh City. Accordingly, films made in the North are regarded as more artistic than those produced in the South, which are viewed as more market-oriented. This bears out in the ways in which films like Đặng Nhật Minh's *Đừng Đốt* [*Don't Burn*] (2009) and Bùi Thạc Chuyên's *Chơi Vơi* [*Adrift*] (2010) receive more critical attention, both locally and internationally. Such perceptions about northern and southern cultural productions are shaped by the two regions' entanglements with foreigners and foreign capital.[32]

In Vietnamese film historiography, scholars note that the birth of a nationalist Vietnamese cinema roughly coincides with the birth of a postcolonial nation, an independent nation sited in Hà Nội.[33] After 1945, the Democratic Republic of Việt Nam established several decrees that allowed for the making of state-sponsored films. In 1953, Hồ Chí Minh signed into law a piece of legislation that declared Vietnamese cinema had two tasks: (1) to build socialism; and (2) to struggle for the liberation of the South for the reunification of country.[34] Solidified by northern Việt Nam's victory over the French in 1954, the postcolonial state took further steps to ensure that film would be a major culture industry in the years that followed. 1957 saw the opening of the first Vietnamese film journal, *Điện Ảnh,* and two years later, the North opened its first film school (Hà Nội Cinema School) and movie engineering plant. In 1959, a major film studio, Xưởng Phim Việt Nam Studio (Việt Nam Film Studio), was established.[35] This same year, the country's first independently produced film, *Chúng Tôi Muốn Sống* [*Together on the Same River*], was released. Historically important, Together was a movie about the reunion of two lovers symbolic of the reunification of North and South Việt Nam.

In the wartime South, however, the situation was different. As Sarah Rouse explains, "Most full-length features distributed in the Republic of

Vietnam were imported from Nationalist China, the U.S., India, Japan, and France."[36] During the American War, the main financers of southern Vietnamese films came to be the US government and private donors. The Republic of Việt Nam's production companies included the Republic's Army Film Service, the USIS (US Information Service), the National Motion Picture Center, and Freedom Films. The chief output during wartime was documentaries and newsreels, with feature films rarely being made because of their high production costs.[37] Feature films that were made featured a distinctly anticommunist angle. Philippe Dumont, for example, speaks briefly of *Chúng Tôi Muốn Sống* [*We Want to Live*] (1956) and *Người Tình Không Chân Dung* [*Warrior, Where Are You?*] (1971) and their ideological content. Dumont notes that after 1975, films made with American funding and cooperation were kept in secret.[38] To this day, southern Vietnamese films remain "systematically misjudged or ignored" and are rarely found in the country's film archives and catalogues.[39]

Since *Đổi Mới,* the state has allowed for more collaborations between Việt Nam, the diaspora, and other countries in relation to film. Many of these collaborations now take place in Hồ Chí Minh City, the film industry's center for investment possibilities with respect to production and exhibition.[40] A series of recent laws has further helped to facilitate these developments. In 2002, the state allowed for the establishment of private production companies in Việt Nam. In 2007, it also set a quota for how many Vietnamese films (20 percent of the total) would screen in theaters nationwide.[41] Other laws pertaining to citizenship and visas affect the ways in which the film industry has been infused with transnational capital and talent. Overseas Vietnamese can now stay in the country for up to five years, provided they obtain a visa in order to live and work there. In 2008, Việt Nam amended its citizenship laws to allow diasporans to hold dual citizenship. Such changes in the bureaucratic, legal, and administrative ways of making films form an integral aspect in analyzing the transnational structures of Vietnamese cinema.

These market forces and political conditions also help to explain the rise of Vietnamese comedies centered in Hồ Chí Minh City. Since the late 1990s, popular film comedies feature the themes of body switching and identity swapping in a city that serves as the country's center of capital flow and desire. *Khi Đàn Ông Có Bầu* [*When Men Get Pregnant*] (2006) and *Đẻ Mướn* [*Hired Birth*] (2007) focus on the reproductive functions of women and feature the thematic of both imagined and real body swappings. In the former, hysterical men are imagined to be pregnant, and in the latter, a career-driven older woman hires, at great cost, a young woman to serve as her surrogate. It is ultimately revealed in *Hired Birth* that her husband is sterile and has lied about it. Both films manifest latent anxieties about Vietnamese male identity and sterility during times of terrific tumult, as they show that under capitalism, it is mostly male subjects who undergo major crises, both bodily and existentially. Comedic films such as these reflect an illiberal panic regarding the prominent role of women in the workplace and labor force since Đổi Mới has been established.

In contrast, *Souls on Swings* steers away from female reproductive capacities and delves more deeply into male sexualities. If Hồ Chí Minh City has been figured as a feminized portal for impurities, epitomized by the figure of the female prostitute, the same city in this film becomes a masculinized backdrop for homosexuality and the homoerotics of male bodies that switch. Set in a sewage tunnel, nightclub, butcher's shop, and mental asylum, the film's emphasis on the scatological and abject is pronounced throughout. In these spaces, the lower half of the male body is most visibly marked as being compromised. After the body-switch, Trương Ba's body, which now houses the butcher's soul, undergoes a series of bodily humiliations that involve his penis (he is kneed by his wife and slides down on a pole only to hurt himself) and buttocks (there is much talk about going to the bathroom and flatulence). At times barely covered with a magazine or a woman's skirt, Johnny Trí Nguyễn's lower body parts are constantly alluded to as symbols for his character's changed and compromised masculinity.

With its substantial potty humor, Nguyễn Quang Dũng's film tries to undo several taboos about the body and sex. Called "unhygienic" by one Vietnamese film critic, the film operates as pure theater in its staging of bodily transgressions.[42] In this respect, *Souls* contains some subversive elements because it enables viewers to engage in a collective fantasy about the inversion of sexual identity as well as of class and gender. By overturning notions of authority, the film demonstrates that patients run the asylum, women dominate their milieus, and gay men find true happiness in the end. Most effectively, this farcical comedy reverses binary oppositions; in the world of the film, men are passive while women are active, and homosexual men are defined by masculine strength while heterosexual women are sexually assertive. Rather than uphold heterosexual patriarchy, the male bodies that switch in *Souls* are extremely vulnerable to punishment and defilement. They are subject to the vagaries of a pint-sized magician and the whims of women, namely the wife and a female psychiatrist who sadistically discipline the men in both familial and institutional contexts. The construct of heterosexuality is also decentered in the end of the film, when Trương Ba comes out as a gay man. The film concludes with a final body switch: Trương Ba finds his rightful body and chooses a male friend, Quang Vinh, as his lover. The coming-out narrative for hypermasculine subjects like Trương Ba overturns the notion that masculinity can only be coupled with heterosexuality.

Through the theme of body switching and mistaken identity, director Nguyễn emphasizes how identities in Việt Nam are constructed, fluid, and shape-shifting. Touched by the occult, which is controversial in itself because of the state's former ban on superstitious practices,[43] characters inhabit each other's bodies with great promiscuity. Revolving around the fantasy of role-playing, *Souls on Swings* opens up a space for a multiplicity of subjectivities to be visible. As Elizabeth Cowie argues, visibility functions as a mechanism of fantasy, "making visible, present, of what isn't there, or what can never *directly* be seen."[44] Fantastically, the male body in *Souls* becomes an open vehicle that realizes mobile subject positions. In the most hyperbolic fashion, the film's use of the male body makes visible the performativity of gender and the elasticity of sexuality.

Subversion and Affirmation in the Grotesque Body

Instead of focusing on women's body parts as in *When Men Get Pregnant* and *Hired Birth*, this film intently explores the Bakhtinian notion of the "lower bodily stratum" of the male body, locating in this nether region the aspects of vulgar comedy that mark the film's carnivalesque tone. Examining the body's degradation in the literature of Rabelais, Bakhtin discusses how official conventions of a spiritual, highly aestheticized body were deliberately overturned in medieval folk culture. Consequently, "all that was considered private and sacred to the intact body was shamelessly parodied, its inner sanctums made public."[45] Bakhtin also observes that folk culture sought to undo official culture and its customs through the staging of carnival and ritual spectacles: "[It] celebrates temporary liberation from the prevailing truth and established order. Carnival marks the suspension of all hierarchies, ranks, privileges, norms, and prohibitions."[46] Appropriately enough, in a film that relentlessly parodies official culture and the notion of prohibitions, there is an explicit focus not only on men's penises but also on their buttocks. Throughout the film, "inner sanctums [that] are made public" are represented within the space of men's bathrooms especially. Several bathroom scenes involve men and show how the violability of their bodies revolves around exposure, revelations, defecation, and homosocial bonding.

Bathroom humor and men's urinals thus serve an integral component of the film's comic and homoerotic texture. One of the first scenes that takes place in the bathroom is when Sang Thịt (the butcher) finds his soul is the body of Trương Ba (the ladies' man). His new identity unbeknownst to him, he squats—rather than sits—on the Western-style toilet (thus signaling the butcher's lack of refinement) and proceeds to go to the bathroom. The soundtrack includes grunts and sounds of flatulence that render the performance both comical and vulgar. The scene's scatological humor is also derived from the viewer's knowledge that the urbane character of Trương Ba, as played by Johnny Trí Nguyễn, has switched bodies with the butcher. Relying upon the idea of incongruity, the comic effect is based on reversing the spectator's expectation of the normative: rakish and debonair, Trương Ba would not be so crude and buffoonish, especially when played by Johnny Trí Nguyễn. With the soul of the butcher inside him, Trương Ba's highly aestheticized body is therefore brought low in this scene, constituting the first "gross-out moment" of many in the film (see Fig. 5–3).

As Geoff King notes on the mechanisms of comedy, such transgressions about the body are specifically designed to test cultural boundaries and restrictions.[47] The testing of cultural boundaries bears out in the moments that follow this scene of defecation. The butcher's confusion about who he is and what body he inhabits is compounded by the fact that he is very dumb. The butcher-as-Trương Ba gazes into the bathroom mirror. Only after a few minutes does he then slowly realize his body is not his own. It is also much later that he discovers that as Trương Ba, he is Quang Vinh's gay lover while in the bathroom. This is a fact he had not realized even though Quang Vinh leans in to try to kiss him when they wake up together in an earlier scene. The moment that Quang Vinh attempts to kiss him is parodically staged with the same music and two-shot composition that frames the scene in *Long-Legged Girls* when Khoa and Hoàng face each other and almost kiss. This scene serves as a sly reference to Vũ's earlier film, demonstrating how some Vietnamese comedies quote one another in a humorous relay of citation. Most of all, when Trương Ba realizes he is in the body of another, transgression and revelation are followed by a very intimate encounter between men.

Later in the film, another bathroom scene emphasizes a similar kind of homoerotic revelation. As Judith Halberstam has written on the men's bathroom, "[It] constitutes both an architecture of surveillance

FIGURE 5.3. The bathroom and the lower bodily stratum of the male body. From the film *Hồn Trương Ba Da Hàng Thịt* (*Souls on Swings*) © 2006. HK Film.

and an incitement to desire, a space of homosocial interaction and of homoerotic inversion."[48] Situated on the hospital grounds, the setting of which intensifies the sense of surveillance that the men undergo, this bathroom establishes a moment of not only homosocial interaction but also homoerotic bonding. The two men discover that their bodies have been switched, and frantically they try to find a solution to their dilemmas. They come up with the idea that they will get each other out of the mental asylum by playing "normal" and thus by performing the gendered identities that accompany their mismatched bodies. In the process, the men confront each other and reveal more details of themselves, their bodies, and their past in an intimate fashion. Through its dialogue and slapstick humor, this scene functions to highlight the homoerotic overtones of their bodily exchange. This fact is further accented in the ways that because of their body-switch, the two men realize they share a relationship with the same woman, Thị, the butcher's wife. Halberstam also notes that it is the "bathroom . . . that comes to represent domestic order, or a parody of it, out in the world."[49] As demontrated in this critical moment between men, their crossed identities and role reversals overturn the domestic order within which they play cuckolded men and rakish playboys. This scene emphasizes the porosity of their gendered identities and reveals the constructedness of the roles they are made to perform in the space of the private and public.

But while the lower regions of the male body provide a "parody of official reason,"[50] the mouth of the woman's body serves as an unnatural site of oral and auditory horror in more conventional ways. The open orifices of Thị's mouth and nose appear in close-up shots of her face throughout the film, while her speaking parts—which include screeching, screaming, yelling, crying, and spewing—all underline the ways in which she is supposed to be threatening and castrating in many scenes. Dressed in gaudy clothes and garish makeup, Thị smothers Trương Ba-as-the butcher with kisses and suffocates him with her embraces; in horror, he struggles to get away because her bad breath and smelly armpits. It is not coincidental that the same actress who plays Thúy in *Long-Legged Girls* is cast here as the insufferable wife, the embodiment of a shrill femininity. Playing against type, the actress, Minh Thư, deliberately downplays the sweet persona of her character in Vũ's film. The casting choice lends an intertextual quality to *Long-Legged Girls* and *Souls on Swings* and underscores the continuity of talent that brings the two films together.

Similarly, the sadistic female psychiatrist (played by popular singer Phương Thanh, known for her husky voice) is also defined by her sexually domineering demeanor. A psychiatrist dressed in knee-length black boots, her enveloping mouth barks orders all day at her patients, but coos lovingly to Trương Ba because she is attracted to him. The connection between her mouth, sex, and feasting is made apparent in a comic moment that relies on a sight gag for its comedic effect.[51] In this scene, Trương Ba is lying on his back, thrashing about as if in pain, while the viewer hears slurping noises that suggest the doctor is performing oral sex on Trương Ba. The camera pulls out to reveal the full scenario: she is sucking ravenously on a bowl of noodles rather than on his body, a sexual innuendo that works through the deployment of sound and gestures as well as in the camera's tracking movement. As both the doctor and Thị demonstrate, women's voracious appetites are never sated when they play the role of monstrous women. As such, these characters highlight the misogyny underlying images of the female grotesque. As Mary Russo suggests, the "carnivalized woman . . . is an image that, however counterproduced, perpetuates the dominant (and in this case misogynistic) representation of women by men."[52]

The film ends on a further note of misogyny and heterosexism, despite its best intentions and the message of acceptance with which it concludes. The film's conclusion forecloses the possibility of a feminist and queer resolution to the gender and sex inversions that it heretofore attempts to establish. While identities are in flux and subject positions shift throughout the film, sexual difference is celebrated with a bodily transformation that allows for only gay men to come together. The film's conclusion confirms this once the daisy chain of body swapping finally ends with a major climax. Swinging as if on a pendulum from gender to gender, sexual orientation to sexual orientation, the switching of bodies ends with a tearful yet joyous reunion between two gay men. Trương Ba's male lover, Quang Vinh, swaps with the body of Trương Ba's socialite girlfriend, Thanh Thanh. When this final switch happens, she is delighted as she jumps on a platform and moves her hands over her "feminine" curves suggestively. Quang Vinh's wish to become a woman has been granted, but in order for this final switch to occur, Thanh Thanh's soul and Quang Vinh's queer body must disappear. In discarding the woman's soul and the "out" queer male body, the film advocates for a bodily transformation for the effete character of Quang Vinh and allows viewers to "see" heterosexual coupledom as part of its narrative resolution. Until this point, the coming together of two men on the screen—symbolically between the butcher and the lothario and literally between Quang Vinh and Trương Ba—is key for reading Vietnamese queerness in films that feature "trans-body" thematics.[53] Ultimately, however, the film maintains a preservation of separate identities that adheres to a Cartesian mind-body split. Beyond the film's diegesis, this preservation of identities dovetails with current political discourses about sexuality, most notably, the government's stance on the fixity of a transsexual identity. The state has recently allowed for transsexuals to claim a new identity, provided their psychological and physical selves are *clearly* at odds.[54] At present, bisexuals, gays, and lesbians are not accorded the same privilege.

With some irony, then, *Souls* reflects the state's unambivalent attitudes toward sex operations and the issue of sexual identity. Denouncing male homosexuality as a fad, or as a false choice between the real and fake, state officials would rather regulate sexual identities and the identification of sexual subjects through a distinction between the two sexes; either you are a woman or a man.[55] During a time marked by neoliberal economic reforms, the state perhaps imagines itself as decidedly liberal in redefining identity in this way, but such legislation also stands in sharp contrast to the crackdown of dissident bodies that occurred during this time period.[56] The state's actions and the film's gestures toward embracing difference can be perceived as commendable, but they operate within a highly limited framework. While the film usefully proposes a popular, lowbrow insurgency against official culture in its comedic staging of carnival, difference is nonetheless congealed by the film's end. Both the film's and the state's understanding of sexual identity is premised upon a neoliberal promise; that is, how the confusion surrounding one's sexual identity can be corrected with surgery because a bodily transformation is all that is needed. In this sense, one's sex and sexual orientation are conflated, tethered to the notion that sexual identities are essential, true, and preordained. Such an ending reminds viewers of the ways that carnival exists only as "authorized transgression,"[57] and that the genre of comedy can itself be both subversive and affirmative of social norms.[58]

As a reflection of these social norms, the film concludes with a shot of Trương Ba's red sports car. The use of the male body in the sports car again suggests a mobile sexual subjectivity and a cosmopolitan identity that the film wants to claim for itself. The malleable body serves as a metaphor for political and economic transformation in twenty-first-century Việt Nam. We propel forward to the future in Trương Ba's sleek red car, which embodies Johnny Trí Nguyễn's star persona (see Fig. 5–4). Read in this way, Trương Ba is a sign of urbanity and modernity, emphasized as such by the fact that he is played by Vietnamese American actor Johnny Trí Nguyễn. The following analysis looks at the multivalent sign of Nguyễn's body and his body of work.

Embodying Vietnamese American Transnationalism: Stardom, Allure, and the Diasporic Male Body

The robust consumption of Vietnamese popular culture in Việt Nam and the diaspora contests the ways that "culture" has been defined by the Vietnamese state as only propagandist and populist in nature. With the rise of fandom and stardom in Việt Nam and the diaspora today, the interconnections between the popular and the political have also been revised. Thomas and Heng assert that in Việt Nam a culture of celebrity is emergent within a media culture that has shifted from a depersonalized public sphere to one dominated by popular media.[59] In this culture, "celebrities, all popular icons, are meaningful because they are hieroglyphs, instantiations of the worlds in the making, of tastes, ideologies and relations of power in the wider social environment of the Vietnamese people."[60] Reading Nguyễn's star turn as a "hieroglyph," we can see the ways that the film commodifies his crossover allure as a diasporic singer, stunt actor, and male performer. Prior to being cast in *Souls*, Nguyễn was known as a Vietnamese American singer for the Vân Sơn Production Company, which produces extravaganzas featuring dancing, singing, and comedy. These shows are extremely popular both in

FIGURE 5.4. The star vehicle for Vietnamese American actor Johnny Trí Nguyễn. From the film *Hồn Trương Ba Da Hàng Thịt (Souls on Swings)* © 2006. HK Film.

the homeland and among the diaspora. However, it was not until he starred in the breakout film, *Dòng Máu Anh Hùng [The Rebel]* (2007), that Nguyễn achieved celebrity status in Việt Nam. As a sign, Nguyễn brings an intertextual value to his Vietnamese-made films, a resonance that emphasizes the desired qualities of modernity and mobility that his body houses and his diasporic subjectivity consolidates. That Nguyễn is more a star in Việt Nam than in the diaspora speaks to how notions of intimacy with Việt Nam's former foreign others—like those in the diaspora—have also been recently transformed. Underlying his celebrity status is Vietnamese youth culture's attraction to media stars and their attachment to globalized identities. As Nguyen Mai Loan notes, Vietnamese commercial cinema attempts to capitalize on these attachments in targeting filmgoers, who are between the ages of twenty and thirty,[61] and in featuring attractive stars and exotic locales.[62]

Souls on Swings participates in the discourse of stars and celebrities both textually and intertextually. As Richard Dyer explains in *Heavenly Bodies*, "star images are always extensive,"[63] whereby stars are produced through intersecting discourses about the stars and their films in interviews, critical reviews, as well as public appearances. Indeed, stars speak to the desires that an audience wants to locate in that particular "heavenly body." The making of Johnny Trí Nguyễn as a star image can be found in the ways that he has appeared in many different films and is regularly featured in Vietnamese-language media, oftentimes as the subject of scandal and gossip. After *Souls on Swings*, Johnny Trí Nguyễn has stayed in Việt Nam to make a string of films with local and diasporic directors: *The Rebel* (2007), *Saigon Eclipse* (2007), *Nụ Hôn Thần Chết* [*Kiss of Death*] (2008), *Chơi Vơi* [*Adrift*] (2009), and *Bảy Rồng* [*Clash*] (2010). Besides his film career, Nguyễn is also known for having a scandalous relationship with Ngô Thanh Vân, his costar from *The Rebel*. At the time they met, he was married with two children. He is now divorced and living with Ngô, the stories of which have made the rounds in terms of tabloid gossip in both Việt Nam and the diaspora.

Despite or because of this negative press, Vietnamese American Johnny Trí Nguyễn embodies a kind of cosmopolitanism assumed to be a part of the diaspora. Ashley Carruthers maintains that the "cosmopolitan aura" of diasporic cultural productions and by extension, the celebrities within them is "dependent on the absence and distance of the diaspora."[64] Nguyễn's star power thus resonates with Vietnamese audiences, since he is Vietnamese and diasporic, "like" Vietnamese and "unlike" them; he symbolizes the diaspora and its absent presence in the homeland. In this way, he personifies the star quality that Richard Dyer argues is intrinsic to the manufacturing of stars as he is both "ordinary and extraordinary," both "authentic and ideal."[65]

After *Souls*, director Nguyễn Quang Dũng further played on this notion of difference and similarity when he cast Nguyễn in another film. In it, Nguyễn is a good-natured demon in the immensely popular *Nụ Hôn Thần Chết* [*Kiss of Death*] (2008). For both *Souls on Swings* and *Kiss of Death*, the director draws on spectatorial knowledge of Nguyễn's body of work as a diasporic actor. Most saliently, *Kiss of Death* places Nguyễn in a role that self-consciously draws upon this duality as well as his otherworldliness. As the clear-skinned son of the devil, Nguyễn's good looks are comically ironized when his underworld family describes him as "ugly" and unremarkable. This film is also saturated with metacinematic puns and self-consciously plays on Nguyễn's past roles in Hollywood, Asian, and Vietnamese films. The film signifies on Nguyễn's action-hero persona; his character saves damsels-in-distress and rescues a busload of people from falling off the bridge. In a sequence featuring computer digital technology, the characters visually pun on Charlie Nguyễn's *The Rebel* and the Wachowski Brothers' *The Matrix* (1999) when they perform martial arts in the film's action scenes. Thus far, Nguyễn's roles in

Vietnamese and diasporic Vietnamese films draw upon his star persona as a transnational action-film hero.

For distributors, Nguyễn's body functions as a hieroglyph and a highly commodifiable sign as well. As part of their marketing and packaging strategies, DVD covers for his films showcase his body. For example, an image of Nguyễn's bare torso and gleaming smile, flanked by the smaller figures of his female costars in the background, adorns the back of the film's DVD cover for *Souls*. The title of the film covers his lower abdomen, so that one's eyes are immediately drawn to his chest. On his torso are words that proclaim in Vietnamese: "This film is Nguyễn's first collaboration with a Vietnamese film production." As Nigel Thrift argues in relation to the material practices of selling glamour, "every surface communicates."[66] As pure surface image, then, Nguyễn's suggestive picture on the DVD is devised to communicate his sexuality and identity, which become translated across different contexts as both modern and cosmopolitan.

Queering the Homeland and Diaspora

Long-Legged Girls and *Souls on Swings* visualize a "postsocialist humanity" for Việt Nam's "desiring subjects," one that is anchored in technology and the visual.[67] This chapter has focused on the flow of "low" Vietnamese popular culture, but I do not intend to celebrate uncritically a postmodern, globalized, and sexualized identity that travels across borders freely. Rather, the emphases on temporality, space, and sexuality present in *Long-Legged Girls* and *Souls on Swings* are locally specific and speak to a key segment of the Vietnamese population today. Since *Đổi Mới*, state discourse around sex and sexuality is in concert with Vietnamese comedies about desire and queer romance, all of which are fantastically recombined with the thematic of the occult and the use of digital technology to attract a more youthful demographic. These films narrate a particular story about queerness and otherness in the homeland. Exploring the impact of collaborative practices, the chapter has interrogated the kind of cultural work enacted when these filmic texts move across boundaries and borders.

Following Gayatri Gopinath's work on queer diasporic cinematic representations, I end my discussion of Vũ's and Nguyễn's films by placing the "impossible desires" engendered by *Long-Legged Girls* and *Souls on Swings* within different contexts—in this case, Việt Nam and the diaspora—to further explore their effects.[68] While such moments of queer desire are fleeting, these expressions are especially potent within an official context in Việt Nam that sees homosexuality primarily as a pathological sickness that has been imported from the West. Although the films can certainly play up the fears of Western contamination that might result from Việt Nam's "open door" policy, they also create new viewing positions from which to contemplate the contemporaneity of Việt Nam, notably through the framework of gender and sexuality. *Long-Legged Girls* and *Souls on Swings* project the libidinal and erotic desires of a youthful population in Việt Nam, a move rarely activated in Vietnamese cinema.

When screened outside of Việt Nam, *Long-Legged Girls* and *Souls on Swings* disrupt the Western paradigm of gay identity politics, as they demonstrate the ways in which the Vietnamese configure constructions of sexuality and private and public space differently. For example, the intimate "play" between Khoa and Hoàng and Trương Ba and Quang Vinh relies on a culturally bound form of homoeroticism in Việt Nam, one publicly displayed, tactile, and sensual, especially within a "tolerant" heterosexist society.[69] Codes of Vietnamese masculinity in the public space are tied to men's social positions as husbands and fathers in a relational and societal hierarchy; as such, they are not related to sexual identity per se.[70] Rather than "come out of the closet" within a binary of visibility and invisibility, which has hegemonically been defined as *the* gay experience by the West, queer subjects in Việt Nam redefine normativities and renegotiate their identities within the public and private differently.[71] The films present to viewers a spectrum of intimate gestures that occur between the sexes, enacted and performed within public spaces and private rooms. Given how the films envisage a range of homosocial and homoerotic acts in such spaces, what are the implications for the films' viewing subjects in multiple contexts?

For diasporans, queering the modern Vietnamese home overturns the reified notion that the homeland is invested with an anteriority and authenticity that the diaspora can only mirror as a false copy. Narratives about Vietnamese queerness in the diaspora destabilize the ways in which "Vietnam" is often viewed outside of Việt Nam through the lens of tragedy and trauma. Starkly different from dominant Western representations of Việt Nam as primarily a "country of war," images of a modern Hồ Chí Minh City predominate in these films. They show a certain image of Việt Nam to itself and the diaspora, presenting to audiences a glittering city made over by transnational corporations and joint ventures with countries like Korea and Japan. Through the films' elision of Việt Nam's history of war, this global city reverberates with joint-productions and economic collaborations that mark Việt Nam's twenty-first-century economy. These works establish a renovated identity for the country and its inhabitants and move away from the discourse of war that usually becomes affixed to cultural productions hailing from the country.

Despite some of their problematic representations regarding gender and sexuality, the very categories the films want to centralize and ironize, *Long-Legged Girls* and *Souls on Swings* allow us to envision the mechanisms by which young cultural producers increasingly deploy film to express the role that sexuality plays in their lives within postsocialist Việt Nam. As a result of these new representations, cotemporal readings of homeland and diasporic cultures must include the analytics of gender and sexuality. As Louisa Schein discusses, we need to emphasize the pluralization of eroticisms that occurs in both homeland and diaspora. Studying the figure of the native woman in isolation would be to ignore the ways in which "homelands . . . are also concrete sites both for capitalist accumulation and for erotic entanglements."[72] Through the operations of fantasy, films by Nguyễn and Vũ imagine "erotic entanglements" that are not directly visible or dealt with in Vietnamese public discourses. Adding to this dynamic of visibility is the fact that homosexuality in Việt Nam has not yet been codified, since homosexuality has "never been illegal in Vietnam."[73] Because homosexuality is murkily defined, within this field of social relations, different subjectivities in the country can go unmarked under a repressive regime and thus clear a space for the contestation of hegemonically defined gendered and sexed identities. Though not an ideal space, and certainly not one that represents a sexual Utopia as "Asia" is sometimes figured, it is important to note that for the Vietnamese state, this field of social relations is exceedingly difficult to delimit and manage. A recent case involving two lesbians demarcates these productive tensions.

In 1998 in the Mekong Delta, two women, Cao Tiên Duyên, twenty, and Hồng Kim Hương, thirty, were married in a public ceremony with about one hundred guests in attendance.[74] At first, the local authorities denied the certification of marriage but did not know what else to do with the two women. Three months later, the National Assembly decided to ban gay marriages. Soon after in June, local officials visited the two women's home and emerged with a signed affidavit stating that the women would agree to no longer see each other. The appalling punishment was exacted because of the ceremony's public nature and the two women's need for the visible and legal recognition of their relationship within the communal and civic domains. Authorities were more disturbed, it seems, by the visibility of the event, the public attention it claimed, and the civic rein-scriptions it demanded, than by the act itself. At a basic level, this event exposes the sheer invisibility of lesbians and indecipherability of female desire within Vietnamese medical discourses and studies on Vietnamese sexuality, dominated as they are by analyses of prostitution, sex traffick-ing, and HIV/AIDS. However, it also illustrates that queer subjects are still very much under state surveillance and that disciplinary measures certainly exist for those who defy social and cultural codes, if not legal regulations. The women's desire for visibility in this case cannot be seen as an ascription to a Western model of "coming out." Rather, it dem-onstrates instead how queer subjects in Việt Nam, marked by class and restricted as heteronormative national subjects in the public space, are currently negotiating the prospect of cultural visibility and performing gender in varying spaces. As highly consumable commodities, *Long-Legged Girls* and *Souls on Swings* tap into this discourse of sexuality and reorient the politics of consumption by carrying out important cultural and political work that is especially timely in the wake of *Đổi Mới* and the state's prescriptions about sexuality and youthful behavior.

Precisely because these types of films are understood to be shallow forms of cultural performance, their popularity represents expressions of popular taste that defy official definitions of Vietnamese culture in both homeland and diaspora. In this way, Vietnamese popular cul-ture is a worthy point of study because, as Timothy Brook and Hy Van Luong observe, the state's past appropriations of culture already serve the state's nationalist interests.[75] Upon the critical terrain of unofficial and popular culture, moreover, feminist cultural critics can attend to acts that are illegible to cultural elites. When it comes to lesbian desires, these acts are, as of yet, also unlegislatable to national publics. Based on such ellipses, critics can interrogate the materials of culture, as they offer "imagined alternatives to the status quo," to use Felicity Nussbaum's words.[76] Nussbaum further argues, "[A] project [of a materialist feminist politics] requires a model of ideology which acknowledges contradiction within it in order to allow subjects to misrecognize themselves in pre-vailing new ideologies and to intervene in producing new knowledge."[77]

In this "model of ideology," gender and sexuality must serve as an interlinked optic through which one reads and recognizes the political makeup of subjects; such categories impact the ways in which subjects are hailed by the community and the nation-state within the public sphere. Consequently we recognize that the state and the community have the power to collaborate in regulating desire within their spheres of influence, particularly in matters of the body, sex, and gender. As an extension of this discussion, the Conclusion examines how post-*Đổi Mới* Việt Nam and a postwar diaspora discipline subjects within real and imagined borders. In such community and national formations, heteropatriarchal nationalism is foundational to the maintenance of power.

Conclusion: Family Politics and the Art of Collaboration

Peter Davies concludes his book *Dangerous Liaisons: Collaboration and World War Two* with a discussion of the Nazi collaborator, Maurice Papon, who was freed from prison in 2002, following his ten-year sentence for sending French Jews to concentration camps during World War II. After working exhaustively through the nuances of collaboration in Europe during WWII, Davies ends with a simple proposition: "Perhaps the legacy of collaboration is as significant as the story of collaboration."[1] My conclusion affirms Davies's statement. *Treacherous Subjects* begins with the story of collaboration that limns the histories of many Vietnamese families. It ends by speaking to the postwar legacy of collaboration, the haunting effects of which are material and linger in the lived experiences of the Vietnamese and the diaspora.

The legacy of collaboration is alluded to in the absences and presences that mark the picture of my family that was taken by a local news reporter in Butler, Pennsylvania, when we first came in 1975. My mother is not the only member of my family absent from the picture; two of my sisters are missing in this photo as well. Indeed, in looking through all my family's photo albums, I cannot find a truly complete family portrait; someone is always missing and deeply missed.[2] Even so, reunions have occurred for my family. An older sister, after having spent nine months in a refugee camp in Guam, arrived in the United States in 1990. These missing parts in the lives of whole families are one of the war's lasting legacies. Premised upon such afterimages of war, *Treacherous Subjects* places great emphasis on these intervals to account for those who have been left out and left behind. To paraphrase Tim O'Brien, the things we carry are these family ties.

Through literary and filmic examples, this book has explored familial ties that bind, focusing on the politics of collaboration and their discursive relation to betrayal and loyalty. The cultural productions examined here reference collaboration to discuss the colonial history and postcolonial reality of Việt Nam. Themes of collaboration index the political imaginaries of the Vietnamese and Vietnamese diaspora, signaling the ways in which artists understand Việt Nam's history. Through the lens of collaboration, we witness how the portrait of Vietnamese and Vietnamese diasporic cultural production alludes to a familial narrative and the many fissures arising from war, occupation, and displacement that mark it. This book has interrogated the disciplining practices integral to the formation and maintenance of the constructions of family, community, and nation within Việt Nam and the diaspora. In the postwar era, the state and community denounce some women artists as traitors while celebrating men as auteurs. Such a perspective overlooks how assumptions about authorship and auteurship can prevent audiences and critics from acknowledging the actual practices of collaboration that many male artists engage in. Conversely, this view also dismisses the validity or even the possibility of artistic collaborations that are feminist and queer in nature, which I have explored in the book's later chapters.

The book has shown the extent to which the acts of inclusion and exclusion enacted by these collaborations are not only proscriptive but also prescriptive for those subjects who stand outside the norms of ideal citizenry, defined as industrious, respectful, and heterosexual. *Treacherous Subjects* names these gendered traitors of the national family both in Việt Nam and the diaspora as being mostly women and queer subjects whose sexuality is seen as deviant, unruly, and nonprocreative. Numerous Others—religious and political minorities, mixed-race peoples, and ethnic minorities—remain outside of this symbolic order as well, all with the potential to be treacherous subjects. The effacement of certain subjects from the portrait of the national family occurs within the borders of the nation-state—Việt Nam, France, and the United States—and within the bounds of a diasporic community.

Treacherous Subjects investigates the cultural politics of collaboration to counter the forms of heterosexist patriarchy and nationalism underpinning denunciations or celebrations of collaborative acts. I enunciate this challenge through what I call trans-Vietnamese feminism. I conclude by reiterating my design for a feminist mode of analysis and collaborative practice, using artist Hanh Thi Pham's work as further reinforcement of a need to "reframe the family"—to borrow from the title of one her works—and rethink group membership and belonging, however painful this process may be. David Eng's recent work on queer diasporas is also central here. Working against an insistent gesture to forget race in contemporary US discourses, Eng emphasizes the importance of refusing the impulse "to recuperate lost origins, to recapture the mother or motherland, and to valorize dominant notions of social belonging and racial exclusion."[3] Drawing from Eng's eloquent appeal to consider "other forms of family and kinship . . . and other relations of affect and desire,"[4] I discuss Pham's queer, feminist work as a counter to the dominant narratives of Vietnamese American politics, which police not only women's bodies but also shape the narratives and rituals of what we are supposed to forget and remember.

As with Trinh T. Minh-ha's *Surname Viet Given Name Nam*, Pham's oeuvre and collaborations are imperative in understanding how a trans-Vietnamese feminist critique embeds itself in art and collaborative practices. Using herself as a subject, her body as a medium of critique, Pham's artwork targets a form of heteropatriarchy entrenched in Vietnamese, Vietnamese American, and US cultures. It is because of her multilayered critiques that art and cultural critics have seized upon her work and commented on its moving imagery. As Erica Lee describes, Pham "manages to take ideas [of Vietnamese American womanhood] and rework them; or rather, make them work for her, celebrating herself, women and our strength."[5] Similarly Peter X. Feng argues that Hanh Thi Pham attempts to "convey the ways young Vietnamese women are interpellated by Vietnamese and US ideologies about women's roles."[6] Most forcefully, in looking at Pham's "badness," Elaine Kim contends that Pham's subversive art "focuses on women and celebrates female sexual desire with images of her own nude body."[7]

Besides centralizing what Pham calls her "transsexual body,"[8] she also engages in powerfully symbolic collaborative acts. Pham joins forces with Richard Turner, a white male artist, in works like *Along the Streets of Knives*. As part of this six-part installation, specifically in a piece entitled *Détente/ Dieu Dinh*, Pham stages the animosity that underlies US-Vietnamese relations during the war. Metaphorizing these relations as a penis-exposed Uncle Sam who proffers money to a Vietnamese woman (Pham herself) in a white *áo dài*, Pham sees the collusion between the South Vietnamese and US military in violently gendered and sexualized terms. Nakedly represented as exploitative, the unequal relations of power between the United States and South Vietnamese carry over into the ways that Vietnamese Americans relate to Americans after the war. According to Pham, this is an aspect that Vietnamese Americans do not want to have visualized or highlighted. The selectivity of narratives that becomes foregrounded within a communal public is part of the dialectic of remembering and forgetting. As Pham intimates in her interviews with art scholar Margo Machida, the Vietnamese American community was incensed by these images; consequently, they "chased [her] out of the place."[9] The "outrage" against her work signals a past and present pattern of behavior within a community of anticommunists when it comes to feminist art and collaborative practices:[10] factions of this community "out" women as traitors when women are perceived to be translating Vietnamese American refugees' histories inaccurately or inappropriately.[11] The community's "outing" of female traitors points to "the exchange value of shame . . . the basic capital that circulates in the symbolic economics of nationalism," as Elaine Kim and Chungmoo Choi observe in another context.[12]

Within this economy of nationalism, women are disciplined in a way that speaks to how they often figure in the diasporic and national imaginations. The patriarchal conception of community and nation operates on the dialectic turn that women are both inside and outside, as simultaneously defender of and offender to nationhood. Such is the "style" with which nationalist collectives imagine themselves and their parameters.[13] As Mary Douglas proposes, "what is viewed as dangerous fosters a sense of bonding within a social body, which responds to danger by seeing it as dirty and then expelling it."[14] Centering on women's sex and sexuality, protests against women by anticommunist Vietnamese Americans show how the community's borders are managed by way of public punition. Positioned in between US and Vietnamese nationalistic narratives of the war, this community lacks cultural power within a national or international context, but it nonetheless maintains a symbolic order from which members can be cast out, particularly if they are seen as collaborating with the enemy or with outsiders. This heteropatriarchal nationalism, rooted in both homeland and diaspora, points to the "limits of kinship" as the bases for forming political solidarities across homeland and diaspora.[15] Hanh Thi Pham's feminist, queer work speaks to this impulse as she embodies both the collaborator and traitor in the community.

An understanding of Vietnamese American community politics is pertinent here. Operating through social practices and rituals that emphasize belonging and exclusion, the Vietnamese American community responds to a loss of power twice demonstrated: once in the actual loss of the Republic of Việt Nam, and then in the ways in which "Vietnam" has been rewritten by a US national culture. A community of anticommunist Vietnamese Americans deploys "restorative nostalgia" to redraw the boundaries of the diaspora.[16] The decrees and the rituals accompanying this nostalgia are strongly enforced. To remember is to remember the Huế massacre, the reeducation camps, and the many lives lost during the harrowing escape from Việt Nam in the aftermath of war. It is also to remember the southern Vietnamese nation before the fall of Sài Gòn, as well as the cultural displacements of being a refugee and of being cast in another country soon after 1975. Because of these displacements, Karin Aguilar-San Juan argues that "strategic memory projects" are crucial for Vietnamese Americans and their desire to form a collective identity and to build communities, particularly because such projects defend against the United States's racist tendencies to misrecognize the Other.[17] Tying memory projects to a sense of place, Aguilar-San Juan lucidly contends, "Staging events and designating monuments that commemorate the war from a refugee-as-heroic ally perspective are memory projects that challenge the impulse of U.S. veterans to look down upon South Vietnamese veterans as 'losers.'"[18]

Aguilar-San Juan and others are importantly recreating in their scholarship an archive of the ways Vietnamese American communities commemorate place against an erasure of their history within US history.[19] For Vietnamese Americans, such projects are essential. Critiques against US historical amnesia lie at the center of many of the Vietnamese American community's multilateral and complex efforts to remember. To animate and reanimate the ghosts of war within the United States, as Thu-Hương Nguyễn-Võ eloquently argues, is absolutely vital for Vietnamese Americans to resist the United States's appropriation of the meaning of the Vietnam War.[20] In a similar vein, Thuy Vo Dang also asserts that anticommunism is a multi-valent cultural discourse, one that functions to "carv[e] a space in the U.S. and [bear] witness to a history that cannot be erased by mainstream America."[21] This is a project of commemoration that gathers further meaning when we consider the liminal status of Vietnamese Americans within the United States, where their subjectivity is defined by victimhood and through acts of US imperialism. Yen Le Espiritu critically notes that it is only within a discourse of anticommunism that Vietnamese Americans, "as objects of United States rescue fantasies," even register as subjects within US national culture.[22] As Kim Nguyen puts it, "Public efforts to remember the Vietnam War offer social recognition to Vietnamese American subjects whose agency is constrained to reiterate a conservative relationship to communist Vietnam and authenticate an empowered connection to American imperialism."[23] The loss of agency on the part of the Vietnamese American refugee subject drives Yen Le Espiritu to further argue that scholars must imbue the term "refugee" with "social and political critiques that critically call into question the relationship between war, race, and violence, then and now."[24]

Such critiques of US imperialism underlie this book as well. I further contend that at the same time we critique US racism, we also need to be critical of the Vietnamese American community's efforts to construct their own discourse about citizenship and cultural membership, one that complies with the binaristic logic of being "with" or "against" one's community or nation. Based on acts of defining certain groups or people as Others to the community, this culturally nationalistic discourse works, above all, to normalize gender and sexuality, regulate the behaviors of the community and its members, and construct a particular narrative about the Vietnamese past. If the past is thus reconstructed by Vietnamese Americans in order to concretize a sense of futurity for themselves within the United States, feminist scholars must investigate the mandates for this elemental passage from past to future. In this passage, heteropatriarchy plays a crucial role in the nationalist narratives of both dominant society and minority communities. The actual and symbolic regeneration of Vietnamese diasporic community and Vietnamese nationhood, for example, rests on the fixity of gender roles and the constructs of heterosexuality. The fantasy of communal and national coherencies depends upon a stable referent—that of women's procreative bodies and women's inherent ability to pass on tradition. The consequences for women who do not deliver on these promises include public denouncements, accusations of betrayal, and other corrective measures. Trans-Vietnamese feminism questions the intersecting constructs of family, community, and nation in order to decenter their naturalization within both homeland and diasporic cultures. To use Paul Gilroy's words, it also posits "other possibilities" in the making of political ties.[25]

Countering the idea that anticommunists are somehow stuck in the past, however, I would like to suggest that anticommunist activists show that they are situated very much in the present time when they demonstrate through protest, particularly against the repression of freedom and democratic thought in contemporary Việt Nam. As C. N. Le evinces, anticommunist factions recalibrate their politics and political strategies each time Việt Nam changes its relations with governments like the United States.[26] Gisèle Bousquet relays a similar set of concerns for the Vietnamese French, for whom homeland politics are more urgent than domestic French politics.[27] Protestors demonstrate, for example, against what they see as an aggressive infiltration of monies (in the form of investments) and bodies (in the form of students) that arrive from Việt Nam. Their protests also continue to confront Việt Nam's official narratives of how the war was waged and won. In particular, Vietnamese American anticommunists critique the ways that the Vietnamese state tries to reach out to the diaspora for investment, while at the same time, restricting free speech and religious beliefs in the country.

Set against the strengthened economic collaborations between Việt Nam and countries like the United States and France, there is, therefore, a resilient desire, characterized by Le as a "fight,"[28] on the part of an overseas community to inscribe acts of remembrance that impress upon successive generations the need to continue these struggles against communism in Việt Nam, even if it means acting against one's own community members. As Như-Ngọc Ông and David Meyer write on Vietnamese American protest movements, when Vietnamese Americans protest against other Vietnamese Americans, a process of metonymy takes place whereby the protestors believe that the protested are proxies for the Vietnamese government and the Communist Party.[29] In forming a collective identity through social action such as protesting, protestors demonstrate an anxious investment in the past but also in their community's future—the next generation—in rooting out what is ideologically suspect. In all of its manifold expressions, anticommunism within the Vietnamese American community needs to be placed within the historical and political coordinates of the American War in Việt Nam. Most of all, anticommunist sentiment in America must be understood as a direct outcome of US war policies and the government's betrayal of South Việt Nam.

Globalizing developments, as well as these shared legacies of war and division, connect the homeland and diaspora ever more intimately today. Encompassing an interdisciplinary mode of analysis, trans-Vietnamese feminism centralizes such intimate, global linkages between Việt Nam and the diaspora. A trans-Vietnamese feminist reading practice thus explores contemporary Việt Nam and the diaspora within the same temporal and spatial nodes. While not coequal in terms of economic capital and symbolic power, both homeland and diaspora are invested in making culture and in expanding their markets. Both homeland and diaspora traffic in images of nostalgia about the past and the future, deploying familial rhetoric and gendered bodies to concretize the affective dimensions of what was and what could be. It follows that we must critique both homeland and diaspora for recreating imagined communities through the language of family and the feeling of kinship. At the junctures of production and reception, this book has examined these processes of inclusion and exclusion through a trans-Vietnamese feminism that takes into consideration the transnational flows of capital and culture underlying relations between homeland and diaspora. Throughout the book, I have argued that these flows are buttressed by laboring bodies whose work is collaborative, yet is often overlooked or denigrated precisely for being collaborative, especially when these laborers are women. The book's objective has been to critique the kinds of heteropatriarchal nationalism that are entrenched within formations of community and nation-state. The book also means to revise the meaning of collaborative practices from a transnational feminist perspective.

Collaborations, whether aesthetic or political, involve working with outsiders or engaging in liaisons that are seen as betrayals to a family, a nation, or a diaspora. In response to such betrayals, homeland and diaspora are vested in disciplining subjects who are not docile within the bounds of imagined communities, and as this book has stressed, such disciplining is articulated through the rhetoric of family. Trans-Vietnamese feminism underscores the need to deconstruct such rhetoric, particularly when it stresses nationalist, patriarchal, and heterosexist constructions of the family. *Treacherous Subjects* has sought to interrogate the family's emplacement in community and national discourses, where the family serves as the foundation of Vietnamese creation myths, linguistic traditions, gender relations, ideas of economic sustainability, and social relations. The image of a cohesive family is the fundamental mechanism that powers nationalistic narratives for the Vietnamese in the homeland and diaspora. Rewriting the story of collaboration, feminists can interrogate "the family as a site of contradictions"[30] and decenter its authority as a discursive construction. To take apart the symbolics of family is to agree with Angela Y. Davis's claims for feminist methodologies that "impel us to explore contradictions and to discover what is productive about these contradictions. These are methods of thought and action that urge us to think things together that appear to be entirely separate and to disaggregate things that seem to naturally belong together."[31]

In recognizing the constructedness of family in its fragments, feminists comprehend the ways that loss may be generative.[32] The work of trans-Vietnamese feminism needs to unseat the familial ideal as a trans-historical signifier for wholeness and completion, yet, ungrounding symbolic family ties does not have to connote loss. For example, one does not have to feel the loss of familial ties or the ungrounding of "home" as a result. To identify loss as part of a nation's and a community's constitution is to see that critical potentialities lie ahead, vitalized by "new forms of possibility and new forms of intellectual and political intervention," as Dorinne Kondo has argued about Asian American art and activism.[33] This book asserts that collaborative acts represent a "continuous engagement with loss and its remains."[34] Understanding collaboration in feminist terms is one way to engage with the past and form communal bonds that cross political boundaries.

Grounded in the future tense, trans-Vietnamese feminism activates the kind of collaborative work that is already found and to be found in artistic and political coalitions, formations that traverse geographical territories and ideological divides. As feminists, sustaining our sense of solidarity with others must be a form of politics that fundamentally challenges colonialism, imperialism, and war, and the structures of classism, racism, sexism, and heterosexism that reinforce such systems. I envision a trans-Vietnamese feminism that works across difference, but one that is not indifferent to questions of loss, history, and power between homeland and diaspora. It is a vision of feminist solidarity to which I feel the strongest kinship. This book has served as an extension of this sentiment: *Treacherous Subjects* is driven by the feminist potential of collaboration and seeks to reconfigure family politics within a transnational frame.

Notes

Introduction

1. Brook, "Collaboration in the History of Wartime East Asia."

2. Denise Ferreira Da Silva speaks about the US wars in Việt Nam and Iraq through the political act of naming. My objective in tracing the discursivity of terms like "hero" and "traitor" and its impact is similar to Da Silva's gesture to look at the power of names and of naming. See Da Silva, "Tale of Two Cities."

3. In this postcolonial historiography, a "narrative of unassailable coherence" was constructed to present a monolithic and singular Việt Nam, despite the many divisions that marked the politics of the time (3). Pelley, *Postcolonial Vietnam*.

4. Pelley calls this prescriptive rhetoric on the part of official historians a "pattern of urging," which used "the pedagogical power of commemorative texts and events" to explain Vietnamese history (13). Pelley, *Postcolonial Vietnam*.

5. Collaboration is defined as cooperation with the enemy within the realms of the everyday, political, military, and economic. As David Barrett argues, "Working with the enemy [is] motivated by a variety of reasons, whether out of self-interest or for sheer survival but not out of ideological commitment to an enemy's cause" (8). Barrett, "Occupied China and the Limits of Accommodation." On the other hand, collaborationism, as Bertram Gordon argues, is an ideological alignment (19). Gordon, *Collaborationism in France*. Neo-collaborations, in the words of William Pomeroy, describe present-day agreements between the US government and its former colony like that of the Philippines. Pomeroy, *Philippines*. Historical accounts of WWII collaboration are numerous and insightful. On Europeans and the Nazi regime, see Taylor, *Between Resistance and Collaboration*; Bennett, *Under the Shadow of the Swastika*; and Bowen, *Spaniards and Nazi Germany*. On Chinese and Korean collaborations with the Japanese, see Barrett and Shyu, *Chinese Collaboration with Japan*; Fu, *Passivity, Resistance, and Collaboration*; Caprio, "Loyal Patriot? Traitorous Collaborator?"; and Han, "On the Question of Collaboration in South Korea."

6. Carter, "Subject Elite," 211.

7. On the use of *quốc ngữ*, the script was a sign of cultural betrayal, but as Pelley maintains, when "radical anticolonialists began to regard it as a revolutionary tool, they sought to suppress its tainted past" (39). Pelley, *Postcolonial Vietnam*. David Marr's study also looks at *quốc ngữ* as the currency for anticolonial sentiment. See chapter 4 of Marr, *Vietnamese Tradition on Trial*.

8. Osborne, *French Presence in Cochinchina and Cambodia*, 99.

9. Bayly, *Asian Voices in a Postcolonial Age*, 63.

10. Carter, "Subject Elite," 226.

11. Womack, "Remakings of a Legend," 37.

12. Vella, "Aspects of Vietnamese History," 55.

13. Bradley, *Imagining America*, 25.

14. Bayly, *Asian Voices in a Postcolonial Age*, 210.

15. For more on Phan Bội Châu and women, see chapter 6 of Marr, *Vietnamese Tradition on Trial*.

16. Wynn Wilcox writes that after 1945, "there was a change in the historical interpretation of hybrid figures, based on the degree to which they [were] polluted by their contact with the West" (204). As Wilcox argues, state resistors like Hồ Chí Minh and collaborators were actually hybrid and cosmopolitan, and that histories surrounding such figures were often rewritten in order to draw "a sharp distinction between those in power and others of similar hybrid background, and those who vied for power, lost, and [were] now 'collaborators'" (202). Wilcox, "Hybridity, Colonialism, and National Subjectivity."

17. Oscar Salemink also looks at the nationalist rhetoric of the family that Hồ Chí Minh used (264). In Salemink's article, however, he examines the rhetorical dimensions of the national family as they relate to ethnic minorities. See Salemink, "Embodying the Nation."

18. In an important letter addressed to his southern compatriots in May 1946, Hồ Chí Minh proclaimed, "The five fingers are of unequal length but they are united in the hand." The historical context for this proclamation was complex. Before departing for France to negotiate for national independence, Hồ needed to encourage southerners to continue to fight for national reunification. A year earlier, Hồ had established the Democratic Republic of Việt Nam (DRV) in Hà Nội, but at the time, southern Việt Nam was still under French colonial authority. On this event, see chapter 10 of Duiker, *Hồ Chí Minh*.

19. Philip Taylor writes cogently on northern political discourses about Sài Gòn, which portrayed this city as a site of an influx of foreigners, goods, and of "neocolonial poison" during the war (122). The elimination of these toxins after the war was a major objective for the newly installed communist government in 1975. Taylor, *Fragments of the Present*.

20. Films made about southern Việt Nam during the war depicted ARVN soldiers as decadent and corrupt. In such films as *Chị Tư Hậu* [*Sister Hau*] (1963), they are to blame for the region's downfall. See also Levy, "ARVN as Faggots "; Woodman, "Hollywood War of Wills."

21. Ironically, as Mark Bradley notes, this feminized version of Việt Nam, porous and susceptible to communist influence, is what motivated US policymakers to declare the war on the Democratic Republic of Việt Nam after 1954 (77). Bradley, *Imagining Vietnam and America*.

22. Nguyễn Du's nineteenth-century epic poem is made up of 3,254 verses in the *lục bát* form (6–8 meter). A lengthy account of a young woman's travails, the core of the narrative displays a woman's filial piety. To free her father from jail, Thúy Kiều becomes a prostitute. Despite being kidnapped, cheated, and sold into brothels soon after, she continually sacrifices herself for the sake of her family. Written in *chữ nôm*, a vernacular script of Vietnamese based on Chinese ideograms, Nguyễn Du's text is

understood to be an allegory for Việt Nam and its struggles with colonialism and foreign domination. I discuss Nguyễn's work in Chapter 4 especially.

23. Thông, "Introduction to *The Tale of Kiều*," 29.

24. Balibar, "Racism and Nationalism," 48.

25. Barbieri and Bélanger, *Reconfiguring Families in Việt Nam*, 2.

26. On *Đổi Mới*, see Boothryoud and Nam, *Socioeconomic Renovation in Việt Nam*; Irvin, "Vietnam: Assessing the Achievements of *Doi Moi*"; Vu, "Vietnam's Economy from 1989 to 1995." On the impacts of *Đổi Mới* on gender, see Fahey, "Vietnam's Women in the Renovation Era"; Luong. "Gender Relations"; and Werner and Bélanger, *Gender, Household, State*.

27. See Chan, *Vietnamese American 1.5 Generation*.

28. Freeman, "*Doi Moi* Policy," 178.

29. On the management of femininity in postwar Việt Nam, see Pettus, *Between Sacrifice and Desire*; and Nguyễn-Võ, *Ironies of Freedom*.

30. Alexander Woodside calls Việt Nam's recent turn toward valorizing a precolonial past "neo-traditionalism" (71). Woodside, "Struggle to Rethink the Vietnamese State."

31. See "Politburo's Resolution on Viet Kieu."

32. See Nguyễn, "Những Kẻ Phản Bội" [Traitors], and Lê's article, "'Better Dead than Red.'" I discuss the politics of treason amongst Vietnamese Americans in the Conclusion.

33. I am thinking of Le Ly Hayslip, a female author whom I discuss in Chapter 2, and Trường Trần, the owner of Hi-Tek Video whose picture of Hồ Chí Minh in his store sparked weeks of protests in Westminster, California, in 1999. Although I do not delve into Trần's case in particular, I talk about the specifics of gender as it pertains to Vietnamese American politics and protests in the Conclusion.

34. Discussing the political organizing of a group called Việt Tân, C.N. Lê notes,"[Its] evolution toward pursuing a more moderate agenda mirrors the general trend in the Vietnamese American community" (197). Lê, "'Better Dead than Red.'"

35. In the Vietnamese language, diacritical marks are crucial to spelling and definition. I have used diacritical marks throughout the book except in regards to the names of Vietnamese diasporic people. They often drop the diacritical marks in rendering their names, and I do the same if they have done so, as in the case of writer Le Ly Hayslip and director Tony Bui. Other artists and authors also put their names in a particular sequence—with the first name coming first and the last name following. (In Vietnamese, it is often the surname and precedes the first name.) As a general rule, I have chosen to spell their names the way I have seen them spelled in their books or films. I have tried to follow this principle with Vietnamese and Vietnamese diasporic critics as well.

36. For more on the Madison controversy, see Sherbert, "Madison's Last Stand"; John Vu, "To Recall or Not"; and Hoàng Lân Nguyễn, "Little Saigon Name."

37. Alexander, "Erotic Autonomy," 65.

38. Peterson, "Sexing Political Identities," 38.

39. Kwon, "Evacuating the History of Collaboration."

40. Heonik Kwon discusses how the vexed terms of "traitor" and "collaborator" were discursive positions that had real material consequences for those branded as such during the American War. Kwon, "Co So Cach Mang."

41. Collaboration studies have shaped my ideas about the history and effects of collaboration. Writing on Chinese collaborators during Japanese occupation, Timothy Brook emphasizes the moral complexities of living under a foreign power. Ronald Robinson's seminal "political theory of collaboration" looks at the efficacy of

indigenous collaborators to explain the processes of the European empire's expansion and its later demise (118). See Brook, *Collaboration*; and Robinson, "Non-European Foundations."

42. See Rivera, "Việt Nam." On the "betrayal of the past," Andrew Lam discusses the ways that betrayal marks the war and its aftermath. See Lam, "Thirty Five Years After the War." Patricia Pelley explains the sense of betrayal that the Vietnamese feel in this way: "Given the degree to which the interests of foreign capital govern Vietnamese today, many Vietnamese are haunted by the thought that the horrendous loss of life and vast ecological damage they have endured over the past fifty years merely set the stage for what they are witnessing today: the reappearance of a wealthy capitalist elite, the reemergence of extraordinary poverty, and the reminder that the destiny of Vietnam is only partially controlled by the Vietnamese" (Pelley, *Postcolonial Vietnam*, 5).

43. Bow, *Betrayal and Loyalty*, 3.

44. Along the same lines as Bow's work, Crystal Parikh's recently published *An Ethics of Betrayal* deals with Asian American as well as Latino/a cultural productions.

45. I reference here monographs that analyze the cultural representations of singular groups. On the Vietnamese French, see Blum-Reid, *East-West Encounters*; Jack Yeager, *Vietnamese Novel in French*; and Nguyen, *Vietnamese Voices*. On Vietnamese Americans, see Christopher, *Viet Nam War, American War*. On Vietnamese literature, see these texts in English: Durand and Nguyen, *Introduction to Vietnamese Literature*; Nguyen, *Vietnamese Literature*; Thông, "Literature and the Vietnamese." On Vietnamese film, see Ngô, *Modernity and Nationality in Vietnamese Cinema*; and Trinh, *30 Years of Vietnam's Cinema Art*.

46. My emphasis on the transnational is aligned with Christina Schwenkel's book, *The American War in Contemporary Vietnam*. Looking at memorials, photographs, and tourist sites, Schwenkel's work insightfully argues for an understanding of the "specific operations of power and knowledge in the transnational co-production and management of history" (18). Schwenkel relates these coproductions of history to the postwar memory projects of the Americans and Vietnamese. Schwenkel, *American War*.

47. See also Barry, *Vietnam's Women in Transition*; Tétreault, "Women and Revolution in Vietnam."

48. Eisen, *Women and Revolution in Viet Nam*, 9.

49. Christine Pelzer White also critiques Eisen's text and others for constructing a sense of international sisterhood, premised upon a "tendency to romanticize women's role in national liberation armed struggle and to see it as an index of women's liberation rather than see it either as a defense of traditional values or as a sign of desperation" (351). White, "Promissory Notes." More recently, Inderpal Grewal in *Transnational America* also points to the logic of morality in narratives of global feminism, which construct "American women as saviors and rescuers of 'oppressed women'" (150). Grewal, *Transnational America*.

50. Speaking to women's past empowerment and present loss of entitlements, Sandra C. Taylor's book *Long-Haired Warriors* documents the struggles of northern Vietnamese women soldiers in the War against the Americans. Along the same lines, Karen Gottschang Turner and Phan Thanh Hao's *Even the Women Must Fight* draws upon the history of women warriors and critiques the current conditions under which Vietnamese women must live. Together, these books comment on the state's betrayal of women and its promise of equality, asserting that this betrayal is especially

deplorable because of the ways in which northern Vietnamese women had fought so valiantly for the nation. Taylor, *Long-Haired Warriors*; and Turner and Phan, *Even the Women Must Fight*.

51. On the limits of such scholarship, Lisa Long claims, "A colonizing view of Southeast Asian women nurtured in the name of military action can blind one to the strengths of individual women and of a woman's history operating within political and cultural frameworks deemed less progressive" (27). Long, "Contemporary Women's Roles."

52. Nathalie Nguyen's book on diasporic women's narratives offers a counterbalance to the northern accounts of "long-haired warriors." She documents the lives of southern Vietnamese women officers in the Republic of Việt Nam's Armed Forces (RVNAF). See chapter 3 of Nguyen, *Memory Is Another Country*.

53. See Hue-Tam Ho Tai, "Faces of Remembering and Forgetting." For critiques of woman-as-nation, see Kandiyoti, *Identity and Its Discontents*; and Yuval-Davis and Anthias, *Woman-Nation-State*.

54. Similarly, Barley Norton notes that while "research on gender in Vietnamese has proliferated since the 1990s, less attention has been paid to the influence of cultural practices on gender ideologies and the constructions of gender in Vietnam" (55). Norton, "'Hot-Tempered Women' and 'Effeminate Men.'"

55. See Soucy, "Vietnamese Warriors, Vietnamese Mothers."

56. See Bui, "Vietnamese Woman in Vietnam's Process of Change."

57. Tran, "Beyond the Myth of Equality," 121.

58. See Le, "National Identity and Gender Characteristics in Vietnam," 5. See also Le Thi Nham Tuyet, *Images of the Vietnamese Woman in the New Millennium*. For more on the 3 submissions and 4 virtues, see Cong-Huyen, "Traditional Roles of Women."

59. Brownell and Wasserstrom argue that texts dealing with the failures of the Communist Chinese Party tend to "treat 'Chinese women' as belonging to a single basic category" (8). Brownell and Wasserstrom, "Theorizing Femininities and Masculinities."

60. Marr, "Concepts of the Self," 774.

61. See also Werner, "Gender Matters."

62. See Berlant, *Queen of America Goes to Washington*; Manalansan, *Global Divas*; Patton and Sánchez-Eppler, *Queer Diasporas*; Warner, *Fear of a Queer Planet*; and Puar, *Terrorist Assemblages*.

63. Peterson, "Sexing Political Identities," 39.

64. Parker et al., *Nationalisms and Sexualities*, 2.

65. Mohanty, *Feminism Without Borders*, 2.

66. On this point, I am influenced by the work of Desai, *Beyond Bollywood*, and Gopinath, *Impossible Desires*.

67. Chow, *Primitive Passions*, 195.

68. Desai, Bouchard, and Detournay, "Disavowed Legacies and Honorable Thievery," 46.

69. Espiritu, "We-Win-Even-When-We-Lose," 337.

70. Dao, "What's Going On," 90.

71. Norindr, *Phantasmatic Indochina*, 153.

72. Bourdieu, *Field of Cultural Production*, 7.

73. Various scholars have critiqued the problems of grafting a Western model onto the "Third World." See Mohanty, "Under Western Eyes"; Ong, "Gender and Labor Politics of Postmodernity"; Chow, *Writing Diaspora*.

74. Grewal and Kaplan, "Introduction: Transnational Feminist Practices and Questions of Postmodernity," 4. The authors critique the ways that postmodernism is seen as "an aesthetic or cultural debate rather than a political one" (3). Instead of postmodernism, they use the term *postmodernity*, which is "marked by a rise of postmodernism cultural forms, the emergence of more flexible modes of capital accumulation, and a new round of 'time-space compression' in the organization of capitalism" (4). Grewal and Kaplan argue that postmodernity is a useful and necessary concept for investigating the uneven flows of culture under globalization.

75. Ibid., 12.

76. Ibid., 24.

77. Karell, *Writing Together, Writing Apart*, 21.

78. On the historical construction of authorship, see Ede and Lunsford, *Singular Texts/Plural Authors*. Women academics who engage in collaborative practices do so for both practical and political reasons. Engaging in collaboration means advancing a radical restructuring of how scholars and writers are evaluated. See Singley and Sweeney, "In League with Each Other"; Doane and Hodges, "Writing from the Trenches"; Sclau and Arenal, "Escribiendo Yo"; and Kaplan and Rose, "Strange Bedfellows."

79. Writing on collaborations between men in Renaissance drama, Jeffrey Mastern explains, "Collaboration is a dispersal of author/ity, and not a mere doubling of it" (19). Mastern, *Textual Intercourse*.

80. Swarr and Nagar, "Introduction: Theorizing Transnational Feminist Praxis," 2.

1 / Manufacturing Feminine Virtue

1. On tourism in Việt Nam, see Kennedy and Williams, "Past Without the Pain."

2. Vietnamese American Charlie Nguyen's action film, *The Rebel* (2007), is a recent movie that makes clear how gendered forms of collaboration resonate as an important theme for diasporic cultural producers. Shot in Việt Nam and received well in the United States and in Việt Nam, the film revolves around moles, collaborators, and traitors during French colonialism. Most intriguing is Sỹ, the villain who is also a métis and the son of a Vietnamese concubine. In contrast to his mother's sexual collaboration, the film spectacularly celebrates her opposite, the heroic rebel Võ Thanh Thúy (played by Vietnamese singer/actress Ngô Thanh Vân). The lone woman in the film who is not tainted by sexual treason, Võ skillfully fights for national independence against the French, embodying nationalist loyalty and familial piety. The film also extratextually gestures toward issues of betrayal and collaboration through its modes of production, as Charlie Nguyen had to work within the confines of a state-monitored film industry. On the gender politics of the film, see Hamilton, "Renovated."

3. As Tran explains, "La douceur nous nourrit; mais c'est parfois au prix de non-dits et d'aveux" [Softness nourishes us, but at the cost of what is unspoken and undeclared] (my translation) (qtd. in Piazzo, "Lê goût du Trần Anh Hùng quand il est mûr," 1).

4. The 1.5–generation refers to Vietnamese children who were born in Việt Nam and who immigrated to other countries as small children.

5. A form of state participation by the French and Vietnamese governments strongly underwrites Tran's feature films. *Scent* was coproduced by Lazennec, SFP, and La Sept, and sponsored by the governmental organizations of the Centre National de la Cinématographie and the Ministère de la Culture et de la Communication. His second film, *Cyclo,* was coproduced by private international companies like Salon (a Hong Kong-based company) and television production company Canal+, and partially funded by French and Vietnamese state-run institutions such as the Centre National de la Cinématographie and Giải Phóng Film Studios, respectively. Finally, *Vertical Ray* was a coproduction with the German firm ZDF, the Vietnamese state-sponsored production company, Hãng Phim Truyện, as well as with Lazennec and Canal+.

6. Blum-Reid, *East-West Encounters,* 84.

7. On Vietnamese refugees in France after 1975, see Hein, *States and International Migrants*; Raymond, "French Culture and the Politics of Self-Esteem." Vietnamese French sociologist Lê Huu Khoa also delves into Vietnamese immigration to France and traces it historically, from the early twentieth century up to the post-1975 era. See Lê, "Les Vietnamiens en France."

8. Cooper, *France in Indochina,* 196.

9. After 1988, the French government enacted several laws restricting immigration and the processes of citizenship. For a discussion of these laws, see Fysh, *Politics of Racism.*

10. "Ostentatious" visibility is a factor in the recent banning of the wearing of religious symbols. Although couched in terms of French secularism, the ban represents a rejection of the public recognition of "difference" within the French polity. Before Jacques Chirac signed the ban into law in 2003, the "Headscarf Affair" originally erupted in a 1989 incident involving three Muslim girls, who were denied entry to their secondary school in Creil because they had worn their headscarves to class. Debates raged about the cohesion of a French national identity in the aftermath of the controversy. For more on the controversy, see Fysh, *Politics of Racism in France.* The organization, *SOS Racisme,* was established to help get the girls reinstated. The decline in the popularity of the French Communist Party and decreased voter loyalty to a singular political party contributed to the rise of Jean-Marie Le Pen of the anti-immigrant National Front Party during the same time. For more on *SOS Racisme,* see Hargreaves, *Immigration, Race, and Ethnicity.* On Jean-Marie Le Pen, see Body-Genrot and Schain, "National and Local Politics."

11. Norindr, *Phantasmatic Indochina,* 1.

12. On "heritage" films, see Powrie, "Heritage, History and 'New Realism.'"

13. Ang, "Hegemony-in-Trouble," 25.

14. Harris and Ezra, "Introduction: The French Exception," 1.

15. On these historic changes in French cinema, see Jeancolas, "Reconstruction of French Cinema." On the global politics of French films, see Hayward, "National Cinemas and the Body Politic."

16. Powrie, "Heritage," 2. For more on the GATT Agreements, see Miller, "Crime of Monsieur Lang"; Strode, "France and EU-Policy Making on Visual Culture"; and Hayward, *French National Cinema.*

17. Katz, *Film Directing Shot by Shot,* 260.

18. Hargreaves, "Writing for Others," 116.

19. Tarr, "French Cinema," 60.

20. Ibid., 63.

21. Loutfi, "Imperial Frame," 25.

22. Information on the French box-office receipts for *Scent* is archived at the Bibliothèque du Film in Paris, France.

23. US box-office receipts for this film can be found on the Internet Movie Database, which is available at http://www.imdb.com/title/tt0107617/business. Accessed May 5, 2000.

24. In Tran's words, "le plan-séquence permet de lier les choses, de passer—toujours en douceur—d'une idée à une autre" [The "plan-séquence" allows for a connection between things, of passings—always through softness—from one idea to another] (my translation)] (2). See Génin, "Une Intense Douceur."

25. Cheng, "Tran Anh Hung and the Scents of Vietnam," 5.

26. Comparing the films *Scent* and *Indochine*, Michèle Bacholle argues Mùi in *Scent* is endowed with a maternal spirituality, which renders her a more profound character than Camille in *Indochine* (956). By contrast, Camille in *Indochine* serves as a faceless cipher for communist ideology. See Bacholle, "Camille et Mùi."

27. Tran's visual and thematic motifs are further reinforced by continuity; he uses the same producer (Christophe Rossignon), actors (his wife, among others), composer (Tôn Thất Tiết) and cinematographer (Benoit Delhomme) in three of his feature films.

28. Neale, *Cinema and Technology*, 17.

29. This plays out in Tran's *Vertical Ray of the Sun* (2000) as well where men and women's domains are not only separate but also carry different valences in respect to notions of labor and leisure. The men in the film are mobile and active in the production and consumption of art, whereas their wives are, not unhappily, yoked to their role as maternal guardians of the bourgeois home. The husbands' identities are tied to their role as artists much in the ways that maternalism defines women's essential qualities in the film.

30. *Vietnamese Women in the Eighties*, 63.

31. On the double burden that women perform, see Yarr, "Gender and the Allocation of Time."

32. Blum-Reid, *East-West Encounters*, 82.

33. Seth Mydans details the reception of the film in Việt Nam. A representative for the government's Cinema Department, Đỗ Duy Anh, denies that the film was banned, but argues that Vietnamese censors would not "permit violence, sex, or 'films that damage the policies of the Government and Party, [nor] films that turn Việt Nam against another country or films that demean the morals of society'" (20). See Mydans, "In Hanoi."

34. Đặng Nhật Minh, Interview with Author, August 15, 2002.

35. Though *Scent* was warmly embraced in Việt Nam, film critic, Ngô, contends of *Cyclo*: "[It] is not a Vietnamese film, even though it talks about Vietnamese life" (quoted in Mydans 20). See Mydans, "In Hanoi."

36. In his essay, Paul Narkunas makes the same point as I do. However, while Narkunas is at pains to draw out the history of Hồ Chí Minh City, he flattens out those cultural specificities comprising the differences between Los Angeles and Hồ Chí Minh City (156). Narkunas, "Streetwalking in the City."

37. Analyzing *Cyclo* and *Scent*, Michèle Bacholle views the images of fruit as components of the director's sensual visual style. In contrast to my position, Bacholle

argues that pregnant women in the films are collectively figured as the "nation in gestation" (172). Bacholle, "Tran Anh Hung's Orphan Tales."

38. Do and Tarr, "Outsider/Insider Views," 60.

39. On "heroic mothers," see Tai, "Faces of Remembering."

40. See Nguyen, "Making History with Tony Bui."

41. See Balzar, "Vietnam and Culture," 4.

42. On Hollywood war films and American masculinity, see Jeffords, *Re-Masculinization of America*.

43. In her reading of *Madame Butterfly* and *Indochine*, Marina Heung discusses the American defeat in Việt Nam, which produced in the collective psyche "an insistent, even obsessive, revalorization of the patriarchal nuclear family" (161). See Heung, "Family Romance of Orientalism."

44. Speechwriter Peggy Noonan actually coined this phrasing, which George H. W. Bush used in his 1989 inaugural speech. In the speech, the phrase is worded in the following way: "It is to make kinder the face of the Nation and gentler the face of the world." A transcription of this speech can be found at the website http://www.bartleby.com/124/pres63.html. Accessed February 2, 2010.

45. Sturken, *Tangled Memories*, 123.

46. On technology and melodrama in the first Persian Gulf War, see Wiegman, "Missiles and Melodrama."

47. Jeffords, *Hard Bodies*, 13.

48. See Michael Rogin's insightful analyses of Reagan's politics of demonology in his book, *Ronald Reagan the Movie*.

49. Chow, *Writing Diaspora*, 29.

50. Ibid., 41.

51. I borrow the term, "looking relations," from Jane Gaines and her essay on white privilege and acts of looking in film. Gaines, "White Privilege and Looking Relations."

52. See the interview with the filmmaker at http://www.filmfestivals.com/berlin99/html/us/interv1.htm. Accessed April 15, 2005.

53. Branigan, "Point-of-view Shot," 674.

54. For a different take on how Bui privileges the female gaze, see Janette, "Look Again."

55. In an interview, Bui reveals that "fake" flowers were necessary because the real ones kept wilting from the heat. Similar to the construction behind the lotus pond, the fake flowers, as simulacra, are supposed to stand in for the true essence of Việt Nam, yet the material constraints of filming in Việt Nam posed significant problems. See Briggs, "Tony Bùi Looks East from West."

56. Heath, *Questions of Cinema*, 44.

57. As former Head of the Cinema Department, Lại Văn Sinh puts it, "Émigrés living far from their country of birth cannot fully understand its customs or its moral, aesthetic and cultural values" (qtd. in Dumont, 55). Yet, as Philippe Dumont notes, some overseas films are ironically catalogued as "Vietnamese" films nonetheless (55). Dumont, "The Multiple Births of Vietnamese Cinema."

58. Within a different framework, Sumita Chakravarty focuses on the figure of the courtesan in Hindu films from postcolonial India. She makes the case that the prostitute figure can be a site of ambivalence and a "searing indictment of social hypocrisy and exploitation" (304). See Chakravarty, *National Identity*.

59. Naficy, *Accented Cinema*, 6.

60. Production notes for *Cyclo* can be found in Sylvie Blum-Reid's chapter on the film (specifically on page 82). See also Béhar, "'Xich-Lo' Press Conference." Tim Larimer's article in *Time Magazine* also notes the ways that the Vietnamese government monitored the filming of *Three Seasons*. See Larimer, "Vietnam Visions."

61. Ngo, "Opening to the World," 216.

62. Ibid.

63. Jeanette Roan makes a similar point in her study of US films, which have been shot on location in Asia. She contends that even before the moment of filming, "the travel that shooting on location necessitates is thus often shaped by national and international policies and may be undertaken by considerable numbers of people, all of whom must contend with the challenges entailed by being on location, away from home" (15). Roan, *Envisioning Asia*.

64. In gauging the reception for Tony Bui's film in the United States, I rely on the ways that he was featured in the book, *25 Years of 25 Vietnamese Americans*. See Nguyen's "Making History with Tony Bui." It should be also be noted that Bui's and Tran's feature films kicked off the first biennial Vietnamese International Film Festival held in Southern California in 2003.

2 / Colonial Histories, Postcolonial Narratives

1. See book reviews of both texts. Shipler, "Child's Tour of Duty"; Bundesen, "Vietnam"; and Nguyen, "Hayslip's Story about Forgiveness."

2. Dizon, "Expatriates Vent Anger," B5.

3. Ibid.

4. Ibid.

5. Bow, *Betrayal and Other Acts*, 11.

6. Bhabha, *Location of Culture*, 54.

7. Bow, *Betrayal and Other Acts*, 133.

8. Lê, *Slander*, 4.

9. Women who bore Amerasian children and their children (colloquially called "bụi đời," or "dust of life") were maltreated in postwar Việt Nam. See Nguyen, "Eurasian and Amerasian Perspectives"; Valverde, "From Dust to Gold"; and McKelvey, *Dust of Life*. This painful history has also been referenced in a number of films, for example, Tiana Thi Nga's *From Hollywood to Hanoi* (1993) and Dolgin and Franco's *Daughter from Danang* (2002).

10. In August 2005, the California State Assembly proposed that an award be given to Hayslip for her humanitarian efforts in Việt Nam. Later this award was pulled. According to the *San Diego Reader*, the Asian Pacific Islander Caucus changed its mind about giving the award to her. Reporter Joe Deegan notes that Hayslip and others suspect California Assemblyman Trần Thái Văn from Orange County blocked the award, a charge Trần denies. Deegan, "Old Wounds."

11. Jin, *Writer as Migrant*, 31.

12. Green et al., "Introduction: Women Writing Beyond the Hexagon," xi.

13. Ibid., xi. On language and postcolonial women's writing, see also Lionnet, *Postcolonial Representations*.

14. Lê's book, *Les Trois Parques*, also deals with these issues. Despite parallels between *Les Trois Parques* and *Calomnies*, I group *Voix* and *Lettre Morte* with *Calomnies* because of the stylistic and thematic similarities that draw these three texts together.

15. On the works of Linda Lê, see also Nguyen, *Vietnamese Voices*; Chiu, "'Open Wound'"; Favre, "Linda Lê: Schizo-Positive"; Pech-Ollier, "Consuming Culture"; and Do, "Entre Salut et Damnation," and "From Incest to Exile."

16. On its website, Christian Bourgois Éditeurs lists the biographies of their writers and their works. Most of their output is literary texts, but they also publish critical essays by theorists like Hannah Arendt and translations of literary works by acclaimed contemporary authors, such as William Vollman and Hanif Kureishi.

17. At last count, Linda Lê has produced thirteen works of fiction and two critical books, most of which have appeared under the aegis of major publishers like Aux Éditions Julliard, Christian Bourgois, and Presses Universitaires de France.

18. On the comparisons between Lê and Duras, see especially Winston, *Postcolonial Duras*; and Chirol, "Histoires de Ruines."

19. See, for example, Selao, "Folie et Écriture"; and Delvaux, "Linda Lê and the Prosthesis of Origin."

20. Selao, "Folie et Écriture," 192.

21. See Roberts, "Vietnamese Voice"; Do, "From Incest to Exile"; Étienne, "Linda Lê ou les jeux de l'errance"; and Favre, "Linda Lê: Schizo-Positive?" on these themes in Lê's work.

22. In Yeager's conclusion of his book, *Vietnamese Literature in French*, he laments that this group of writings lacks a distinctive literary voice today. He attributes this to the acculturation of the Vietnamese into French culture, the process of which dilutes their unique perspective and historical background (162). See Pelaud, "Métisse Blanche"; and Barnes, "Linda Lê's *Voix*," for critiques of Yeager's work.

23. Maryse Fauvel notes in passing that Lê's work speaks to "une identité française multiethnique et multiculturelle, caracteristique des années 80–90 en France at au cœur de nouveau débat sur l'intégration culturelle" (130) [a French multiethnic and multicultural identity, characteristic of the 80s-90s in France and which lies at the heart of the new debates on cultural integration] (my translation). Fauvel attempts to situate Lê's work within the cultural context of France in the 1980s and 1990s, but it is not fully developed. Fauvel, "Scènes d'Intérieur."

24. Cooper, *France in Indochina*, 184.

25. Gino Raymond observes that France's actions after the war ended were highly symbolic; such acts were "the last dramatic examples of France's consistent attempt to use her colonies to sustain a certain idea of France" (66). Raymond, "French Culture and the Politics of Self-Esteem."

26. Hargreaves, *Immigration, 'Race,' and Ethnicity*, 17.

27. Balibar, *Race, Nation, Class*, 21.

28. Rye and Worton, *Women's Writing in Contemporary France*, 5.

29. Horowitz, "Immigration and Group Relations," 5.

30. See Cloonan and Postel, "Celebrating Literature."

31. Cloonan, "Literary Scandal," 28.

32. Cloonan, "'Les Grands Écrivains,'" 51.

33. Central to this discussion are also definitions of literature and literary value for a French reading culture as well as for France's academic institutions. Looking at writings by immigrant women, Winnifred Woodhull writes, "In France today, 'literariness' is widely assumed to be critical of existing political discourses and social practices" (45). Woodhull, "Ethnicity on the French Frontier." Along the same lines,

literary critic Manthia Diawara critiques the French literary establishment for ignoring the vibrant strains of Francophone literature. Diawara argues for the placement of key ethnic players themselves within the field of production—as educators, reviewers, and editors (143). Diawara, "Francophone and the Publishing World."

34. Hargreaves, "Contribution of North," 149.

35. Woodhull, "Ethnicity," 48.

36. Kidd and Reynolds contend, "Multiculturalism is viewed by many French people as representing a dangerous kind of 'ghettoization,' which they see as the pattern in countries like Britain and the United States" ("Introduction" 5).

37. Hargreaves, "Post-Colonial Problematic in France," 116.

38. Huggan defines the "postcolonial exotic" as a form of commodity fetishism that dovetails with the rise of postcolonial studies and the consumption of postcolonial literatures in the West (28). Huggan, *Postcolonial Exotic*.

39. See website at http://www.christianbourgois-editeur.com. Accessed April 30, 2000.

40. Selao, "Folie et Écriture," 200.

41. In French, the word "éditeur" can mean both publisher and editor. Given Lê's play with language throughout the book, it is clear she draws upon this ambiguity.

42. Lê, *Calomnies*, 45. Subsequent references to the French-language text will be noted as *Calomnies*. The English version comes from Esther Allen's translation, published under the title *Slander*. Lê, *Slander*, 22. Subsequent references to the English-language text will be noted as *Slander*.

43. Lê, *Slander*, 101.

44. Lê, *Calomnies*, 31. Lê also references US films like Carol Reed's *Odd Man Out* (1947) and Fritz Lang's *Moonfleet* (1955). Her allusions to such films serve a strong diegetic function. Both films by Reed and Lang feature characters who experience persecution, alienation, and exile, figures with whom the narrator feels emotionally aligned.

45. Ibid., 70.

46. Ibid., 32. Lê, *Slander*, 23.

47. See Bacholle, "Exiled Woman's Burden"; and Chirol, "Histoires de Ruines," for analyses of these paternal figures.

48. Lê, *Calomnies*, 33. Lê, *Slander*, 23–24.

49. Lê, *Slander*, 103.

50. Lê, *Calomnies*,144.

51. Lê, *Slander*, 120.

52. Lê, *Calomnies*, 30.

53. Lê, *Slander*, 20.

54. Lê, *Calomnies*, 79.

55. Lê, *Slander*, 64–65.

56. Lê, *Slander*, 143.

57. Lê, *Calomnies*, 59. Lê, *Slander*, 47.

58. Lê, *Slander*, 106.

59. Lê, *Calomnies*, 43.

60. Lê, *Slander*, 33.

61. Ibid., 33.

62. Leslie Barnes discusses Lê's *Voix: Une Crise* along the same lines as I do. In *Voix*, a group called the "Organization" makes demands upon her work. Barnes asserts that the Organization may also allude to a diasporic community that would

reject her work for being too individualistic (124). Barnes, "Linda Lê's *Voix*." For me, the "Organization" is also a pointed reference to Carol Reed's film noir, *Odd Man Out*, which is cited in *Calomnies* as well.

63. Ching Selao and Maryse Fauvel separately speak to the vexed relations between host and guest. Both critics evocatively look to France's reputation as a country that historically grants asylum to refugees in relation to Lê's work. Similar to my work here, Selao also notes the ways in which the word "asylum" in French (as in English) has a double meaning (197). See Selao, "Folie"; Fauvel, "Scènes."

64. For more on the representations between the past and present as represented by the uncle and niece, respectively, see Chirol, "Histoires de Ruines."

65. Lê, *Calomnies*, 17, 9.

66. These regenerative beginnings can also be found at the end of *Voix: Une Crise* and *Lettre Morte*, where the narrator takes solace in solitude and daybreak.

67. Lê, *Calomnies*, 181.

68. Allen, "Afterword," 153.

69. Genette, *Paratexts*, 2.

70. Huggan, *Postcolonial Exotic*, 1.

71. Brouillette. *Postcolonial Writers*, 59.

72. "Elle...retranscrite [le passé] dans un langage si incisif, qu'on oublie parfois qu'elle renvoie aussi à l'indicible, à l'absence, au non-vécu, à l'oubli, bref au *paradis perdu*: le Vietnam." Chirol, "Histoires de Ruines," 103.

73. I borrow the phrase "fear and fascination" from Milton Osborne's book. See Osborne, "Fear and Fascination in the Tropics."

74. See Norindr, *Phantasmatic Indochina*.

75. Kaplan, *Questions of Travel*, 119.

76. Ibid.

77. In a book of literary criticism, *Tu écriras sur le bonheur*, entitled as an injunction ostensibly to the ethnic writer, Lê describes *littérature deplacée* as a body of work that is strongly exilic in nature. For Lê, exile is not only a physical displacement but a psychological and literary dislocation as well (330). Lê, *Tu écriras sur le bonheur*.

78. Kang, *Compositional Subjects*, 45.

79. Leslie Bow discusses the ways Asian American women are cultural traitors to their race if they align themselves too closely with white feminism and a white readership. These problems arise from the famous debate over Maxine Hong Kingston's work. See Leslie Bow, "For Every Gesture of Betrayal." For more on these debates, see Lim, "Tradition of Chinese American Women's Life-Stories"; Cheung, "Woman Warrior versus the Chinaman Pacific"; and Wong, "Autobiography as Guided Chinatown Tour?"

80. Bow claims that an emphasis on collaboration would "position Hayslip as merely an ethnographic dupe" (134). See Bow, *Betrayal and Other Acts*.

81. Chan, *Vietnamese American 1.5 Generation*, 63.

82. On Vietnamese women's emigration to the United States, see Võ, "Managing Survival."

83. On education in the refugee camps, see Kelly, "To Become an American Woman."

84. See DuBois, "Constructions Construed."

85. On model minorities in popular and political cultures, see Lee, *Orientals*; and Osajima, "Asian Americans as the Model Minority."

86. Hein, *States and International Migrants*, 43.

87. Berlant, *Queen Goes to America*, 8.

88. In 1991, after the end of the first Persian Gulf War, George H.W. Bush famously proclaimed, "By God, we've kicked the Vietnam syndrome once and for all. . . . The specter of Vietnam has been buried forever in the desert sands of the Arabian Peninsula." See Bush, "Address to the Nation Announcing Allied Military Action in the Persian Gulf, January 16, 1991," 44.

89. I draw from Ann Anagnost's reconceptualization of the term, "past-time." In terms of the nation, a national past-time is the "propensity for continually looking backward in order to face the future" (2). See Anagnost, *National Past-Times*.

90. Jeffords, *Re-Masculinization of America*, 53.

91. On Reagan's "politics of demonology," see Rogin, *Ronald Reagan*.

92. Georges Gusdorf discusses the ways in which autobiography centralizes man at the center of his literary universe (48). Feminist literary theorists have since deconstructed Gusdorf's masculinist and universalist model of autobiography. Gusdorf, "Conditions and Limits of Autobiography." For critiques of his work, see Smith and Watson, *De/Colonizing the Subject*; Brodzki and Schenk, *Life/Lines*; Culley, *American Women's Autobiography*.

93. See Lejeune, *On Autobiography*; and Eakin, *Fictions in Autobiography*.

94. Klein, "Historical Memory," 23.

95. Brooks, *Melodramatic Imagination*, 15–16.

96. Ibid., 26.

97. Robert Sayre contends that the American autobiography presents an idea of America as a project of American civilization (167). See Sayre, *Autobiography and the Making of America*.

98. Brooks, *Melodramatic Imagination*, 157.

99. Hayslip, *When Heaven and Earth*, 131.

100. Ibid., 220–26.

101. Ibid., 50.

102. Gledhill, "Pleasurable Negotiations," 82.

103. Hayslip, *When Heaven and Earth*, 101.

104. Ibid.

105. Doane, "Melodrama and Temporality," 70.

106. Hayslip, *Child of War*, 330.

107. Ibid., 223.

108. Ibid., 329.

109. Berlant, *Queen Goes to America*, 25.

110. Ibid., 25.

111. Ibid., 29.

112. Ibid., 27.

113. Hayslip, *Child of War*, 7.

114. Ibid., 34.

115. Ibid., 265–66.

116. Ibid., 266.

117. Ibid.

118. Ibid.

119. Ibid.

120. Ibid., 300.

121. Ibid., 214.

122. Ibid., 304.

123. Ibid., 193.

124. Ibid., 195.

125. Ibid.

126. Ibid., 4.

127. Ibid., 214.

128. Ibid., 300.

129. In an interview with Khanh Ho, Le Ly Hayslip emphasizes that her will to write was born of wartime experiences and rooted in a deep sense of injustice (107). See Ho, "Le Ly Hayslip."

130. Hayslip, *Child of War*, 304.

131. Though the writers of the books never state they are sisters, I have deduced this from similarities found in their narratives. These two books are different from Hayslip's in terms of their style of writing and class backgrounds. The Nguyễn sisters' family was a part of the southern Vietnamese middle class before they arrived to the United States. Narratively, their works are not full of the emotional crescendos marking Hayslip's books. As of yet, their books have not been reprinted.

132. *Fallen Leaves* was published by the Yale Center for International and Area Studies, while *The Rubber Tree* was published by McFarland & Company. McFarland & Company publishes mostly nonfiction.

133. In a book on the making of *Heaven and Earth*, Hayslip's description of Oliver Stone relies on familial metaphors. "And soul, I believe, is what Oliver's movies are all about . . . Oliver has given us many strong 'sons' this way. I am pleased and honored that, with *Heaven and Earth*, he has now also raised a daughter worthy of his warrior's heart" (110). See Singer, *Making of Oliver Stone*.

134. Trương, "Vietnamese American Literature," 237.

135. Bow, *Betrayal and Other Acts*, 35.

136. Christopher, *Viet Nam War, The American War*, 27.

137. See Kim, *Asian American Literature*; and Cheung, "Re-Viewing Asian American Literature," on this problematic especially.

138. On ethnic literature and the issue of "consent or descent," see Wong, "Autobiography as Guided Chinatown Tour?"

139. In New Horizon's *25 Years of 25 Vietnamese Americans*, the magazine reports on twenty-five Vietnamese Americans who have made the most important contributions to the Vietnamese American community. There is no mention of Le Ly Hayslip, nor of the organizations she has founded, the East Meets West Foundation and Global Village Foundation.

140. Dorland, "Le Ly Hayslip," 89.

141. Alarcón, "Traddutora, Traditora," 111.

142. Moraga, "From a Long Line," 176.

143. Visweswaran, "Betrayal," 92.

144. Trinh, *Woman Native Other*, 28.

3 / Heroes and Traitors

1. Dương Thư Hương, Interview with Author, July 20, 2004.

2. Đặng Nhật Minh, Interview with Author, August 1, 2003. Đặng expresses the same sentiment in Marchetti's article on Vietnamese melodramas. Marchetti, "Excess and Understatement," 63.

3. I found the label "communist whore" in Party documents I received from Nina McPherson, Dương's English-language translator. I am very grateful to Nina McPherson for her willingness to help with my research. Zachary Abuza also mentions that Dương Thu Hương was labeled a "dissident whore" (25). See Abuza, *Renovating Politics in Contemporary Vietnam*.

4. As McPherson has written online, Dương's list of achievements and literary and human rights awards are numerous. See McPherson, "Duong Thu Huong."

5. Đặng Nhật Minh has made five major films about women: *Bao Giờ Cho Đến Tháng Mười* [*When the Tenth Month Comes*] (1984), *Cô Gái Trên Sông* [*Woman on the Perfume River*] (1987), *Trở Về* [*The Return*] (1994), *Thương Nhớ Đồng Quê* [*Nostalgia for the Countryland*] (1996), and *Đừng Đốt* [*Don't Burn*] (2009). All of these films constitute an important part of the country's film canon.

6. Ngô, *Modernity and Nationality*, 82.

7. Vietnamese blockbusters like *Gái Nhảy* [*Bar Girls*] (2003) fare better at the box office than films like *Ký Ức Điện Biên Phủ* (2004) [*Memories of Dien Bien Phu*] and Đặng's latest film, *Đừng Đốt* [*Don't Burn*]. See Helen Clark, "Wartime Movie a Slow Burner."

8. Foucault, "Language, Counter-Memory, and Practice," 123.

9. Niranjana, *Siting Translation*, 49.

10. Simon, "Translating the Will to Knowledge," 106.

11. Venuti, *Scandals of Translation*, 65.

12. Ibid., 48.

13. Rainer Nagele looks at the "echoes of translation" (4) and argues that in reading translations, we should read "the interstitial space between texts, between languages" (10). Nagele, *Echoes of Translation*.

14. On questions of gender and translation, see Simon, *Gender in Translation;* Chamberlain, "Gender and the Metaphorics of Translation"; Mehrez, "Translation and the Postcolonial Experience"; and Niranjana, *Siting Translation*.

15. Founded in 1974, *des Femmes* was originally called *Édition des Femmes*. Later, it was taken over by Antoinette Fuque and supported by the psychoanalytic collective, *Psych et po*. The publishing house, which included a library and devoted itself to publishing women's feminist writings, was later renamed *des Femmes*.

16. Dương, *Những Thiên Đường Mù*, 11. My translation follows. Subsequent references to the original Vietnamese text will be noted as *Những Thiên*.

17. On this ambiguity in the Vietnamese language, see Luong, "Discursive Practices and Power Structure."

18. Dương, *Les paradis des aveugles*, 17. Subsequent references to the French-language text will be noted as *Les paradis*.

19. Simon, *Gender in Translation*, 19.

20. Dương, *Paradise of the Blind*, 14. Subsequent references to the English-language text will be noted as *Paradise*.

21. Surprisingly, there are few academic essays on Dương. For an early work, see Tai, "Duong Thu Huong and the Literature of Disenchantment." Other academic reviews privilege Dương as a feminist. See Young, "Human Sacrifices"; and Blodgett, "The Feminist Artistry." While William Searle does not label Dương's work as explicitly feminist, Searle does read her work in line with other women writers who focus on "women warriors." See Searle, "Women, Vietnamese, Other."

22. Dương, *Những Thiên*, 159.

23. In this respect, the French and Vietnamese versions reflect one another fairly closely, while the English-language translation is different from either the Vietnamese or French text because it has removed many descriptive details and some minor characters. Consequently this version is much more compact in its focus on the narrative and in maintaining a linear structure. For example, Dương uses a filmic metaphor to initiate a scene in which her protagonist remembers her maternal grandfather in flashback (13). The French version replicates the metaphor (20) but the English-language text omits it altogether. I asked Nina McPherson about some of these editing choices. She replied that there is a lot of editing and cutting involved in any act of translation. Interview with Author, March 28, 2007.

24. Dương, *Les paradis*, 197.

25. Dương, *Paradise*, 130.

26. Dương, *Những Thiên*, 82.

27. Dương, *Les paradis*, 109.

28. Dương, *Paradise*, 74.

29. Dương, *Những Thiên*, 138.

30. Dương, *Les paradis*, 173.

31. Dương, *Paradise*, 115.

32. In Vietnamese, Dương writes: "Nhưng số phận đã ưu đãi họ. Họ đã được đầu thai dưới một mái nhà bằng an, ít bão gió" (*Những Thiên*, 298).

33. On publishing in France, see Lottman, "French Publishing"; "Publishing without Paris"; and "Publishing à la Française."

34. See Julie C. Suk's observations, which reflect mine when I browse through Paris's many bookstores. Suk, "Resident Tourist."

35. In an interview with Dương, she explained to me that her picture was taken when she had just been released from prison. This may explain why she appears so gaunt in the photo. Interview with Author, July 2004.

36. Dương, *Những Thiên*, 272; Dương, *Les paradis*, 327; Dương, *Paradise*, 213.

37. When I asked Dương about this issue, she said that she was not aware of the changes. Interview with Author, July 20, 2004.

38. Dương, *Những Thiên*, 272.

39. Dương, *Les paradis*, 327.

40. Dương, *Paradise*, 213.

41. On *Bar Girls*, see articles by Do, "*Bar Girls* and *Street Cinderella*"; Do and Tarr, "Insider and Outsider Views"; and the final chapter of Nguyễn-Võ's *Ironies of Freedom*. For an overview of Vietnamese cinema and the "blockbuster," see Worthy, "Striking Home."

42. Vietnamese film critic Ngô Phương Lan also sees this film as a decisive moment for contemporary Vietnamese cinema. Not only was the country undergoing a "renovation," but cinema itself was also being revived. See Ngô, *Modernity and Nationality*.

43. See Charlot, "Vietnamese Cinema: Powers of the Past."

44. Vu, "Dang Nhat Minh," 120.

45. See Pettus, *Between Memory and Desire*.

46. Bradley, "Contests of Memory," 215.

47. Turim, *Flashbacks in Films*, 2.

48. Ibid., 18.

49. Brooks, *Melodramatic Imagination*, 4.

50. Bradley, "Contests of Memory," 213.

51. Ibid.

52. Charlot, "Vietnamese Cinema," 39.

53. Vu, "Dang Nhat Minh," 120.

54. Alexander, "Erotic Autonomy," 64.

55. McMahon, "Gender, Paradoxical Space, Critical Spectatorship," 108.

56. Brooks, *Melodramatic Imagination*, 4.

57. Ehrlich, *Journalism in the Movies*, 180.

58. Marchetti, "Excess and Understatement," 64.

59. Charlot, "Vietnamese Cinema," 38.

60. Võ, "Memories that Bind," 201.

61. When asked recently whether or not he was happy that CNN had nominated his film as one of the "Best of Asia," Đặng lamented the fact that his 1984 film, *When the Tenth Month Comes*, is more known internationally than domestically. http://www.lookatvietnam.com/2008/09/dang-nhat-minh-happy-with-cnns-selection.html. Accessed November 1, 2008.

62. Ngô, *Modernity and Nationality*, 82.

63. On the images of women in contemporary Việt Nam, see Tai, "Faces of Remembering"; Pettus, *Between Sacrifice and Desire*; and Fahey, "Vietnam's Women in the Renovation Era."

64. Renov, "Hollywood's Wartime Women," 10.

65. Ibid.

66. Nguyễn-Võ, *Ironies of Freedom*, 276.

67. Boudarel, "Intellectual Dissidence,"164.

68. Abuza, *Renovating Politics*, 53.

69. David Marr states that ironically, a similar trend occurred in South Vietnam from 1954–1963 during the dictatorial rule of anticommunist President Ngô Đình Diệm. After reunification in 1975, Marr writes, the "stern northern system of media controls was applied to the South" (3). In his study of contemporary Vietnamese media, Russell Heng also finds that Vietnamese media practices are founded upon Leninist ideals and shaped by Stalinist practices. See Heng, "Media in Vietnam."

70. Healey, "Laments of Warriors' Wives," 42.

71. For an overview of these three writers, see Healy, "Literature in Transition." For more on the publishing industry in Việt Nam, see Linh, "Introduction"; Hồ, "Creative Writers and the Press."

72. Abuza, *Renovating Politics*, 66.

73. Nguyễn-Võ, *Ironies of Freedom*, 65.

74. Ibid., 68.

75. Abuza, *Renovating Politics*, 112.

76. Ninh, *World Transformed*, 10.

77. In his essay, "Mono-Organizational Socialism and the State," Carlyle Thayer maintains that the Vietnamese government is predicated on a "mono-organization socialism," whereby all of the governmental organs are controlled by a small group of people within a one-party system. Thayer, "Mono-Organizational Socialism." In contrast to this claim, researchers like Benedict Kirkvliet contend that Việt Nam's government has become more fragmented and decentralized in recent years. In such a climate, sites of resistance are created in these gaps of control, even under heavy state surveillance. See Kirkvliet, "Authorities and the People." Other articles note the ways different classes of Vietnamese people negotiate with the government and resist some of the state's control over social activities, such as frequenting karaoke bars and performing religious rituals. See Koh, "Negotiating the Social State"; and Malarney, *Culture, Ritual and Revolution in Vietnam.*

78. Dương Thu Hương, Interview with Author, July 20, 2004.

79. I am influenced by Aihwa Ong's concept of flexible strategies here. As Ong argues, these "flexible strategies" describe how the state governs with great mutability in an era of globalization. She relates "transnational strategies to systems of governmentality – in the broad sense of techniques and codes for directing human behavior – that condition and manage the movements of popultions and capital" (6). Looking at the flexible strategies of the individual and the government, Ong states, "[both] develop a flexible notion of citizenship and sovereignty as strategies to accumulate capital and power" (6). See Ong, *Flexible Citizenship.*

80. Bow, *Betrayal and Other Acts,* 3.

81. Abu-Lughod, "Romance of Resistance," 42.

82. Ibid.

4 / Traitors and Translators

1. Longfellow, "Great Dance," 343.

2. Scholarship on Trinh's films is extensive. In addition to the critics and works referenced in this chapter, see Nam, "Recounting History"; and Turner, "Documentary Friction."

3. Chow, *Primitive Passions,* 185.

4. In her discussion on films, Rey Chow draws on Walter Benjamin's essay, "The Task of the Translator," wherein Benjamin comments on the importance of displaying "the fragmentedness of the original" in the echoes that follow (76). See Chow, *Primitive Passions;* and Benjamin, "The Task of the Translator."

5. Mimura, *Ghostlife of Third Cinema,* 75.

6. Lawrence, "Women's Voices in Third World Cinema," 417.

7. In speaking about the Vietnamese American reception of the film, Trinh states, "what the women were facing here was not just the interviewer but a whole community of Vietnamese exiles, especially Vietnamese men or those who claim authoritative knowledge of the culture. . . . Everything that came out was a way of addressing the community" (57). Trinh, *Cinema Interval,* 57.

8. Ibid., 257.

9. Ibid.

10. Naficy, *Accented Cinema,* 72.

11. Trinh, *Cinema Interval,* 10.

12. Mark Bradley discuses how in the 1920s, French collaborators like Phạm Quỳnh

"sought to canonize Kiều" as a way to justify [their] collaboration with the French, while anticollaborationists argued that "Kiều was a reprobate who 'drift[ed] on streams of foul desire'" (215). See Bradley, "Contests of Memory." As Kim Ninh remarks, soon after the establishment of the Democratic Republic of Việt Nam (DRV), headed by Hồ Chí Minh, intellectuals began to evaluate the story of Kiều in terms of class (36) and applied a Marxist approach to the text (60). See Ninh, *World Transformed*.

13. Trinh, *Framer Framed*, 80.

14. Along the same lines, Herman Rapaport argues that Trinh stages "precarious objectifications" of difference in her film and her book, *Woman, Native, Other* (100). Rapaport, "Deconstruction's Other."

15. Trinh, *Framer Framed*, 208.

16. Feng, *Identities in Motion*, 198.

17. Trinh, *Framer Framed*, 123.

18. Ibid., 207.

19. Ibid., 22.

20. Appadurai, *Modernity at Large*, 7.

21. Vân, *Vietnam*, 100, 171.

22. Ibid., 100 (my translation).

23. Ibid., 99, 133.

24. Ibid., 60, 149.

25. Ibid., 191.

26. Ibid., 173.

27. Ibid., 130–31 (my translation).

28. Appadurai, *Modernity at Large*, 31.

29. Mai's words are recited in the film by Trinh T. Minh-ha.

30. Gracki, "True Lies," 49.

31. Ibid., 50.

32. In fact, Women Make Movies has distributed all of Trinh's films: *Reassemblage* (1982), *Naked Spaces: Living is Round* (1985), *Shoot for the Contents* (1991), *A Tale of Love* (1995), *The Fourth Dimension* (2001), and *Night Passage* (2004).

33. Peckham, "*Surname Viet Given Name Nam*," 238.

34. Trinh, *When the Moon Waxes Red*, 29.

35. Trinh's notion of "speaking nearby" is an ethical way of representing the Other. In turn, it is instructive to emphasize the speaker and for viewers to "listen" nearby. See Trinh and Chen, "Speaking Nearby."

36. Nichols asks, "Why, for example, give such emphasis on the failures of the Communist government when neither it nor American-style democracy provides a context in which patriarchal oppression can be overcome?" (253–54). See Nichols, *Representing Reality*.

37. Parreñas-Shimizu, "Sex Acts," 1388.

38. For example, Cassie Premo contends that Trinh T. Minh-ha offers an unproductive critique, one that is not a viable blueprint for speaking of difference for postmodern feminism. Premo, "When the Difference Becomes Too Great." Against such a position, I see that Trinh tries to "undo the I" and points to a construction of many subjectivities all at once. See Trinh, *Woman, Native, Other*. On Trinh's rhetorical strategies, which emphasize empathetic connotation rather than emphatic argumentation, see Jarratt, "Beside Ourselves."

39. Taylor, *Archive and the Repertoire*, 15.

40. Wallis, "Questioning Documentary," 60.

41. A full transcript of the film alludes to this moment. See Trinh, *Framer Framed*, 80.

42. Rapaport, "Deconstruction's Other," 102.

43. See Sara Suleri's critique of both Trinh T. Minh-ha and bell hooks in terms of language. Suleri, "Woman Skin Deep." Similarly, Feroza Jussawalla questions Trinh's language—specifically, Trinh's use of the term "hybridity." Jussawalla, "South Asian Diaspora Writers."

44. Jane Desmond looks at Trinh's *Reassemblage* and *Naked Spaces*. Desmond argues that these two films, which deal mainly with African women, reify the Other. Desmond, "Ethnography, Orientalism and the Avant-Garde Film."

45. Trinh, *Framer Framed*, 165.

46. On the veiling metaphors found in this film, see McCormick, "Veiling Practices."

47. Nhi T. Lieu, "Remembering 'The Nation,'" 147.

48. Trinh, *Framer Framed*, 194.

49. Ibid. On the women's clothing and preferred settings, see also chapter 6 of Feng's *Identities in Motion*, where he argues that Trinh assents to ethnic commodification (201).

50. Cvetkovich, *Archive of Feelings*, 7.

51. Yen Le Espiritu, "Vietnamese Women in the United States," 311.

52. Ibid., 312.

53. Nguyễn-Vo, "Forking Paths," 170.

54. Nguyen, *Memory Is Another Country*, 5.

55. Ibid., 9.

56. Taylor, *Archive*, 3.

57. On the issue of repetition and difference, Trinh states, "Repetition here is not just the automatic reproduction of the same, but rather the production of the same with and in differences" (114). Trinh, *Framer Framed*.

58. Ibid., 169.

59. Marks, *Skin of the Film*, 243.

60. Trinh, *Cinema Interval*, 11.

61. Ibid., 257.

62. Ibid.

63. Ibid., 187.

64. Ahmed, *Politics of Emotion*, 111.

65. Trinh, *Cinema Interval*, 228.

66. Ibid., 10.

67. Ibid., 173.

68. See Nguyen, "Classical Heroine."

69. See Beevi, "Passing of Literary Tradition"; and Nguyen, "Representing Reconciliation."

70. Trinh, *Cinema Interval*, 79.

71. Boudarel, "Kieu or the Misfortunes of Virtue," 40.

5 / Betraying Feminine Virtue

1. While I use the term "low" and "high" to describe the divide between cultural productions in Việt Nam, I do so with an understanding that such terms resonate more clearly as classificatory designations within Western culture industries and are more meaningful

pline of cultural studies in the West. For overviews of popular cultural
ks by Storey, *Cultural Studies and the Study of Popular Culture* and Fiske,
ular. On gender and the distinctions between "high" and "low" cultures,
ding the Romance; Stacey, *Star Gazing*; and Ang, *Watching Dallas.*

2. In 1999, several noted Vietnamese films were screened at UCLA. On the campus, there were some protestors who objected to a few of the Vietnamese films and the supposed communist propaganda contained within them. More recently, however, at a screening of Đặng Nhật Minh's film, *When the Tenth Month Comes*, at UCI in 2007, there were no protestors. Đặng has since toured his films at numerous American universities.

3. See "Film Wins Big Distribution Deal."

4. *Long-Legged Girls* earned nearly VNĐ 7 billion (over US$445,000) in ticket sales. See "Evolving Film Industry." The concept of the blockbuster in Việt Nam is new, but increasingly used to describe in English-language media the phenomenon of commercially profitable films. The first "blockbuster" in Việt Nam's film history was Lê Hoàng's *Gái Nhảy* (2002), or *Bar Girls*, which made US$1 million at the box office. Mangat, "Sex and Drugs Sell."

5. On the state and youths in Việt Nam, see Marr, "Vietnamese Youth in the 1990s"; and Valentin, "Politicized Leisure."

6. de Lauretis, *Alice Doesn't*, 37.

7. After *Souls on Swings*, Nguyễn has stayed in Việt Nam to make a string of films with local and diasporic directors: *Dòng Máu Anh Hùng* [*The Rebel*] (2007), *Saigon Eclipse* (2007), *Nụ Hôn Thần Chết* [*Kiss of Death*] (2008), *Chơi Vơi* [*Adrift*] (2009), and *Bẫy Rồng* [*Clash*] (2010). See Chu, "Vietnam's Economy Lures Some Who Left in the 1970s."

8. The latest film collaborations are made by Vietnamese American directors, who work with Vietnamese and diasporic actors and producers, and shoot on location in Việt Nam. These films include *Để Mai Tính* [*Fool for Love*] (2010), *Chuyện Tình Xa Xứ* [*Passport to Love*] (2009), *14 Ngày Phép* [*14 Days Off*] (2009), and *Khi Yêu Đừng Quay Đầu Lại* [*Don't Look Back*] (2010).

9. Appadurai discusses how a reimagining of the political is possible through technology, or what he calls a mediascape (35). Appadurai, *Modernity at Large*.

10. Director Vũ Ngọc Đãng reportedly spent VND 550 million, or US$35,000, on advertising alone, a first in Vietnamese cinema. See "Evolving Film Industry."

11. Hamilton, "Renovated," 143.

12. For more on the debates on commercial cinema in Việt Nam, see "Thị Trường Điện Ảnh Việt Nam"; Tran, "*Bar Girls* Raise Hell in Vietnam"; Hương Hòai, "Loay Hoay Thị Trường và Phim Nghệ Thuật."

13. See "Evolving Film Industry."

14. Popular websites for cinephiles in Việt Nam reference two major sites: moviesboom.com and filmcriticvn.com. Their websites can be found at http://www.moviesboom.com/ and http://filmcriticvn.org. Accessed May 15, 2005, and January 10, 2010.

15. Thomas and Heng, "Stars in the Shadow," 288.

16. I refer to classic Vietnamese films, such as *Em Bé Hà Nội* [*Girl from Hanoi*] (1970), which relies on flashbacks to narrate a tragic past, most distinctly from a young girl's perspective. Another important film that uses flashbacks extensively is Đặng Nhật Minh's *Woman on the Perfume River*, which I examine in Chapter 3.

17. See Jameson, *Postmodernism*.

18. On similar points about sexuality and the city, see Gammeltoft, "Being Special for Somebody."

19. Carruthers, "National Identity, Diasporic Anxiety," 136.

20. Berry, "Happy Alone?" 188.

21. Nguyen and Thomas, "Post-Socialist Women," 144.

22. In Vietnamese, the lyrics do not have the same punning effect as in English, but they are still suggestive. The throbbing tempo of the song and the husky tones in which the Vietnamese singer intones the words speak to the song's sexual overtones. In Vietnamese, the lyrics of the song are: "như là/như là/ ta ước mơ đêm ngày có đôi chân dài nào ghé thăm/Để ta yêu đương."

23. In Vietnamese, the song lyrics are: "Những đôi chân dài em đến đây bao lần/ Dù trong giấc mơ cũng là cho ta biết ơn em rồi."

24. On MTV videos and dreams, see Kinder, "Music Video and the Spectator." On how MTV videos appeal to a queer male visual aesthetic, see Drukman, "Gay Gaze."

25. de Lauretis, "Popular Culture, Public and Private Fantasies," 304.

26. Krzywinska, "La Belle Dame Sans Merci?" 103.

27. Mulvey's phrasing is apt in describing how women's bodies are fetishized in this film. Mulvey, "Visual Pleasure and Narrative Cinema," 835.

28. I borrow this phrase from Linda Williams' essay, "When the Woman Looks."

29. Steven Neale's seminal essay, "Masculinity as a Spectacle," is relevant to my discussion about the erotics of the male body, "displayed solely for the gaze of the spectator" in film (13). However, my work is less focused on the paradigm of psychoanalysis that Neale uses in his study of genres like action and western films. Critiquing Neale's work, film theorist Yvonne Tasker similarly argues that Neale relies on the "stability of a gendered binary," which is "understood to be 'universal' or 'transhistorical'" (116). See Tasker, *Spectacular Bodies*.

30. Instead of "Sài Gòn," I use "Hồ Chí Minh City," even though in common parlance, the Vietnamese still use the name "Sài Gòn." By using these two different appellations, I differentiate between the "Sài Gòn" that is associated with war and the past. "Hồ Chí Minh City" connotes for me a post-Đổi Mới Việt Nam.

31. See chapter 1 of Taylor, *Fragments of the Present*.

32. On these perceived differences, Gustafsson writes, "Capitalism has had a longer and firmer hold on southern Vietnam, giving rise to the northern perception that southerners care only about money" (127). Gustafsson, *War and Shadows*.

33. For an overview of Vietnamese cinema, see Trinh, *30 Years*.

34. Trinh, *30 Years*, 28.

35. Dumont, "Multiple Births," 46.

36. Rouse, "South Vietnam's Film Legacy," 214.

37. Ibid., 215.

38. Dumont, "Multiple Births," 48.

39. Ibid.

40. See article, "Business Opportunities."

41. See the article, "TV, Cinema Show More Vietnam Flicks."

42. Thanh Chung, "*Hồn Trương Ba*: Phim Hài . . . Mất Vệ Sinh."

43. On the state's banning of superstitious practices in Việt Nam, see Gustafsson, *War and Shadows*; Malarney, *Culture, Ritual, and Revolution in Vietnam*; Norton, *Song of the Spirits*; and Fjalsted and Nguyen, *Possessed by the Spirits*.

44. Cowie, "Fantasia," 75.

45. Bakhtin, *Rabelais and His World*, 91.

45. Ibid., 10.

47. King, *Film Comedy*, 67.

48. Halberstam, *Female Masculinity*, 24.

49. Ibid.

50. Bakhtin, *Rabelais and His World*, 39.

51. See Carroll, "Notes on the Sight Gag."

52. Russo, "Female Grotesque," 216.

53. On "trans-body films," see chapter 3 of Straayer, *Deviant Eyes, Deviant Bodies*.

54. On the identity of transsexuals in Việt Nam, see "Gender Change Challenges Traditional Culture"; and "Government Considers Transsexuality."

55. Việt Nam's eminent sexologist, Dr. Trần Bông Son, has claimed, "Homosexuality . . . is influenced by fashion and experimentation" (qtd. in Blanc 664). In relation to this perception, the state has cracked down on homosexuality as a "social evil." Blanc, "Social Constructions of Male Homosexualities in Vietnam"; Laurent, "Sexuality and Human Rights"; Colby et al., "Men Who Have Sex with Men and HIV in Vietnam "; and Khuat Thu Hong, "Study on Sexuality in Vietnam."

56. See articles on Việt Nam's crackdown of dissidents: "Vietnam: Crackdown on Dissent in Wake of WTO and APEC"; and Steinglass, "Vietnam Continues Crackdown on Dissidents."

57. Jenkins and Karnik, *Classical Hollywood Comedy*, 272.

58. King, *Film Comedy*, 8.

59. Thomas and Heng, "Stars in the Shadows," 291.

60. Ibid., 295.

61. Nguyen, "The Boom of Commercial Cinema," 145.

62. Ibid., 148.

63. Dyer, *Heavenly Bodies*, 3.

64. Carruthers, "National Identity, Diasporic Anxiety," 139.

65. Dyer, *Stars*, 24.

66. Thrift, "Material Practices of Glamour," 13.

67. Rofel, *Desiring China*, 3.

68. See Gopinath, *Impossible Desires*.

69. See Laurent, "Sexuality and Human Rights."

70. Ibid., 192.

71. See Manalansan, *Global Divas*.

72. Schein, "Diaspora Politics, Homeland Erotics," 699.

73. See "Frank,"On the Legality of Homosexuality in Vietnam. During French colonialism, neither homosexuality nor homosexual behaviors were actually prohibited. This is still the case today. On the 2002 decree that homosexual is a "social evil" and its effects on young women, see Rydstrøm, "Sexual Desires and 'Social Evils.'"

74. For a report on this incident, see Nguyen et al., "Gay Life Is Persecuted."

75. See Brook and Luong, "Introduction."

76. Nussbaum, "Politics of Subjectivity," 164.

77. Ibid.

Conclusion

1. Davies, *Dangerous Liaisons*, 195.

2. Nathalie Nguyen discusses "lost photographs" and their importance to refugees as "they embody a sense of past place and belonging that is all the more important in the aftermath of displacement. Photographs are also a potent reminder of those who were lost" (11). Nguyen, *Memory is Another Country*. Similarly, as Susan Sontag has written, "A family's photograph albums is generally about the extended family—and often, is all that remains of it" (43). Sontag, "In Plato's Cave."

3. Eng, *Feeling of Kinship*, 14–15.

4. Ibid.

5. Lee, "Breaking through the Chrysalis," 132.

6. Feng, *Identities in Motion*, 130.

7. Kim, "'Bad Women,'" 578.

8. Ibid., 584.

9. Machida, *Unsettled Visions*, 184.

10. Ibid.

11. Here, I refer to the controversies surrounding Le Ly Hayslip and Madison Nguyen. I was also embroiled in these politics. In January 2009, fellow arts organizers and I organized an art exhibit called *F.O.B. II: Art Speaks*. The exhibit featured communist images. Because of these images, we were demonstrated against, called "whores" to our faces, and labeled "thương nữ bất tri vong quốc hận" in print (Triệu 2). This phrase roughly translates as: "businesswomen who are unaware of the people's resentment that the nation has been lost." In using this phrase to denigrate our art exhibit, the author—writer and former soldier Hải Triều—offered a telling analogy that figures women as conduits for commerce. He compared us, the new intellectual class of today, to the destitute prostitutes of yesteryear: both are only interested in selling themselves and in selling out their country during its most difficult times. Thanks to Nguyễn Thị Thu Hương for help on this translation. Hải Triều, "Cờ Máu, Hình Hồ và VAALA tại Nam California," 1–2. For coverage of this event, see Mỹ-Thuận Trần, "Vietnamese Art Exhibit Puts Politics on Display."

12. Choi and Kim, *Dangerous Women*, 5.

13. Anderson, *Imagined Communities*, 6.

14. Douglas, *Purity and Danger*, 2. As Douglas writes: "Ideas about separating, purifying, demarcating and punishing transgressions have as their main function to impose a system on an inherently untidy experience" (5).

15. I borrow this phrasing from the title of David Haines's book, *Limits of Kinship*.

16. Svetlana Boym defines two types of nostalgias. "Reflective nostalgia" understands the past as "ironic, inclusive, and fragmentary" (50), whereas "restorative nostalgia" is "dead serious" in its evocation of a national past to "reconstruct emblems and rituals of home and homeland in an attempt to conquer and spatialize time" (49). Boym, *Future of Nostalgia*.

17. Aguilar-San Juan, *Little Saigons*, 64.

18. Ibid., 77.

19. See also Vu and Dang, "Competing Images."

20. Nguyễn-Võ, "Forking Paths," 170.

21. Thuy Vo Dang, "The Cultural Work of Anti-Communism," 77.

22. Espiritu, "The-We-Win-Even-If-We-Lose-Syndrome," 340.

23. Nguyen, "'Without the Luxury of Historical Amnesia,'" 137.

24. Espiritu, "Towards a Critical Refugee Study," 411.

25. In his critique of black nationalism and its rhetoric of the family, Paul Gilroy discusses how the trope of the family is "defined by ideas about nurturance, about family, about fixed gender roles and generational responsibilities" ("It's a Family Affair," 89). Gilroy ends his essay by asking readers to "remind ourselves that we have other possibilities" (94).

26. Le, "'Better Dead Than Red,'" 204.

27. Bousquet, *Behind the Bamboo Hedge*, 5.

28. Le, "'Better Dead Than Red,'" 207.

29. Ông and Meyer, "Protest and Political Incorporation," 95.

30. Discussing her work, "Beyond the Family Album," feminist photographer Joe Spence describes both herself and the family as "sites of contradiction" (355). Spence, "Beyond the Family Album."

31. Davis, "Vocabulary for Feminist Praxis," 22.

32. As Lily Cho suggests for queer diasporic subjects, loss can be transformative. She writes, "Loss can be carried forward not only as a condition of the future but also as a way of converting the desires of the present for the home" (431). Cho, "Future Perfect Loss."

33. Kondo, "Art, Activism, Asia and Asian Americans," 658.

34. Eng and Kazanjian, "Introduction," 4.

WORKS CITED

Abu-Lughod, Lila. "The Romance of Resistance: Tracing Transformations of Power Through Bedouin Women." *American Ethnologist* 17, no. 1 (1990): 41–55.

Abuza, Zachary. *Renovating Politics in Contemporary Vietnam.* Boulder, CO, and London: Lynne Rienner Publishers, 2001.

Aguilar-San Juan, Karin. *Little Saigons: Staying Vietnamese in America.* Minneapolis: University of Minnesota, 2009.

Ahmed, Sara. *The Cultural Politics of Emotion.* New York: Routledge, 2004.

Alarcón, Norma. "Traddutora, Traditora: A Paradigmatic Figure of Chicana Feminism." In *Scattered Hegemonies: Postmodernity and Transnational Feminist Practices,* edited by Inderpal Grewal and Caren Kaplan, 110–33. Minneapolis: University of Minnesota Press, 1994.

Alexander, M. Jacqui. "Erotic Autonomy as a Politics of Decolonization: An Anatomy of Feminist and State Practice in the Bahamas Tourist Economy." In *Feminist Genealogies, Colonial Legacies, Democratic Futures,* edited by Chandra Talpade Mohanty and M. Jacqui Alexander, 63–100. New York: Routledge, 1997.

Allen, Esther. "Afterword: Linda Lê's Slander." In *Slander,* 153–56. Lincoln: University of Nebraska Press, 1996.

Anagnost, Ann. *National Past-Times: Narrative, Representation, and Power in Modern China.* Durham, NC: Duke University Press, 1997.

Anderegg, Michael. "Introduction." In *Inventing Vietnam: The War in Films and Television,* edited by Michael Anderegg, 1–14. Philadelphia, PA: Temple University Press, 1991.

Anderson, Benedict. *Imagined Communities.* London and New York: Verso, 1983.

Ang, Ien."Hegemony-In-Trouble: Nostalgia and the Ideology of the Impossible in European Cinema." In *Screening Europe: Image and Identity in Contemporary European Cinema*, edited by Duncan Petrie, 21–31. London: British Film Institute, 1992.

———. *Watching Dallas: Soap Opera and the Melodramatic Imagination*. Translated by Della Couling. London and New York: Routledge, 1982.

Appadurai, Arjun. *Modernity at Large: Cultural Dimensions of Globalization*. Minneapolis and London: University of Minnesota Press, 1996.

Bacholle, Michèle. "Camille et Mui ou du Vietnam dans *Indochine* et *L'odeur de la papaye verte*." *The French Review* 74, no. 5 (2001): 946–56.

———. "The Exiled Woman's Burden: Father Figures in Lan Cao's and Linda Lê's Works." *Sights: The Journal of Twentieth Century/Contemporary French Studies* 6, no. 2 (2002): 267–81.

———. "Tran Anh Hung's Orphan Tales." In *Of Vietnam: Identities in Dialogue*, edited by Jane Bradley Winston and Leakthina Chau-Pech Ollier, 170–79. New York: Palgrave, 2001.

Bakhtin, Mikhail. *Rabelais and His World*. Translated by Helene Iswolsky. Bloomington: Indiana University Press, 1984.

Balibar, Étienne. "Racism and Nationalism." In *Race, Nation, Class: Ambiguous Identities*, edited by Étienne Balibar and Immanuel Wallerstein, 37–67. London and New York: Verso, 1991.

Balzar, John. "Vietnam and Culture: Lessons and Legacies 25 Years After Vietnam; Coming Home Is Never Easy." *Los Angeles Times*, April 16, 2000.

Barnes, Leslie. "Linda Lê's *Voix* and the Crisis of Representation: Alterity and the Vietnamese Immigrant Writer in France." *French Forum* 32, no. 3 (2008): 123–38.

Barrett, David. "Occupied China and the Limits of Accommodation." In *Chinese Collaboration with Japan, 1934–1945*, edited by David Barrett and Larry Shyu, 1–17. Stanford: Stanford University Press, 2001.

Barrett, David, and Larry Shyu, eds. *Chinese Collaboration with Japan, 1932–1945*. Stanford: Stanford University Press, 2001.

Barry, Kathleen, ed. *Vietnam's Women in Transition*. New York: St. Martin's Press, 1996.

Bayly, Susan. *Asian Voices in a Postcolonial Age: Vietnam, India, and Beyond*. Cambridge: Cambridge University Press, 2007.

Beevi, Mariam. "The Passing of Literary Traditions: The Figure of the Woman from Vietnamese Nationalism to Vietnamese American Transnationalism." *Amerasia Journal* 23, no. 2 (1997): 27–54.

Béhar, Henri. "'Xich-Lo' Press Conference at the 1995 New York Film Festival." *Film Scouts Interviews*. http://www.filmscouts.com/scripts/interview.cfm?File=2759. Accessed August 4, 2011.

Benjamin, Walter. "The Task of the Translator." In *The Translation Studies*

Reader, edited by Lawrence Venuti, 15–25. London and New York: Routledge, 2000.

Bennett, Rab. *Under the Shadow of the Swastika: The Moral Dilemmas of Resistance and Collaboration in Hitler's Europe*. New York: New York University Press, 1999.

Berlant, Lauren. *The Queen of America Goes to Washington: Essays on Sex and Citizenship*. Durham, NC: Duke University Press, 1997.

Berry, Chris. "Happy Alone? Sad Young Men in East Asian Gay Cinema." *Journal of Homosexuality* 39, no. 3/4 (2000): 187–200.

Bhabha, Homi. *The Location of Culture*. London and New York: Routledge, 1994.

Blanc, Marie-Eve. "Social Constructions of Male Homosexualities in Vietnam: Some Keys to Understanding Discrimination and Implications for HIV Prevention Strategy." *International Social Science Journal* 57, no. 186 (2005): 661–73.

Blodgett, Harriet. "The Feminist Artistry of *Paradise of the Blind*." *World Literature Today* 75, no. 3/4 (2001): 31–39.

Blum-Reid, Sylvie. *East-West Encounters: Franco-Asian Cinema and Literature*. London and New York: Wallflower Press, 2003.

Body-Gendrot, Sophie, and Martin Schain. "National and Local Politics and the Development of Immigration Policy in the United States and France: A Comparative Analysis." In *Immigrants in Two Democracies: French and American Experience*, edited by Donald L. Horowitz and Gerard Noiriel, 411–38. New York and London: New York University Press, 1992.

Boothryoud, Peter, and Pham Xuan Nam, eds. *Socioeconomic Renovation in Viet Nam: The Origin, Evolution and Impact of Doi Moi*. Singapore: Institute of Southeast Asian Studies, 2000.

Bordwell, David. *Planet Hong Kong: Popular Cinema and the Art of Entertainment*. Cambridge, MA: Harvard University Press, 2000.

Boudarel, George. "Intellectual Dissidence in the 1950s: The Nhan Van-Giai Pham Affair." *The Vietnam Forum* 13 (1991): 154–74.

———. "Kieu or the Misfortunes of Virtue in Vietnamese." *Vietnamese Studies* 3 (1999): 35–51.

Bourdieu, Pierre. *The Field of Cultural Production: Essays on Art and Literature*. New York: Columbia University Press, 1993.

Bousquet, Gisèle. *Behind the Bamboo Hedge: The Impact of Homeland Politics in the Parisian Vietnamese Community*. Ann Arbor: University of Michigan Press, 1991.

Bow, Leslie. *Betrayal and Other Acts of Subversion*. Princeton, NJ: Princeton University Press, 2001.

———. "'For Every Gesture of Loyalty, There Doesn't Have to Be a Betrayal': Asian American Criticism and the Politics of Loyalty" In *Who Can Speak?*

Authority and Critical Identity, edited by Robyn and Judith Roof Wiegman, 30–55. Urbana and Chicago: University of Illinois Press, 1995.

Bowen, Wayne. *Spaniards and Nazi Germany: Collaboration in the New Order.* Columbia and London: University of Missouri Press, 2000.

Boym, Svetlana. *The Future of Nostalgia.* New York: Basic Books, 2001.

Bradley, Mark Philip. "Contests of Memory: Remembering and Forgetting the War in the Contemporary Vietnamese Cinema." In *The Country of Memory: Remaking the Past in Late Socialist Vietnam*, edited by Hue-Tam Ho Tai, 196–226. Berkeley: University of California Press, 2001.

———. *Imagining Vietnam and America: The Making of Postcolonial Vietnam: 1919–1950.* Chapel Hill and London: University of North Carolina Press, 2000.

Briggs, Pamela Beere. "Tony Bùi Looks East from West." *Release Print* 19, no. 1 (1996): 28–36.

Brodzki, Bella, and Celeste Schenck, eds. *Life/Lines: Theorizing Women's Autobiography.* Ithaca, NY: Cornell University Press, 1988.

Brook, Timothy, and Hy Van Luong. "Introduction: Culture and Economy in a Postcolonial World." In *Culture and Economy: The Shaping of Capitalism in Eastern Asia*, edited by Timothy Brook and Hy Van Luong, 1–21. Ann Arbor: University of Michigan Press, 1997.

Brook, Timothy. *Collaboration: Japanese Agents and Local Elites in Wartime China.* Cambridge, MA: Harvard University Press, 2005.

———. "Collaboration in the History of Wartime East Asia." *Japan Focus*, July 4, 2008. http://japanfocus.org/-Timothy_Brook/2798. Accessed August 28, 2010.

Brooks, Peter. *The Melodramatic Imagination: Balzac, Henry James, Melodrama, and the Mode of Excess.* New Haven, CT, and London: Yale University Press, 1976.

Brouillette, Sarah. *Postcolonial Writers and the Global Literary Marketplace* New York: Palgrave MacMillan, 2007.

Brownell, Susan, and Jeffrey Wasserstrom. "Introduction: Theorizing Femininities and Masculinities." In *Chinese Femininities/Chinese Masculinities*, edited by Susan Brownell and Jeffrey Wasserstrom, 1–42. Berkeley, London, and Los Angeles: University of California Press, 2002.

Bui Thi Kim Quy. "The Vietnamese Woman in Vietnam's Process of Change." In *Women in Transition*, edited by Kathleen Barry, 159–66. New York: St. Martin's Press, 1996.

Bundesen, Lynne. "Vietnam: One Woman's Story." *Los Angeles Times*, June 25, 1989, 4.

Bush, George. "Address to the Nation Announcing Allied Military Action in the Persian Gulf, January 16, 1991." In *Public Papers of the Presidents of the United States: George Bush—1991 Book I—January 1 to June 30, 1991.* Washington, DC: U.S. Government Printing Office, 1993.

————. 1986. "Inaugural Addresses of the Presidents of the United States." http://www.bartleby.com/124/pres63.html. Accessed January 21, 2010.

"Business Opportunities: The New Vietnam Film Industry." *Viet Nam a Go Go*, January 15, 2010. http://www.bigbloggle.com/vietnam_agogo/. Accessed August 15, 2010.

Caprio, Mark. "Loyal Patriot? Traitorous Collaborator? The Yun Chiho Diaries and the Question of National Loyalty." *Journal of Colonialism and Colonial History* 7: 3. http://www.press.jhu.edu/journals/journal_of_colonialism_and_colonial_history/. Accessed August 31, 2010.

Carroll, Noel. "Notes on the Sight Gag." In *Comedy/Cinema/Theory*, edited by Andrew Horton, 25–42. Berkeley: University of California Press, 1991.

Carruthers, Ashley. "National Identity, Diasporic Anxiety, and Music Video Culture in Vietnam." In *House of Glass: Culture, Modernity, and the State in Southeast Asia*, edited by Yao Souchou, 119–49. Singapore: Institute of Southeast Asian Studies, 2001.

Carter, Jay. "A Subject Elite: The First Decade of the Constitutionalist Party in Cochinchina, 1917–1927." In *Viet Nam Forum 14: A Review of Vietnamese Culture and Society*, edited by Oliver Wolters. New Haven, CT: Yale University Council on Southeast Asian Studies, 1994.

Chakravarty, Sumita S. *National Identity in India Popular Cinema, 1947–1987.* Delhi: South Asia Books and Oxford University Press, 1993.

Chamberlain, Lori. "Gender and the Metaphorics of Translation." In *The Translation Studies Reader*, edited by Lawrence Venuti, 314–29. London and New York: Routledge, 2000.

Chan, Sucheng. *The Vietnamese American 1.5 Generation.* Philadephia, PA: Temple University Press, 2006.

Charlot, John. "Vietnamese Cinema: First Views." *Journal of Southeast Asian Studies* (1991): 33–62.

Cheng, Scarlet. "Tran Anh Hung and the Scents of Vietnam." *Cinemaya* 24 (1994): 5–7.

Cheung, King-Kok. "Re-Viewing Asian American Literary Studies." In *An Interethnic Companion to Asian American Literature*, edited by King-Kok Cheung, 1–36. Cambridge: Cambridge University Press, 1997.

————. "The Woman Warrior Versus the Chinaman Pacific: Must a Chinese American Critic Choose between Feminism and Heroism?" In *Conflicts in Feminism*, edited by Marianne Hirsch and Evelyn Fox Keller, 234–51. New York: Routledge, 1990.

Chirol, Marie-Magdeleine. "Histoires de Ruines: *Calomnies* de Linda Lê." *French Forum* 29, no. 2 (2004): 91–105.

Chiu, Lily. "'An Open Wound on a Smooth Skin': (Post)Colonialism and the Melancholic Performance of Trauma in the Works of Linda Lê." *Intersections: Gender and Sexuality in Asia and the Pacific* 21 (2009). http://intersections.anu.edu.au/issue21/chiu.htm. Accessed November 23, 2009.

Cho, Lily. "Future Perfect Loss: Richard Fung's *Sea of Blood.*" *Screen* 49, no. 4 (2008): 426–39.

Choi, Chungmoo, and Elaine Kim. "Introduction." In *Dangerous Women: Gender and Korean Nationalism*, edited by Chungmoo Choi and Elaine Kim, 1–8. New York and London: Routledge, 1998.

Chow, Rey. *Primitive Passions: Visuality, Sexuality, Ethnography, and Contemporary Chinese Cinema*. New York: Columbia University Press, 1995.

———. *Writing Diaspora: Tactics of Intervention in Contemporary Cultural Studies*. Bloomington and Indianapolis: Indiana University Press, 1993.

Christopher, Renny. *The Viet Nam War, the American War: Images and Representations in Euro-American and Vietnamese Exile Narratives*. Amherst: University of Massachusetts Press, 1995.

Chu, Kathy. "Vietnam's Economy Lures Some Who Left in the 1970s." *USA Today*, August 18, 2010. http://www.usatoday.com/money/world/2010–08–18–1Avietnam18_CV_N.htm?loc=interstitialskip. Accessed August 18, 2010.

Chung, Thanh. "*Hồn Trương Ba*: Phim Hài . . . Mất Vệ Sinh" [*Hồn Trương Ba*: An unsanitary comedy]. *Việt Báo*, February 12, 2006. http://vietbao.vn/Van-hoa/Hon-Truong-Ba-Phim-hai-mat-ve-sinh/20540574/181/. Accessed July 1, 2006.

Clark, Helen. 2009. "Wartime Movie a Slow Burner at the Box Office." *Monsters and Critics.com*. http://www.monstersandcritics.com/news/asiapacific/news/article_1474753.php/FEATURE_Don_t_Burn_wartime_movie_a_slow_burner_at_the_box_office. Accessed January 1, 2010.

Cloonan, William, and Jean-Philippe Postel. "Celebrating Literature: Literary Festivals and the Novel in 1997." *The French Review* 72, no. 1 (1998): 8–19.

Cloonan, William. "'Les Grands Écrivains' and the Novel in 2000." *The French Review* 75, no. 1 (2000): 38–52.

———. "Literary Scandal, *Fin du Siècle*, and the Novel in 1999." *The French Review* 74, no. 1 (2000): 14–30.

Colby, Donn, Nghia Huu Cao, and Serge Doussantousse. "Men Who Have Sex with Men and HIV in Vietnam: A Review." *AIDS Education Prevention* 16, no. 1 (2004): 45–54.

Cong-Huyen, Ton Nu Thi Nha Trang. The Traditional Roles of Women as Reflected in Oral and Written Vietnamese Literature. PhD Diss., University of California, Berkeley, 1973.

Cooper, Nicola. *France in Indochina: Colonial Encounters*. Oxford and New York: Berg, 2001.

Cowie, Elizabeth. "Fantasia." *m/f* 9 (1984): 70–105.

Culley, Margo, ed. *American Women Autobiography: Fea(s)ts of Memory*. Madison: University of Wisconsin Press, 1992.

"Cultural Policy in the Socialist Republic of Vietnam." http://www.wwcd.org/policy/clink/Vietnam.html. Accessed January 5, 2010.

Cunningham, Stuart, and Tina Nguyen. "Popular Media of the Vietnamese Diaspora." *The Public* 6, no. 1 (1999): 71–92.

Cvetkovich, Ann. *An Archive of Feelings: Trauma, Sexuality and Lesbian Public Culture.* Durham, NC, and London: Duke University Press, 2003.

Da Silva, Denise Ferreira. "A Tale of Two Cities: Saigon, Fallujah, and the Ethical Boundaries of Empire." *Amerasia Journal* 31, no. 2 (2005): 121–34.

"Dang Nhat Minh Happy with CNN's Selection." 2008. *LookatVietnam*, http://www.lookatvietnam.com/2008/09/dang-nhat-minh-happy-with-cnns-selection.html. Accessed December 20, 2008.

Dang, Thuy Vo. "The Cultural Work of Anticommunism in the San Diego Vietnamese American Community." *Amerasia* 31, no. 2 (2005): 65–86.

———. "Mediating Diasporic Identities: Vietnamese/American Women in the Musical Landscape of *Paris by Night*." In *Le Viet Nam au féminin: Viet Nam, Women's Realities*, edited by Gisèle Bousquet and Nora A. Taylor, 337–51. Paris: Les Indes Savantes, 2005.

Đào Hiếu. "Hồn Trương Ba Da Hàng Thịt" [*Souls on Swings*].*Vanchinh.net*, October 1, 2008. http://vanchinh.net/index.php?option=com_content&view=article&id=241:hn-trng-ba-da-hang-tht&catid=37:phe-binh&Itemid=56. Accessed September 13, 2010.

Dao, Loan. "What's Going On with the Oakland Museum's 'California and the Vietnam Era' Exhibit?" *Amerasia Journal* 31, no. 2 (2005): 89–106.

Davies, Carol Boyce. "Collaboration and the Ordering Imperative in Life Story Production." In *De/Colonizing the Subject; the Politics of Gender in Women's Autobiography*, edited by Julia Watson and Sidonie Smith, 3–19. Minneapolis: University of Minnesota Press, 1992.

Davies, Peter. *Dangerous Liaisons: Collaboration and World War Two.* Harlow, UK: Pearson Longman, 2004.

Davis, Angela Y. "A Vocabulary for Feminist Praxis: On War and Radical Critique." In *Feminism and War: Confronting U.S. Imperialism*, edited by Chandra Mohanty, 19–26. London and New York: Zed Books, 2008.

de Lauretis, Teresa. *Alice Doesn't: Feminism, Semiotics, Cinema.* Bloomington: Indiana University Press, 1984.

———. "Popular Culture, Public and Private Fantasies: Femininity and Fetishism in David Cronenberg's *M. Butterfly*." *Signs: Journal of Women in Culture and Society* 24, no. 2 (1999): 303–34.

Deegan, Joe. 2005. "Old Wounds." *San DiegoReader.com*, http://www.sandiegoreader.com/news/2005/aug/25/old-wounds/. Accessed November 15, 2009.

Delvaux, Martine. "Linda Lê and the Prosthesis of Origin." In *Immigrant Narratives in Contemporary France*, edited by Susan Ireland and Patrice J. Proulx, 201–11. Westport, CT: Greenwood Press, 2001.

Desai, Jigna. *Beyond Bollywood: The Cultural Politics of South Asian Diasporic Film.* New York and London: Routledge, 2004.

Desai, Jigna, Danielle Bouchard, and Diane Detournay. "Disavowed Legacies and Honorable Thievery: The Work of the 'Transnational' in Feminist and LGBT Studies." In *Critical Transnational Feminist Praxis*, edited by Richa Nagar and Amanda Lock Swarr, 46–64. Albany: State University of New York Press, 2010.

Desmond, Jane. "Ethnography, Orientalism and the Avant-Garde Film." *Visual Anthropology* 4, no. 2 (1991): 147–60.

Diawara, Manthia. "Francophone and the Publishing World." *Black Renaissance/Renaissance Noire* 3, no. 2 (2001): 143–57.

Dinh, Linh 2000. "Introduction: Writing and Publishing in Vietnam." http://www.theliteraryreview.org/. Accessed May 3, 2005.

Dizon, Lily. "Expatriates Vent Anger at Author, Movie Portrayals." *Los Angeles Times*, January 16, 1994, B1 and B5.

Do, Tess. "*Bar Girls* and *Street Cinderella*: Women, Sex, and Prostitution in Lê Hoang's Commercial Films." *Asian Studies Review* 30 (2006): 175–88.

———. "Entre Salut et Damnation: Metaphores Chez Linda Lê." *French Cultural Studies* 15, no. 2 (2004): 142–57.

———. "From Incest to Exile: Linda Lê and the Incestuous Vietnamese Immigrants." In *France and 'Indochina': Cultural Representations*, edited by Kathryn Robson and Jennifer Yee, 165–78. Lanham, MD: Lexington Books, 2005.

Do, Tess, and Carrie Tarr. "Outsider and Insider Views of Saigon/Hồ Chí Minh City: *The Lover/L'amant, Cyclo/Xich-Lo, Collective Flat/Chung Cu*, and *Bargirls/Gai Nhay*." *Singapore Journal of Tropical Geography* 29 (2008): 55–67.

Doane, Janice, and Devon Hodges. "Writing from the Trenches: Women's Work and Collaborative Writing." *Tulsa Studies in Women's Literature* 14, no. 1 (1995): 51–57.

Doane, Mary Ann. "Melodrama, Temporality, Recognition: American and Russian Silent Cinema." *East-West Film Journal* 4, no. 2 (1990): 69–89.

Dorland, Gilbert. "Le Ly Hayslip." In *Legacy of Discord: Voices of the Vietnam War Era*, edited by Gilbert Dorland, 81–94. Washington, DC: Brassey's Inc., 2001.

Douglas, Mary. *Purity and Danger: An Analysis of Concept of Pollution and Taboo*. London and New York: Routledge, 2004.

Drukman, Steve. "The Gay Gaze, or Why I Want My MTV." In *A Queer Romance: Lesbians, Gay Men, and Popular Culture*, edited by Paul Burston and Colin Richardson, 81–95. London and New York: Routledge, 1995.

Drummond, Lisa, and Helle Rydstrøm, eds. *Gender Practices in Contemporary Vietnam*. Singapore: Singapore University Press, 2004.

DuBois, Thomas A. "Constructions Construed: The Representations of Southeast Asian Refugees in Academic, Popular and Adolescent Discourse." *Amerasia Journal* 19, no. 3 (1993): 1–25.

Duiker, William. *Hồ Chí Minh*. New York: Hyperion, 2000.

Dumont, Philippe. "The Multiple Births of Vietnamese Cinema." In *Vietnam-*

ese Cinema: Le Cinéma Vietnamien, edited by Philippe Dumont and Kirstie Gormley, 44–60. Lyon, France: Asiexpo Edition, 2007.

Dương Thu Hương. Những Thiên Đường Mù: Tiểu Thuyết. Hà Nội: Nhà Xuất Bản Việt Nam, 1990.

———. Les paradis des aveugles. Translated by Phan Huy Đường. Paris: Éditions de Femmes, 1991.

———.Paradise of the Blind. Translated by Nina McPherson and Phan Huy Đường. New York: William Morrow and Company, Inc., 1993.

Durand, Maurice, and Tran Huan Nguyen. An Introduction to Vietnamese Literature. New York: Columbia University Press, 1985.

Dyer, Richard. Heavenly Bodies. New York and London: Routledge, 2003.

———. Stars. London: British Film Institute, 1979.

Eakin, Paul John. Fictions in Autobiography: Studies in the Art of Self-Invention. Princeton, NJ: Princeton University Press, 1985.

Ede, Lisa, and Andrea Lunsford. Singular Texts/Plural Authors. Carbondale and Edwardsville: Southern Illinois University Press, 1990.

Ehrlich, Matthew. Journalism in the Movies. Urbana and Chicago: University of Illinois Press, 2004.

Eisen, Arlene, ed. Women and Revolution in Viet Nam. London: Zed Books, 1984.

Eng, David. The Feeling of Kinship: Queer Liberalism and the Racialization of Intimacy. Durham, NC, and London: Duke University Press, 2010.

Eng, David, and David Kazanjian. "Introduction: Mourning Remains." In Loss, edited by David Eng and David Kazanjian, 1–25. Berkeley, Los Angeles, and London: University of California Press, 2003.

Espiritu, Yen Le. "Towards a Critical Refugee Study: The Vietnamese Refugee Subject in U.S. Scholarship." Journal of Vietnamese Studies 1, nos. 1–2 (2006): 410–33.

———. "Vietnamese Women in the United States: A Critical Transnational Perspective." In Le Viet Nam au féminin: Viet Nam, Women's Realities, edited by Gisèle Bousquet and Nora A. Taylor, 307–21. Paris: Les Indes Savantes, 2005.

———. "'The We-Win-Even-When-We-Lose' Syndrome: United States Press Coverage of the Twenty-Fifth Anniversary of the 'Fall of Saigon.'" American Quarterly 58, no. 2 (2006): 329–52.

Étienne, Marie-France. "Linda Lê ou les jeux de l'errance." Tangence no. 71 (2003): 79–90.

"Evolving Film Industry Faces New Challenges." 2005. Viet Nam News, http://vietnamnews.vnagency.com.vn/showarticle.php?num=03SUN231005. Accessed January 10, 2010.

Fahey, Stephanie. "Vietnam's Women in the Renovation Era." In Gender and Power in Affluent Asia, edited by Krishna Sen and Maila Stivens, 222–49. London and New York: Routledge, 1998.

Fauvel, Maryse. *Scènes d'Intérieur: Six romanciers des années 1980–1990*. Birmingham, AL: Summa Publications, Inc., 2007.

Favre, Isabelle. "Linda Lê: Schizo-Positive?" *Présence Francophone*, no. 61 (2003): 191–202

Feng, Peter X. *Identities in Motion: Asian American Film and Video*. Durham, NC: Duke University Press, 2002.

"Film Makers Clash After 'Bar Girls' Triumphs at Box Office." 2003. *Viet Nam Embassy News*, http://www.vietnamembassy-usa.org/news/story. php?d=20030318111014. Accessed January 10, 2010.

"Film Wins Big Distribution Deal." *Việt Nam News*, August 25, 2006. http://vietnamnews.vnagency.com.vn/Life-Style/Film/156672/Film-wins-big-distribution-deal.html. Accessed August 31, 2008.

Fiske, John. *Reading the Popular*. New York: Routledge, 1989.

Fjelstad, Karen, and Nguyen Thi Hien. *Possessed by the Spirits: Mediumship in Contemporary Vietnamese Communities*. Ithaca, NY: Cornell University Press, 2006.

Forsdick, Charles, and David Murphy. "Introduction: The Case for Francophone Postcolonial Studies." In *Francophone Postcolonial Studies: A Critical Introduction*, edited by Charles Forsdick and David Murphy, 1–14. London: Arnold, 2003.

Foucault, Michel. *Language, Counter-Memory, Practice: Selected Essays and Interviews*. Translated by Donald Bouchard and Sherry Simon. Ithaca, NY: Cornell University Press, 1977.

"Frank." 2000. On the Legality of Homosexuality in Vietnam. GBLF Email Forum. Accessed 1 May, 2005.

Freeman, Donald B. "*Doi Moi* Policy and the Small-Enterprise Boom in Hồ Chí Minh City, Vietnam." *Geographical Review* 86: 2 (1996): 178-198.

Fu, Poshek. *Passivity, Resistance, and Collaboration: Intellectual Choices in Occupied Shanghai, 1937–1945*. Stanford: Stanford University Press, 1993.

Fysh, Peter. *The Politics of Racism in France*. London: MacMillan Press, Ltd., 1998.

Gaines, Jane. "White Privilege and Looking Relations." In *Issues in Feminist Film Criticism*, edited by Patricia Erens, 197–214. Bloomington: Indiana University Press, 1990.

Gammeltoft, Tine. "Being Special for Somebody: Urban Sexualities in Contemporary Vietnam." *Journal of Social Science* 30, no. 3 (2002): 476–92.

"Gender Change Challenges Traditional Culture." *Việt Nam Net Bridge*, February 1, 2006. http://english.vietnamnet.vn/social/2006/02/537764/. Accessed October 13, 2007.

Genette, Gerard. *Paratexts: Thresholds of Interpretation*. Cambridge: Cambridge University Press, 1997.

Génin, Bernard. "Une Intense Douceur." *Télérama* (June 9, 1993): 1–2.

Gilroy, Paul. "It's a Family Affair " In *That's the Joint!: The Hip-Hop Studies*

Reader, edited by Murray Forman and Mark Anthony Neal, 87–94. New York and London: Routledge, 2004.

Gledhill, Christine. "Pleasurable Negotiations." In *Female Spectators: Looking at Film and Television*, edited by Deidre E. Pribram, 64–89. London: Verso, 1988.

Gopinath, Gayatri. *Impossible Desires: Queer Diasporas and South Asian Public Cultures*. Durham, NC, and London: Duke University Press, 2005.

Gordon, Bertram. *Collaborationism in France During the Second World War*. Ithaca, NY, and London: Cornell University Press, 1980.

"Government Considers Transsexuality." *Việt Nam Net Bridge*, October 19, 2007. http://english.vietnamnet.vn/social/2006/02/537764/. Accessed October 23, 2007.

Gracki, Katherine. "True Lies: Staging the Ethnographic Interview in Trinh T. Minh-ha's *Surname Viet Given Name Nam*." *Pacific Coast Philology* 36 (2001): 48–63.

Green, Mary Jean, Karen Gould, Micheline Rice-Maximin, Keith Walker, and Jack Yeager. "Introduction: Women Writing Beyond the Hexagon." In *Postcolonial Subjects: Francophone Women Writers*, edited by Mary Jean Green, Karen Gould, Micheline Rice-Maximin, Keith Walker, and Jack Yeager, ix–xxii. Minneapolis: University of Minnesota Press, 1996.

Grewal, Inderpal. *Transnational America: Feminisms, Diasporas, Neoliberalisms*. Durham, NC: Duke University Press, 2005.

Grewal, Inderpal, and Caren Kaplan. "Introduction: Transnational Feminist Practices and Questions of Postmodernity." In *Scattered Hegemonies: Postmodernity and Transnational Feminist Practices*, edited by Inderpal Grewal and Caren Kaplan, 1–33. Minneapolis: University of Minnesota Press, 1994.

Gusdorf, Georges. "Conditions and Limits of Autobiography." In *Autobiography: Essays Theoretical and Critical*, edited by James Olney, 28–48. Princeton, NJ: Princeton University Press, 1980.

Gustafsson, Mai Lan. *War and Shadows: The Haunting of Vietnam*. Ithaca, NY: Cornell University Press, 2009.

Haines, David. *The Limits of Kinship: South Vietnamese Households: 1954–1975*. DeKalb: Southeast Asia Publications, Center for Southeast Asian Studies, Northern Illinois University, 2006.

Halberstam, Judith. *Female Masculinity*. Durham, NC, and London: Duke University Press, 1998.

Hamilton, Annette. "Renovated: Gender and Cinema in Contemporary Vietnam." *Visual Anthropology* 22, no. 2 (2009): 141–54.

Han, Suk-Jung. "On the Question of Collaboration in South Korea." *Japan Focus*, July 4, 2008. http://japanfocus.org/-Suk_Jung_Han/2800. Accessed August 28, 2010.

Hargreaves, Alec. "The Contribution of North and Sub-Saharan Immigrant Minorities to the Redefinition of Contemporary French Culture." In *Franco-*

phone Postcolonial Studies: A Critical Introduction, edited by Charles Forsdick and David Murphy, 145–54. London: Arnold, 2003.

——. *Immigration, 'Race,' and Ethnicity in Contemporary France*. London and New York: Routledge, 1995.

——. "Writing for Others: Authorship and Authority in Immigrant Literature." In *Race, Discourse, and Power in France*, edited by Maxim Silverman, 111–19. Aldershot, UK: Avebury, 1991.

Hargreaves, Alec G., and Mark McKinney. "The Post-Colonial Problematic in France." In *Post-Colonial Cultures in France*, edited by Alec G. Hargreaves and Mark McKinney, 3–25. London and New York: Routledge, 1997.

Harris, Sue, and Elizabeth Ezra. "Introduction: The French Exception." In *France in Focus: Film and National Identity*, edited by Sue Harris and Elizabeth Ezra 1–9. Oxford and New York: Berg, 2000.

Hayslip, Le Ly, and James Hayslip. *Child of War, Woman of Peace*. New York: Doubleday, 1993.

Hayslip, Le Ly, and Jay Wurts. *When Heaven and Earth Changed Places: A Vietnamese Woman's Journey from War to Peace*. New York: Doubleday, 1989.

Hayward, Susan. "National Cinemas and the Body Politic." In *France in Focus: Film and National Identity*, edited by Sue Harris and Elizabeth Ezra, 97–113. Oxford and New York: Berg, 2000.

Healy, Dana. "Laments of Warriors' Wives: Re-gendering the War in Vietnamese Cinema." *South East Asia Research* 14, no. 2 (2006): 231–59.

——. "Literature in Transition: An Overview of Vietnamese Writing of the Renovation Period." In *The Canon in Southeast Asian Literature*, edited by David Smith, 41–50. Richmond, Surrey: Curzon, 2000.

Heath, Stephen. *Questions of Cinema*. Bloomington: Indiana University Press, 1981.

Hein, Jeremy. *States and International Migrants: The Incorporation of Indochinese Refugees in the United States and France*. Boulder, CO: Westview Press, 1993.

Heng, Russell. "Media in Vietnam and the Structure of Its Management." In *Mass Media in Vietnam*, edited by David Marr, 27–53. Canberra: Department of Political and Social Change, Research School of Pacific and Asian Studies, The Australian National University, 1998.

Heung, Marina. "The Family Romance of Orientalism: From *Madame Butterfly* to *Indochine*." In *Visions of the East: Orientalism in Film*, edited by Matthew Bernstein and Gaylin Studlar, 158–83. New Brunswick, NJ: Rutgers University Press, 1997.

Hồ Anh Thái. "Creative Writers and the Press in Vietnam Since Renovation." In *Mass Media in Vietnam*, edited by David Marr, 58–63. Canberra: Department of Political and Social Change, Research School of Pacific and Asian Studies, The Australian National University, 1998.

Ho, Khanh. "Le Ly Hayslip." In *Words Matter: Conversations with Asian Amer-*

ican Writers, edited by King-Kok Cheung, 105–19. Honolulu: University of Hawai'i Press in Association with UCLA Asian American Studies Center, Los Angeles, 2000.

Hoài Hương. "Loay Hoay Phim Thị Trường Và Phim Nghệ Thuật" [Anxiety regarding commercial and artistic cinema]. *Tuần Vietnam.net*, November 11, 2009. http://tuanvietnam.net/2009–11–10–loay-hoay-phim-thi-truong-va-phim-nghe-thuat. Accessed January 10, 2010.

Hoang Ba Thinh. "Women and Family in Transition." In *Images of the Vietnamese Woman in the New Millennium*, edited by Le Thi Nham Tuyet, 139–92. Hà Nội: Thế Giới Publishers, 2002.

Horowitz, Donald. "Immigration and Group Relations in France and America." In *Immigrants in Two Democracies: French and American Experience*, edited by Donald Horowitz and Gerard Noiriel, 3–35. New York and London: New York University Press, 1992.

Huggan, Graham. *The Postcolonial Exotic: Marketing the Margins*. London and New York: Routledge, 2001.

Irvin, George. "Vietnam: Assessing the Achievements of *Doi Moi*." *Journal of Development Studies* 31, no. 5 (1995): 725–50.

Jameson, Fredric. *Postmodernism, or, the Cultural Logic of Late Capitalism*. Durham, NC: Duke University Press, 1991.

Janette, Michele. "Look Again: *Three Seasons* Refocuses American Sights of Vietnam." *Journal of Vietnamese Studies* 1, nos. 1–2 (2006): 253–76.

Jarratt, Susan. "Beside Ourselves: Rhetoric and Representation in Postcolonial Feminist Writing." In *Crossing Borderlands: Composition and Postcolonial Studies*, edited by Andrea Lunsford and Lahoucine Ouzgane, 110–28. Pittsburgh: University of Pittsburgh Press, 2000.

Jeancolas, Jean-Pierre. "The Reconstruction of French Cinema." In *France in Focus: Film and National Identity*, edited by Sue Harris and Elizabeth Ezra, 13–21. Oxford and New York: Berg, 2000.

Jeffords, Susan. *Hard Bodies: Hollywood Masculinity in the Reagan Era*. New Brunswick, NJ: Rutgers University Press, 1994.

———. *The Remasculinization of America: Gender and the Vietnam War*. Bloomington: Indiana University Press, 1989.

Jin, Ha. *The Writer as Migrant*. Chicago: University of Chicago Press, 2008.

Jussawalla, Feroza "South Asian Diaspora Writers in Britain: 'Home' Versus 'Hybridity.'" In *Ideas of Home: Literature of Asian Migration*, edited by Geoffrey Kaine, 17–37. East Lansing: Michigan State University Press, 1997.

Kandiyoti, Deniz. "Identity and Its Discontents: Women and the Nation." In *Colonial Discourse and Post-Colonial Theory: A Reader*, edited by Patrick Williams and Laura Chrisman, 376–91. New York: Columbia University Press, 1994.

Kang, Laura Hyun Yi. *Compositional Subjects: Enfiguring Asian American Women*. Durham, NC, and London: Duke University Press, 2002.

Kaplan, Caren. *Questions of Travel: Postmodern Discourses of Displacement.* Durham, NC, and London: Duke University, 1996.

Kaplan, Carey, and Ellen Cronan Rose. "Strange Bedfellows: Feminist Collaboration." *Signs* 18, no. 3 (1993): 547–61.

Karell, Linda. *Writing Together, Writing Apart.* Lincoln and London: University of Nebraska Press, 2002.

Karnick, Kristine, and Henry Jenkins. *Classical Hollywood Comedy.* New York: Routledge, 1994.

Katz, Steven D. *Film Directing Shot by Shot: Visualizing From Concept to Screen.* Studio City, CA: Michael Wiese Productions, 1991.

Kelly, Gail Paradise. "To Become an American Woman: Education and Sex Role Socialization of the Vietnamese American Woman." In *Unequal Sisters: A Multicultural Reader in U.S. Women's History,* edited by Vicki L. Ruiz and Ellen Carol DuBois, 554–64. New York: Routledge, 2000.

Kennedy, Laurel B., and Mary Rose Williams. "The Past Without the Pain: The Manufacture of Nostalgia in Vietnam's Tourist Industry." In *The Country of Memory: Remaking the Past in Late Socialist Vietnam,* edited by Hue-Tam Ho Tai, 135–63. Berkeley: University of California Press, 2001.

Kidd, William, and Sian Reynolds. "Introduction: To the Reader." In *Contemporary French Cultural Studies,* edited by William Kidd and Sian Reynolds, 3–9. London: Arnold, 2000.

Kim, Elaine. *Asian American Literature: An Introduction to the Writings and Their Social Context.* Philadelphia, PA: Temple University Press, 1982.

———. "'Bad Women': Asian American Visual Artists: Hanh Thi Pham, Hung Liu, and Yong Soon Min." *Feminist Studies* 22, no. 3 (1996): 573–602.

Kinder, Marsha. "Music Video and the Spectator: Television, Ideology, and Dream." *Film Quarterly* 38, no. 1 (1984): 2–15.

King, Geoff. *Film Comedy.* London and New York: Wallflower Press, 2002.

Kirkvliet, Benedict J. Tria. "Authorities and the People." In *Postwar Vietnam: Dynamics of a Transforming Society,* edited by Hy Van Luong, 27–53. New York: Institute of Southeast Asian Studies, 2003.

Khuat Thu Hong. "Study on Sexuality in Vietnam: The Known and Unknown Issues." Hà Nội: The Population Council, The Regional Working Papers No. 11, 1998.

Klein, Michael. "Historical Memory, Film, and the Vietnam Era." In *From Hanoi to Hollywood: The Vietnam War in American Film,* edited by Linda Dittmar and Gene Michaud, 19–40. New Brunswick, NJ: Rutgers University Press, 1997.

Koh, David. "Negotiating the Social State in Vietnam Through Local Administrators: The Case of Karaoke Shops." *Sojourn: Journal of Social Sciences in Southeast Asia* 16, no. 2 (2001): 279–305.

Kondo, Dorinne. "Art, Activism, Asia, and Asian Americans." In *Contemporary Asian America: A Multidisciplinary Reader,* edited by Min Zhou and James Gatewood, 636–64. New York: New York University Press, 2000.

Krzywinska, Tanya. "La Belle Dame Sans Merci?" In *A Queer Romance: Lesbians, Gay Men, and Popular Culture*, edited by Paul Burston and Colin Richardson, 99–110. London and New York: Routledge, 1995.

Kwon, Heonik. "Co So Cach Mang and the Social Network of War." In *Making Sense of the Vietnam Wars*, edited by Mark Bradley and Marilyn Young, 199–216. Oxford: Oxford University Press, 2008.

———. "Excavating the History of Collaboration." *Japan Focus*, July 4, 2008. http://www.japanfocus.org/-Heonik-Kwon/2801. Accessed August 28, 2010.

Lam, Andrew. "Thirty Five Years After the War, Betrayal is Vietnam's Story." April 27, 2010. http://www.redroom.com/blog/andrew-q-lam/thirty-five-years-after-the-war-betrayal-vietnams-story. Accessed May 1, 2010.

Larimer, Tim. "Vietnam Visions," *Time Magazine*. http://www.time.com/time/world/article/0,8599,2054260,00.html. Accessed August 4, 2011.

Laurent, Erick. "Sexuality and Human Rights: An Asian Perspective." *Journal of Homosexuality* 48, nos. 3/4 (2005): 163–225.

Lawrence, Amy. "Women's Voices in Third World Cinema." In *Multiple Voices in Feminist Film Criticism*, edited by Diane Carson, Linda Dittmar, and Janice Welsh, 406–20. Minneapolis: University of Minnesota Press, 1994.

Le Huu Khoa. *Les Vietnamiens en France: Insertion et Identité*. Paris: Editions L'Harmattan, 1985.

Le Thi. "Women, Marriage, Family and Gender Equality." *Vietnam Social Sciences* 2, no. 36 (1993): 21–33.

Le Thi Nham Tuyet. "National Identity and Gender Characteristics in Vietnam." *Vietnam Social Sciences* 5, no. 67 (1998): 31–65.

Le Thi Nham Tuyet et al., eds. *Images of the Vietnamese Woman in the New Millennium*. Hà Nội: Thế Giới Publishers, 2002.

Le Van Phung, La Nham Thin, and Le Thi Nham Tuyet. *Gender and Development in Vietnam*. Hà Nội: Nhà Xuất Bản Khoa Học Xã Hội, 1995.

Le, C. N. "'Better Dead Than Red': Anti-Communist Politics Among Vietnamese Americans." In *Anti-Communist Minorities in the U.S.: The Political Activism of Ethnic Refugees*, edited by Ieva Zake, 189–210. New York: Palgrave-MacMillan, 2009.

Lê, Linda. *Calomnies*. Paris: Christian Bourgeois Editeur, 1993.

———. *Les trois Parques*. Paris: Christian Bourgois Editeur, 1997.

———. *Lettre Morte*. Paris: Christian Bourgois Editeur, 1999.

———. *Slander*. Translated by Esther Allen. Lincoln: University of Nebraska Press, 1996.

———. *Tu écriras sur le bonheur*. Paris: Presses Universitaires de France, 1999.

———. *Voix: Une crise*. Paris: Christian Bourgois Editeur, 1998.

Lee, Robert. *Orientals: Asian Americans in Popular Culture*. Philadelphia, PA: Temple University Press, 1999.

Lefevere, André. "Mother Courage's Cucumbers: Text, System, and Refraction in a Theory of Literature." In *The Translation Studies Reader*, edited by Lawrence Venuti, 233–49. London and New York: Routledge, 2000.

Lejeune, Philippe. *On Autobiography*. Translated by Katherine Leary. Vol. 52. Minneapolis: University of Minnesota Press, 1989.

Levy, Charles. "ARVN as Faggots: Inverted Warfare in Vietnam." In *Men's Lives*, edited by Michael S. Kimmel and Michael A. Messner, 183–97. New York: MacMillan Publishing Company, 1992.

Lieu, Nhi T. "Remembering 'The Nation' Through Pageantry: Femininity and the Politics of Vietnamese Womanhood in the Hoa Hau Ao Dai Contest." *Frontiers: A Journal of Women's Studies* 21, nos. 1/2 (2000): 126–51.

Lim, Shirley Geok-Lin. "The Tradition of Chinese American Women's Life Stories: Thematics of Race and Gender in Jade Snow Wong's *Fifth Chinese Daughter* and Maxine Hong Kingston's *The Woman Warrior*." In *American Women's Autobiography: Fea(s)ts of Memory*, edited by Margo Culley, 252–67. Madison: University of Wisconsin Press, 1992.

Lionnet, Françoise. *Postcolonial Representations: Women, Literature, Identity*. Ithaca, NY, and London: Cornell University Press, 1995.

Long, Lisa. "Contemporary Women's Roles through Hmong, Vietnamese and American Eyes." *Frontiers: A Journal of Women's Studies* 29, no. 1 (2008): 1–36.

Longfellow, Brenda. "The Great Dance: Translating the Foreign in Ethnographic Film." In *Subtitles: On the Foreignness of Film*, edited by Atom Egoyan and Ian Balfour, 335–53. Cambridge, MA: MIT Press, 2004.

Lottman, Herbert. "French Publishing: A Fast Portrait." *Publishers Weekly*, January 29, 1996, 43–46.

———. "Publishing à la Française " *Publishers Weekly*, June 1, 1990, S6–S16.

———. "Publishing Without Paris." *Publishers Weekly*, September 14, 1992, 45–54.

Loutfi, Martine Astier. "Imperial Frame: Film Industry and Colonial Representation." In *Cinema, Colonialism, and Postcolonialism*, edited by Dina Sherzer, 20–29. Austin: University of Texas Press, 1996.

Luong, Hy Van. "Discursive Practices and Power Structure: Person-Referring Forms and Sociopolitical Struggles in Colonial Vietnam." *American Ethnologist* 15, no. 2 (1988): 239–53.

———. "Gender Relations: Ideologies, Kinship Practices, and Political Economy." In *Postwar Vietnam: Dynamics of a Transforming Society*, edited by Hy Van Luong, 201–23. New York: Institute of Southeast Asian Studies, 2003.

Machida, Margo. *Unsettled Visions: Contemporary Asian American Artist and the Social Imaginary*. Durham, NC, and London: Duke University Press, 2008.

Malarney, Shaun Kingsley. *Culture, Ritual, and Revolution in Vietnam*. Honolulu: University of Hawai'i Press, 2002.

Manalansan, Martin F., IV. *Global Divas: Filipino Gay Men in the Diaspora.* Durham, NC, and London: Duke University Press, 2003.

Mangat, Mona. "Sex and Drugs Sell." *Eastern Horizons* 14, June 2003. http://www.unaids.org.vn/event/sexndrugs.htm. Accessed September 21, 2010.

Marchetti, Gina. "Excess and Understatement: War, Romance, and the Melodrama in Contemporary Vietnamese Cinema." *Genders* 10 (1991): 47–74.

Marks, Laura U. *The Skin of the Film: Intercultural Cinema, Embodiment, and the Senses.* Durham, NC, and London: Duke University Press, 2000.

Marr, David. "Concepts of 'Individual' and 'Self' in Twentieth-Century Vietnam." *Modern Asian Studies* 34, no. 4 (2000): 769–96.

———. *Vietnamese Tradition on Trial, 1920–1945.* Berkeley: University of California Press, 1981.

———. "Vietnamese Youth in the 1990s." *The Vietnam Review* 2 (1997): 288–354.

Mastern, Jeffrey. *Textual Intercourse: Collaboration, Authorship, and Sexualities in Renaissance Drama.* Cambridge: Cambridge University Press, 1997.

McCormick, Adrienne. "Veiling Practices, Invisibility, and Knowledge Production in the Documentary Films of Trinh T. Minh-ha, Barbara Hammer, and Lourdes Portillo." In *Visual Media and the Humanities: A Pedagogy of Representation,* edited by Kecia Driver McBride, 357–99. Knoxville: University of Tennessee, 2004.

McKelvey, Robert S. *The Dust of Life: America's Children Abandoned in Vietnam.* Seattle and London: University of Washington Press, 1999.

McMahon, Kathryn. "Gender, Paradoxical Space, and Critical Spectatorship in Vietnamese Film: The Works of Đặng Nhật Minh." In *Trans-Status Subjects: Gender in the Globalization of South and Southeast Asia,* edited by Sonita Sarjer and Esha Nigoyi De, 108–25. Durham, NC: Duke University Press, 2002.

McPherson, Nina. "Duong Thu Huong." *WikiVietLit: VNLP: Viet Nam Literature Project.* http://www.vietnamlit.org/wiki/index.php?title=Duong_Thu_Huong. Accessed February 1, 2009.

Mehrez, Samia. "Translation and the Postcolonial Experience: The Francophone North African Text." In *Rethinking Translation: Discourse, Subjectivity, Ideology,* edited by Lawrence Venuti, 120–38. London and New York: Routledge, 1992.

Miller, Toby. "The Crime of Monsieur Lang: GATT, the Screen, and the New International Division of Cultural Labour." In *Film Policy: International, National, and Regional Perspectives,* edited by Albert Moran, 72–84. London and New York: Routledge, 1996.

Mimura, Glen. *Ghostlife of Third Cinema: Asian American Film and Video.* Minneapolis: University of Minnesota Press, 2009.

Mohanty, Chandra Talpade. *Feminism Without Borders: Decolonizing Theory, Practicing Solidarity.* Durham, NC: Duke University Press, 2003.

———. "Under Western Eyes: Feminist Scholarship and Colonial Discourses."

In *Third World Women and the Politics of Feminism*, edited by Chandra Tal-pade Mohanty, Ann Russo and Lourdes Torres, 51–80. Bloomington and Indianapolis: Indiana University Press, 1991.

Moraga, Cherríe. "From a Long Line of *Vendidas*: Chicanas and Feminism." In *Feminist Studies, Critical Studies*, edited by Teresa de Lauretis. Bloomington: Indiana University Press, 1986.

Mulvey, Laura. "Visual Pleasure and Narrative Cinema." In *Narrative, Apparatus, Ideology: A Film Theory Reader*, edited by Philip Rosen, 833–45. New York: Columbia University Press, 1986.

Mydans, Seth. "In Hanoi, an Austere Film Diet." *The New York Times*, September 1, 1996, 20.

Naficy, Hamid. *An Accented Cinema: Exilic and Diasporic Filmmaking*. Princeton, NJ: Princeton University Press, 2001.

Nagele, Rainer. *Echoes of Translation: Reading Between Texts*. Baltimore, MD, London: Johns Hopkins University Press, 1997.

Nam, Soo-Young. "Recounting 'History': Documentary as Women's Cinema." *Asian Journal of Women's Studies* 7, no. 1 (2001): 80–110.

Narkunas, Paul J. "Streetwalking in the Cinema of the City: Capital Flows through Saigon." In *Cinema and the City: Film and Urban Societies in a Global Context*, edited by Mark Shiel and Tony Fitzmaurice, 147–57. Oxford: Blackwell Publishers Ltd., 2001.

Neale, Steven. *Cinema and Technology: Image, Sound, Colour*. Bloomington: Indiana University Press, 1985.

———. "Masculinity As Spectacle: Reflections on Men and Mainstream Cinema." *Screen* 24, no. 6 (1983): 2–16.

Ngô Phương Lan. "Opening to the World." In *Vietnamese Cinema: Le Cinéma Vietnamien*, edited by Philippe Dumont and Kirstie Gormley, 214–17. Lyon, France: Asiexpo Edition, 2007.

———. *Modernity and Nationality in Vietnamese Cinema*. Ygyakarta, Indonesia: JAFF, NETPAC and Galangpress 2007.

Nguyen Mai Loan. "The Boom of Commercial Films." In *Vietnamese Cinema: Le Cinéma Vietnamien*, edited by Philippe Dumont and Kirstie Gormley, 144–52. Lyon, France: Asiexpo Edition, 2007.

Nguyễn Thị Thu-Lâm, Edith Kreisler, and Sandra Christenson. *Fallen Leaves: Memoirs of a Vietnamese Woman from 1945 to 1975*. Boston: Yale Center for International and Area Studies, 1989.

Nguyễn Thị Tuyết Mai, and Monique Senderowicz. *The Rubber Tree*. Jefferson, NC: McFarland & Company, Inc., 1994.

Nguyen Vu Viet-Huong. "Making History with Tony Bui." In *New Horizons: 25 Vietnamese Americans in 25 Years*, edited by Nguyen Thi Diem Huyen and Nguyen Thi Thuy, 24–29. San José, CA: New Horizons, 2000.

Nguyễn-Võ Thu-Hương. "Forking Paths: How Shall We Mourn the Dead?" *Amerasia* 31, no. 2 (2005): 157–75.

——. *The Ironies of Freedom: Sex, Culture, and Neoliberal Governance in Vietnam*. Seattle: University of Washington Press, 2008.

Nguyen, Bich Thuan, and Mandy Thomas. "Young Women and Emergent Postsocialist Sensibilities in Contemporary Vietnam." *Asian Studies Review* 28 (2004): 133–49.

Nguyễn Hoàng Lân. "The Little Saigon Name is a Big Deal," *New American Media*, January 12, 2008. http://news.newamericamedia.org/news/view_article. html?article_id=ab55620bcc7341de8ad57d49e4d24b16. Accessed December 11, 2009.

Nguyen, Kim. "'Without the Luxury of Historical Amnesia': The Model Postwar Immigrant Remembering the Vietnam War through Anticommunist Protests." *Journal of Communication Inquiry* 34, no. 2 (2010): 134–50.

Nguyen, Nathalie. "A Classical Heroine and Her Modern Manifestation: *The Tale of Kieu* and Its Modern Parallels in *Printemps Inachevé*." *The French Review* 73, no. 3 (2000): 454–62.

——. "Eurasian and Amerasian Perspectives: Kim Lefèvre's *Métisse Blanche* (White Métisse) and Kien Nguyen's *The Unwanted*." *Asian Studies Review* 29, no. 2 (2005): 107–22.

——. *Memory Is Another Country: Women of the Vietnamese Diaspora*. Santa Barbara, CA: ABC-CLIO, LLC, 2009.

——. *Vietnamese Voices: Gender and Cultural Identity in the Vietnamese Francophone Novel*. DeKalb, IA: Southeast Asia Publications, 2003.

Nguyen, Tien, Lam Tran, and Tom Le. "Gay Life Is Persecuted and Condemned in Vietnam," *Globalgays.com*, July 7, 1999. http://www.globalgayz.com/ country/Vietnam/view/VNM/gay-vietnam-news-and-reports#article1a. Accessed March 25, 2005.

Nguyen, Viet Thanh. "Hayslip's Story About Forgiveness, Growth." *Asian Week*, March 12, 1993. 28.

——. "Representing Reconciliation: Le Ly Hayslip and the Victimized Body." *positions* 5, no. 2 (1997): 605–39.

Nichols, Bill. *Representing Reality: Issues and Concepts in Documentary*. Bloomington: Indiana University Press, 1991.

Ninh, Kim. *A World Transformed: The Politics of Culture in Revolutionary Vietnam: 1945–1965*. Ann Arbor: University of Michigan Press, 2002.

Niranjana, Tejeswari. *Siting Translation: History, Post-Structuralism, and the Colonial Context*. Berkeley: University of California Press, 1992.

Norindr, Panivong. *Phantasmatic Indochina: French Colonial Ideology in Architecture, Film, and Literature*. Durham, NC: Duke University Press, 1996.

Norton, Barley. "'Hot-Tempered' Women and 'Effeminate' Men: The Performance of Memory and Gender in Vietnamese Mediumship." In *Possessed by the Spirits: Mediumship in Contemporary Vietnamese Communities*, edited by Karen Fjelstad and Nguyen Thi Hien, 55–75. Ithaca, NY: Cornell University Press, 2006.

——. *Songs for the Spirits: Music and Mediums in Modern Vietnam*. Chicago: University of Illinois Press, 2009.

Nussbaum, Felicity. "The Politics of Subjectivity and the Ideology of Genre." In *Women, Autobiography, Theory*, edited by Sidonie Smith and Julia Watson, 160–67. Madison: University of Wisconsin Press, 1998.

Ollier, Leakthina Chau-Pech. "Consuming Culture: Linda Lê's Autofiction." In *Of Vietnam: Identities in Dialogue*, edited by Jane Bradley Winston and Leakthina Chau-Pech Ollier, 241–50. New York: Palgrave, 2001.

Ong, Aihwa. "Colonialism and Modernity: Feminist Re-Presentations of Women in Non-Western Societies." *Inscriptions* 3, no. 4 (1985): 79–93.

——. *Flexible Citizenship: The Cultural Logics of Transnationality*. Durham, NC: Duke University Press, 1999.

Ông, Nhu-Ngọc T., and David S. Meyer. "Protest and Political Incorporation: Vietnamese American Protests in Orange County, California, 1975–2001." *Journal of Vietnamese Studies* 3, no. 1 (2008): 78–107.

Osajima, Keith. "Asian Americans as the Model Minority: An Analysis of the Popular Press Image in the 1960s and 1980s." In *Reflections on Shattered Windows: Promises and Prospects for Asian American Studies*, edited by Gary Y. Okihiro, Shirley Hune, Arthur A. Hansen, and John M. Liu, 165–74. Pullman: Washington State University Press, 1988.

Osborne, Milton. "Fear and Fascination in the Tropics: A Reader's Guide to French Fiction on Indo-China." In *Asia in Western Fiction*, edited by Robin Winks and James Rush, 15–174. Manchester, England: Manchester University Press, 1990.

——. *The French Presence in Cochinchina and Cambodia: Rule and Response (1859–1905)*. Ithaca, NY, and London: Cornell University Press, 1969.

Parker, Andrew, Mary Russo, Doris Summer, and Patricia Yaeger. "Introduction: Nationalisms and Sexualities." In *Nationalisms and Sexualities*, edited by Mary Russo Andrew Parker, Doris Summer, and Patricia Yaeger, 1–18. New York: Routledge, 1992.

Parreñas-Shimizu, Celine, and Helen Lee. "Sex Acts: Two Meditations on Race and Sexuality." *Signs: A Journal of Women in Culture and Society* 30, no. 1 (2004): 1385–402.

Patton, Cindy, and Benigno Sánchez-Eppler, eds. *Queer Diasporas*. Durham, NC: Duke University Press, 2000.

Peckham, Linda. "*Surname Viet Given Name Nam*: Spreading Rumors and Ex/Changing Histories." In *Screening Asian Americans*, edited by Peter X. Feng, 235–42. New Brunswick, NJ, and London: Rutgers University Press, 2002.

Pelaud, Isabelle Thuy. "*Métisse Blanche*: Kim Lefèvre and Transnational Space." In *Mixed Race Literature*, edited by Jonathan Brennan, 122–36. Stanford: Stanford University Press, 2002.

Pelley, Patricia. *Postcolonial Vietnam: New Histories of the National Past*. Durham, NC, and London: Duke University Press, 2002.

Peterson, Spike V. "Sexing Political Identities/Nationalism as Heterosexism." *International Feminist Journal of Politics* 1, no. 1 (1999): 34–65.

Pettus, Ashley. *Between Sacrifice and Desire: The Governing of Femininity in Viet Nam.* New York: Routledge, 2003.

Piazzo, Philippe. "Le goût du Trần Anh Hùng quand il est mûr." *Aden* (May 24, 2000).

"Politburo's Resolution on Viet Kieu." *Embassy of the Socialist Republic of Vietnam,* May 11, 2004. http://www.vietnamembassy-usa.org/news/story.php?d=20040511170158. Accessed March 14, 2010.

Pomeroy, William. *The Philippines: Colonialism, Collaboration, and Resistance!* New York: International Publishers, 1992.

Powrie, Phil. "Heritage, History and 'New Realism': French Cinema in the 1990s." In *French Cinema in the 1990s: Continuity and Difference,* edited by Phil Powrie, 1–21. Oxford: Oxford University Press, 1999.

Premo, Cassie. "When the Difference Becomes Too Great: Images of the Self and Survival in a Postmodern World." *Genre* 16 (1995): 183–91.

Puar, Jasbir. *Terrorist Assemblages: Homonationalism in Queer Times.* Durham, NC: Duke University Press, 2007.

Radway, Janice. *Reading the Romance: Women, Patriarchy, and Popular Literature.* Chapel Hill: University of North Carolina, 1984.

Rapaport, Herman. "Deconstruction's Other: Trinh T. Minh-ha and Jacques Derrida." *Diacritics* 25, no. 2 (1995): 98–113.

Raymond, Gino. "French Culture and the Politics of Self-Esteem: The Vietnam Experience." In *America, France, and Vietnam: Cultural History and Ideas of Conflict,* edited by John Roper and Phil Melling, 56–70. Aldershot, England: Avebury, 1991.

Renov, Michael. *Hollywood's Wartime Woman: Representation and Ideology.* London and Ann Arbor, MI: UMI Research Press, 1988.

"Review of *Child of War, Woman of Peace.*" *Publishers Weekly,* November 23, 1992, 48.

Rivera, Javier Delgado. "Viet Nam: The Troubled Ideology," *Global Affairs: An International Relations Magazine* 11. October–November 2008. http://www.globalaffairs.es/en/viet-nam-the-troubled-ideology/. Accessed March 20, 2009.

Roan, Jeanette. *Envisioning Asia: On Location, Travel, and the Cinematic Geography of U.S. Orientalism.* Ann Arbor: University of Michigan Press, 2010.

Roberts, Emily Vaughan. "A Vietnamese Voice in the Dark: Three Stages in the Corpus of Linda Lê." In *Francophone Postcolonial Cultures: Critical Essays,* edited by Kamal Salhi, 331–42. Lanham, MD: Lexington Books, 2003.

Robinson, Ronald. "Non-European Foundations of European Imperialism: Sketch for a Theory of Collaboration." In *Studies in the Theory of Imperialism,* edited by Roger Owen and Bob Sutcliffe, 117–40. London: Longman Group Limited, 1972.

Rofel, Lisa. *Desiring China: Experiments in Neoliberalism, Sexuality, and Public Culture.* Durham, NC, and London: Duke University Press, 2007.

Rogin, Michael Paul. *Ronald Reagan, the Movie and Other Episodes in Political Demonology.* Berkeley: University of California Press, 1988.

Rouse, Sarah. "South Vietnam's Film Legacy." *Historical Journal of Film, Radio and Television* 6, no. 2 (1986): 211–22.

Russell, Catherine. "Beyond Authenticity: The Discourse of Tourism in Ethnographic and Experimental Film." *Visual Anthropology* 5, no. 2 (1992): 131–41.

Russo, Mary. "Female Grotesques: Carnival and Theory." In *Feminist Studies, Critical Studies,* edited by Teresa de Lauretis, 213–29. Bloomington: Indiana University Press, 1986.

Rydstrøm, Helle. "Sexual Desires and 'Social Evils': Young Women in Rural Vietnam." *Gender, Place, and Culture* 13, no. 3 (2006): 283–301.

Rye, Gill, and Michael Worton, eds. *Women's Writing in Contemporary France: New Writers, New Literatures in the 1990s.* Manchester, England, and New York: Manchester University Press, 2002.

Sayre, Robert F. "Autobiography and the Making of America." In *Autobiography: Essays Theoretical and Critical,* edited by James Olney, 146–68. Princeton, NJ: Princeton University Press, 1980.

Schein, Louisa. "Diaspora Politics, Homeland Erotics, and the Materializing of Memory." *positions* 7, no. 3 (1999): 697–729.

Schiffrin, André. "Auteur! Auteur! On Being Published in Paris." *The Chronicle of Higher Education,* September 17, 1999, B7–B8.

Schwenkel, Christina. *The American War in Contemporary Vietnam.* Bloomington and Indianapolis: Indiana University Press, 2009.

Sclau, Stacey, and Electa Arenal. "Escribiendo yo, escribiendo ella, escribiendo nosotras: On Co-Laboring." *Tulsa Studies in Women's Literature* 14, no. 1 (1995): 39–49.

Searle, William. "Women, Vietnamese, Other: The Depiction of Women in Vietnamese Short Fiction." *War, Literature and the Arts* (2001): 314–27.

Selao, Ching. "Folie et Écriture dans *Calomnies* de Linda Lê." *Présence Francophone:* 63 (2004): 189–202.

Sherbert, Erin. "Madison Nguyen's Last Stand," *MetroSantaCruz.com,* December 3, 2008. 6. http://www.metroactive.com/metro/12.03.08/news-0849.html. Accessed January 15, 2010.

Shipler, David. "A Child's Tour." *New York Times,* June 25, 1989, 71.

Simon, Sherry. *Gender in Translation: Cultural Identity and the Politics of Transmission.* London and New York: Routledge, 1996.

———. "Translating the Will to Knowledge: Prefaces and Canadian Literary Politics." In *Translation: History and Culture,* edited by Susan Bassnett and André Lefevere, 110–17. London and New York: Pinter Publishers, 1990.

Singer, Michael. *The Making of Oliver Stone's Heaven and Earth.* Boston: Charles E. Tuttle Company, Inc., 1993.

Singley, Carol, and Susan Elizabeth Sweeney. "In League with Each Other: The Theory and Practice of Feminist Collaboration." In *Common Ground: Feminist Collaboration in the Academy*, edited by Elizabeth Peck and Jo-Anna Stephens Mink, 63–79. New York: State University of New York Press, 1998.

Smith, Sidonie, and Julia Watson, eds. *De/Colonizing the Subject: The Politics of Gender in Women's Autobiography*. Minneapolis: University of Minnesota Press, 1992.

Soucy, Alexander. "Vietnamese Warriors, Vietnamese Mothers: State Imperatives in the Portrayal of Women." *Canadian Woman Studies/Les Cahiers de la Femme* 19, no. 4 (2000): 121–26.

Spence, Joe. " Beyond the Family Album." In *Feminist-Art-Theory: An Anthology 1968–200*, edited by Hilary Robinson, 352–61. Malden and Oxford: Blackwell Publishers, Ltd 2001.

Stacey, Jackie. *Star Gazing: Hollywood Cinema and Female Spectatorship*. London and New York: Routledge, 1994.

Steinglass, Matt. "Vietnam Continues Crackdown on Dissidents." *Scoop World: Independent News*, December 2, 2007. http://www.scoop.co.nz/stories/WO0712/S00088.htm. Accessed March 22, 2008.

Storey, John. *Cultural Studies and the Study of Popular Culture*. Athens: University of Georgia Press, 1996.

Straayer, Chris. *Deviant Eyes, Deviant Bodies: Sexual Re-Orientations in Film and Video*. New York: Columbia University Press, 1996.

Strode, Louise. "France and EU Policy-Making on Visual Culture: New Opportunity for National Identity?" In *France in Focus: Film and National Identity*, edited by Sue Harris and Elizabeth Ezra, 61–75. Oxford and New York: Berg, 2000.

Sturken, Marita. *Tangled Memories: The Vietnam War, the AIDS Epidemic, and the Politics of Remembering*. Berkeley, Los Angeles, and London: University of California Press, 1997.

Swarr, Amanda Lock, and Richa Nagar. "Introduction: Theorizing Transnational Feminist Praxis." In *Critical Transnational Feminist Praxis*, edited by Amanda Lock Swarr and Richa Nagar, 1–23. Albany: State University of New York Press, 2010.

Suk, Julie. "The Resident Tourist: Asian Immigrant Writers in France," *The Back Page*, 1995. http://www.digitas.harvard.edu/~perspy/old/issues/1995/sep/france.html. Accessed December 1, 2000.

Suleri, Sara. "Woman Skin Deep: Feminism and the Postcolonial Condition." In *Colonial Discourse and Post-Colonial Theory: A Reader*, edited by Patrick and Laura Chrisman Williams, 244–56. New York: Columbia University Press, 1994.

Tai, Hue-Tam Ho. "Duong Thu Huong and the Literature of Disenchantment." In *Viet Nam Forum 14: A Review of Vietnamese Culture and Society*, edited by Oliver Wolters. New Haven, CT: Yale University Council on Southeast Asian Studies, 1994.

———. "Faces of Remembering and Forgetting." In *The Country of Memory: Remaking the Past in Late Socialist Vietnam*, edited by Hue-Tam Ho Tai, 167–95. Berkeley: University of California Press, 2001.

Tarr, Carrie. "French Cinema and Post-Colonial Minorities." In *Post-Colonial Cultures in France*, edited by Alec Hargreaves and Mark McKinney, 59–83. London and New York: Routledge, 1997.

———. "Tran Anh Hung as Diasporic Filmmaker." In *France and 'Indochina': Cultural Representations*, edited by Kathryn Robson and Jennifer Yee, 153–64. Lanham, MD: Lexington Books, 2005.

Tasker, Yvonne. *Spectacular Bodies: Gender, Genre, and the Action Cinema*. London and New York: Routledge, 1993.

Taylor, Diana. *The Archive and the Repertoire: Performing Cultural Memory in the Americas*. Durham, NC, and London: Duke University Press, 2003.

Taylor, Keith. *The Birth of Vietnam*. Berkeley and Los Angeles: University of California Press, 1983.

Taylor, Lynne. *Between Resistance and Collaboration: Popular Protest in Northern France, 1940–1945*. New York: St. Martin's Press, Inc., 2000.

Taylor, Philip. *Fragments of the Present: Searching for Modernity in Vietnam's South*. Honolulu: Allen & Unwin and University of Hawaii Press, 2001.

Taylor, Sandra C. *Vietnamese Women at War: Fighting for Hồ Chí Minh and the Revolution*. Lawrence: University of Kansas, 1999.

Tétreault, Mary Ann. "Women and Revolution in Vietnam." In *Vietnam's Women in Transition*, edited by Kathleen Barry, 38–57. New York: St. Martin's Press, 1996.

Thayer, Carlyle A. "Mono-Organizational Socialism and the State." In *Vietnam's Rural Transformation*, edited by B. J. Kervliet and Doug Porter, 39–64. Boulder, CO: Westview Press, 1995.

"Thị Trường Điện Ảnh VN - Chợ Cóc? [Commercial Vietnamese cinema--popular market?]. *Việt Báo News*, October 18, 2006. http://vietbao.vn/Giai-tri/Thi-truong-dien-anh-VN-Cho-coc/55127139/233/. Accessed January 10, 2010.

"Thị Trường Điện Ảnh Việt Nam" [A market-oriented Vietnamese cinema]. *Việt Báo News*, October 18, 2006. http://vietbao.vn/Giai-tri/Thi-truong-dien-anh-VN-Cho-coc/55127139/233/. Accessed January 10, 2010.

Thông, Huỳnh Sanh. "Introduction." In *The Tale of Kiều*. Translated by Huỳnh Sanh Thông, xix–xl. New York: Random House, 1973.

———. "Literature and the Vietnamese." *The Vietnam Forum* 9 (1987): 37–48.

Thomas, Mandy, and Russell Heng. "Stars in the Shadows: Celebrity, Media, and the State in Vietnam." In *House of Glass: Culture, Modernity, and the State in Southeast Asia*, edited by Yao Souchou, 287–312. Singapore: Institute of Southeast Asian Studies, 2001.

Thrift, Nigel. "The Material Practices of Glamour." *Journal of Cultural Economy* 1, no. 1 (2010): 9–23.

Tran Dinh Thanh Lam. 2003. "*Bar Girls* Raise Hell in Vietnam." *Asia Times Online*, http://www.atimes.com/atimes/Southeast_Asia/ED26Ae01.html. Accessed January 10, 2010.

Trần, Mỹ-Thuận. 2009. "Vietnamese Art Exhibit Puts Politics on Display." *Los Angeles Times*, 2009, 1–3. http://articles.latimes.com/2009/jan/10/local/me-vietarts10. Accessed January 10, 2009.

Tran, Nhung Tuyet. "Beyond the Myth of Equality: Daughters' Inheritance Rights in the Lê Code." In *Viet Nam: Borderless Histories*, edited by Nhung Tuyet Tran and Anthony Reid, 121–44. Madison: University of Wisconsin Press, 2007.

Triều, Hải. "Cờ Máu, Hình Hồ và VAALA tại Nam California" [Bloody flag, the picture of Hồ, and VAALA in southern California]. *Vietnam Daily*, January 15, 2009, 1–2. http://www.vietnamdaily.com/index.php?c=article&p=49731. Accessed December 28, 2009.

Trinh Mai Diễm. *30 Years of Vietnam's Cinema Art*. Hà Nội: The Vietnam Film Archives, 1983.

Trinh, T. Minh-ha. *Cinema Interval*. New York and London: Routledge, 1999.

———. *Framer Framed*. New York: Routledge, 1992.

———. *When the Moon Waxes Red: Representation, Gender and Cultural Politics*. New York: Routledge, 1991.

———. *Woman, Native, Other: Writing Postcoloniality and Feminism*. Bloomington and Indianapolis: Indiana University Press, 1989.

Trương, Monique T.D. "Vietnamese American Literature." In *An Interethnic Companion to Asian American Literature*, edited by King-Kok Cheung, 219–46. New York: Cambridge University Press, 1997.

Turim, Maureen. *Flashbacks in Film: Memory and History*. New York and London: Routledge, 1989.

Turner, Karen Gottschang, and Phan Thanh Hao. *Even the Women Must Fight: Memories of War from North Viet Nam*. New York: John Wiley & Sons, Inc., 1998.

Turner, Lynn. "Documentary Friction: Vocal and Visual Strategies in *Surname Viet Given Name Nam*." *Parallax: A Journal of Metadiscursive Theory and Cultural Practices* 3 (1996): 81–93.

"TV, Cinema Show More Vietnam Flicks." *Vietnam Net Bridge*, July 8, 2007. http://english.vietnamnet.vn/lifestyle/2007/07/715505/. Accessed August 16, 2010.

Valentin, Karen. "Politicized Leisure in the Wake of Doi Moi: A Study of Youth in Hanoi " In *Youth and the City in the Global South*, edited by Karen Hansen, 74–97. Bloomington: Indiana University Press, 2008.

Valverde, Caroline. "From Dust to Gold: The Vietnamese Amerasian Experience." In *Racially Mixed People in America*, edited by Maria Root, 144–61. Newberry Park, CA: Sage Publications, Inc., 1992.

Vân, Mai Thu. *Vietnam: un peuple, des voix* Paris: Pierre Horay, 1983.

Vella, Walter F., ed. *Aspects of Vietnamese History.* Hawai'i: University Press of Hawaii, 1973.

Venuti, Lawrence. *The Scandals of Translation: Towards an Ethics of Difference.* London and New York: Routledge, 1998.

"Vietnam: Crackdown on Dissent in Wake of WTO and APEC." *Human Rights Watch*, March 9, 2007. http://www.hrw.org/english/docs/2007/03/09/vietna15466.htm. Accessed March 9, 2007.

Vietnamese Women in the Eighties. Edited by Vietnam Women's Union and The Centre for Women's Studies. Hà Nội: Foreign Languages Publishing House, 1989.

Visweswaran, Kamala. "Betrayal: An Analysis in Three Acts." In *Scattered Hegemonies: Postmodernity and Transnational Feminist Practices*, edited by Inderpal Grewal and Caren Kaplan, 90–109. Minneapolis: University of Minnesota Press, 1994.

Võ, Chương-Đài. "Memories That Bind: Dang Thuy Tram's Diaries as Agent of Reconciliation." *Journal of Vietnamese Studies* 3, no. 2 (2008): 196–207.

Võ, Linda Trinh. "Managing Survival: Economic Realities for Vietnamese American Women." In *Asian/Pacific Islander American Women: A Historical Anthology*, edited by Shirley Hune and Gail Nomura, 237–52. New York: New York University Press, 2003.

Vu, Cam Nhung, and Thuy Vo Dang. "Competing Images: Anti-Communist Protests in Little Saigon." In *30 Years Beyond the War Vietnam, Southeast Asian/American National Conference*. Riverside: University of California, Riverside, 2005.

Vu, John. "To Recall or Not Recall Madison Nguyen?," *New American Media*, May 8, 2008. 5. http://blogs.newamericamedia.org/nam-round-table/1210/to-recall-or-not-recall-madison-nguyen. Accessed January 22, 2010.

Vu, Ngoc Quynh. "Danh Nhat Minh: An Artist's Regard." In *Vietnamese Cinema: Le Cinéma Vietnamien*, edited by Philippe Dumont and Kirstie Gormley, 117–24. Lyon, France: Asiexpo Edition, 2007.

Vu Quang Viet. "Vietnam's Economy from 1989 to 1995." *The Vietnamese Studies* 123 (1997): 7–34.

Wallis, Brian. "Questioning Documentary." *Aperture* 112 (1988): 60–71.

Warner, Michael. *Fear of a Queer Planet: Queer Politics and Social Theory.* Minneapolis: University of Minnesota Press, 1993.

Werner, Jayne. "Gender Matters: Gender Studies and Viet Nam Studies." In *Le Viet Nam au féminin: Viet Nam, Women's Realities*, edited by Gisèle Bousquet and Nora A. Taylor, 19–41. Paris: Les Indes Savantes, 2005.

Werner, Jayne, and Danièle Bélanger, eds. *Gender, Household, State: Đổi Mới in Viet Nam.* Ithaca: Southeast Asia Program Publications, Cornell University, 2005.

White, Christine Pelzer. "Promissory Notes." In *Promissory Notes: Women in the Transition to Socialism,* edited by Sonia Kruks, Rayna Rapp and Marilyn B. Young, 345–53. New York: Monthly Review Press, 1989.

Wiegman, Robyn. "Missiles and Melodrama (Masculinity and the Televisual War)." In *Seeing through the Media: The 1990 Persian Gulf War,* edited by Lauren Rabinovitz and Robyn Wiegman, 171–87: Rutgers, 1994.

Wilcox, Wynn. "Hybridity, Colonialism, and National Subjectivity in Vietnamese Historiography." In *Travelling Concepts: Text, Subjectivity, Hybridity,* edited by Joyce Goggin and Sonja Neef, 201–11. Amsterdam: ASCA Press, 2001.

Williams, Linda. "When the Woman Looks." In *The Dread of Difference: Gender and the Horror Film,* edited by Barry Keith Grant, 15–34. Austin: University of Texas Press, 1996.

Winston, Jane Bradley. *Postcolonial Duras: Cultural Memory in Postwar France.* New York: Palgrave, 2001.

Wong, Sau-ling Cynthia. "Autobiography as Guided Chinatown Tour? Maxine Hong Kingston's *The Woman Warrior* and the Chinese-American Autobiographical Controversy." In *Multicultural Autobiography: American Lives,* edited by James Robert Payne, 246–79. Knoxville: University of Tennessee Press, 1992.

Woodhull, Winifred. "Ethnicity on the French Frontier." In *Writing Identities: Gender, Nation, and Immigration in Contemporary Europe,* edited by Sidonie Smith and Gisela Brinker-Gabler, 31–61. Minneapolis and London: University of Minnesota Press, 1997.

Woodman, Brian J. "A Hollywood War of Wills: Cinematic Representation of Vietnamese Super-Soldiers and America's Defeat in the War." *Journal of Film and Video* 55, nos. 2/3 (2003): 44–58.

Worthy, Kim. "Striking Home: Trends and Changes in Vietnamese Cinema." *CineAction* 64 (2004): 46–53.

Yarr, Linda. "Gender and the Allocation of Time: Impact on the Household Economy." In *Women in Transition,* edited by Kathleen Barry, 110–22. New York: St. Martin's Press, 1996.

Yeager, Jack. *The Vietnamese Novel in French: A Literary Response to Colonialism.* Hanover, NH, and London: University Press of New England, 1987.

Young, Marilyn. "Human Sacrifices: A Review of *Paradise of the Blind.*" *The Women's Review of Books* X: 10–11 (1993): 24–25.

Yuval-Davis, Nira, and Floya Anthias, eds. *Woman-Nation-State.* London: MacMillan Press Ltd, 1989.

Index

ABOUT THE AUTHOR

Lan P. Duong is an Associate Professor in Media and Cultural Studies at the University of California, Riverside.